Twelve Secrets of the Caucasus

Essad-Bey

Essad Bey

Twelve Secrets of the Caucasus

Translated from the German by
G. CHYCHELE WATERSTON

With an Afterword
by TOM REISS

BRIDGES
PUBLISHING

First published 1931
Second Edition 2008

Afterword "The Orient of the Imagination"
Copyright 2008 by Tom Reiss.
All rights reserved.

Book cover: Rosi Weiss, Freiburg/Germany on the basis of the original
American book cover of 1931
Layout and typesetting: Hans-Jürgen Maurer, Freiburg/Germany

All rights of this edition reserved by the publisher.

This book is published by:
Bridges Publishing
Verlag Hans-Jürgen Maurer
P.O. Box 207
79002 Freiburg
Germany

www.bridges-publishing.de

ISBN 978-3-929345-37-7

CONTENTS

Introduction 7

1. Into the Mountains 10
2. The Idyllic Robber's Den 14
3. The Land of Mountains 18
4. Inaccessible Treasures 27
5. The Naked City 35
6. The Caucasian Scimitar 43
7. The Master of Fragrance 48
8. Love 52
9. The Slave Trade 64
10. How to Become a Prince 72
11. The Blood Feud 77
12. Alamut – The Garden of Heaven 87
13. Christians Who Do Not Know the Name of Christ 90
14. Germany in the Mountains 98
15. Civis Romanus Sum 106
16. The Hero of the Mountains 113
17. Lamaroi 122
18. The Village of Poets 135
19. The Empire of the Jews 145
20. How the Caucasus Was Conquered 159
21. Narsan – The Blood of the Giant 174
22. The Castle of Love and Betrayal 187
23. The Art of Healing in the Mountains 194
24. True Stories from Daghestan 201
25. Please Come and Visit Me 209
26. Ruins, Dead Cities, and Churches 218

27. The Cradle of Humanity 227
28. A More or Less Extravagant Conclusion 233

AFTERWORD — »The Orient of the Imagination«
by Tom Reiss 239

INTRODUCTION

The Caucasus – The Pearl of the East!
The ancients called it »the ring of mountains which encircles the earth,
as a marriage ring does a finger,« and today the poets of the East have
named it »the land of tongues and of miracles,« for the languages of
these mountains are innumerable, and the miracles that are related in
these languages are without end.

This book is an attempt to describe that strange and peculiar world
on the basis of my own and of other people's experience.

For thousands of years the Caucasus, that giant wall dividing Asia
from Europe, has been the home of the most interesting of races, the
most adventurous of customs, and the strangest of experiences. Its
incredible history stretches from Prometheus to Stalin, and it is itself a
kind of curiosity shop of world history in its loyal preservation of all
that is no more, all that is outlived and forgotten.

Savage brutality, brigandage, and bloodthirstiness, as well as chivalrous bravery, nobility, and honour distinguish the people of these highlands, and it would be entirely wrong to conceive of them merely as
barbarous and backward cave-dwellers. Professor Marr, one of the most
famous experts on the Caucasian races, has rightly observed that
»there are no savages in the Caucasus, and no races without cultures of
their own.« And this culture is by no means insignificant, even if it does
appear in the form of a spiritual attitude which is somewhat incomprehensible to Europeans, rather than in outward cultural manifestations.

Today the Caucasus is at the crossroads; revolutions and wars are
striking at the foundations of the old patriarchal ways of life. The tribes
which have been confined until now within their valleys, cut off from
the whole world and obliged by force of circumstances to lead the lives

of their forefathers, seem now to be migrating more and more into the broad and fruitful plains of Ciscaucasia. If this bold attempt were to succeed and the people of the mountains were actually to realize their age-long dream and settle in the plains, then at last the proud, piratical Caucasus that still persists today will definitely be conquered, and the old customs, the ancient individuality of life in the mountains, will gradually give place to another order of things. At present this development is incomplete. Europe is already knocking at the door, but so far the door has only been half opened. Anyone who knows the Caucasus realizes also that it may be hundreds of years before the last brigand shall be changed to a peace-loving ploughman, and the romantic life of the hills shall finally have ceased.

But the metamorphosis is gradually being completed. The old order changeth, and even today, as I write these lines, some old mountain custom or other is perhaps being supplanted by a new, sober, commonplace one, from Europe.

But until this incident of world history is at an end (and who knows when it may be fulfilled) the Caucasus remains a miraculous fairyland.

Dark secrets surround its hitherto untrodden summits; unfamiliar races still dwell among its crags and gorges; the old aristocratic chivalry still flowers in all its pristine splendour; and the bold European who dares penetrate into the hills is still uncertain, to this very day, whether he will be received by some mountain hero with hospitality or with bullets.

The races of the Caucasus have no unity. Christian, Mohammedan, Pagan, and Jewish tribes live there cheek by jowl. People of ancient and magnificent culture, like the Georgians, the Armenians, or the men of Azerbaijan, are neighbours of rough tribes like the Khevsurs, the Svanetians, and others. The higher the mountains, the more definite is the influence of the three great cultural races of the Caucasus, and the more characteristic and conservative is the original state of existence.

I have attempted to portray the life of these hill tribes and the customs prevailing among the inhabitants of the god-forsaken gorges and the alpine heights, for it is there especially that the old Caucasus still survives. But it is to be hoped that the exotic character of these ancient highlands will not affect unfavourably the opinion of the European as to my homeland; on the contrary, my picture is intended to facilitate and promote familiarity with the basically different life of the untouched mountains.

A word to unfriendly critics. The author is aware, from personal observation, that there are such things as hospitals and secondary schools for girls in the Caucasus. But things which would be in place in an encyclopaedia will not be found here in a book which has no wish to be confused with the heavy artillery of scholarship.

Berlin, Autumn, 1930
ESSAD-BEY

1.

INTO THE MOUNTAINS

IN HIS YOUTH ISKENDER-KHAN had been a soldier. At least so he said. It is certain that he would have been destined to achieve high military distinction if a capricious fate had not served him a low trick. In his passport stood the words »Iskender-Khan, Nobleman« and underneath it, in brackets, »Illiterate.« Iskender was unable to efface this little word from his passport. The profundities of learning had always filled him with terror, and, since an officer, even in Daghestan, the home of Iskender, must at least be able to sign his name without a mistake, he renounced the fame of his namesake Alexander the Great, of which he had otherwise been assured, and took his departure.

»In these days,« he was wont to say later on, »knights have sunk to the level of scribes. No one plunders hostile villages any more, or steals fat sheep, or seduces the beautiful girls of the enemy. Instead of all that, they sit indoors with their swords blunted, peeping into big books full of ugly black signs. A free knight has no business looking in big books.«

To me Iskender-Khan was always the embodiment of Daghestan's knighthood. His long black moustaches hung menacingly down from his upper lip; his sword and dagger, from which he was never parted, clanked with every step he took; and, of an evening as he drew his dagger peacefully from its sheath to cut himself an extra thick slice of roast mutton, his face never lost that forbidding look of a world conqueror in retirement.

It was true that the offensive remark in his passport ruined his military career, but it did not ruin his reputation among the inhabitants of the gorges of Daghestan. They didn't hold much with bothersome notes in foreign passports. Iskender's gigantic proportions impressed them. And when, mounted high upon his steed, he rode through the villages–the hero himself in full panoply of war–the people bowed down before him and told each other legends of his magnanimity, his strength, and of his knightly prowess.

I myself was always firmly convinced that Iskender-Khan–the peaceful owner of a village in Daghestan– was better suited to be a gallant brigand than a common officer. And when I asked him: »Iskender, how many people have you slain? How many maidens have you carried off?« he seemed to understand that a negative retort would not be commensurate with his dignity. »Very many,« he answered proudly, and to this day I am not sure whether his words did not contain more of truth than he himself would care to admit. Many things were murmured about Iskender-Khan, many things not entirely compatible with his position as the father of a family and the owner of a village.

His family was a large one, though he had but one wife, to whom, like a true carpetknight, he remained strictly faithful. This woman was a Lesghian, also from Daghestan, and she brought to the marriage a certain tendency towards European civilization, as well as an unparalleled fertility. This tendency, however, narrowed itself down to the fact that every time she was expecting a child (an event which occurred pretty nearly every winter) she came down from the mountains into the plain of Azerbaijan in order that she might fulfil her wifely duties in Baku amid the questionable peace of the oil community.

At the very moment when I myself saw the light of the oil town of Baku for the first time, she brought a son into the world who was given the name of Ali-Bey. My mother was sickly, and the strong Lesghian woman was chosen by my father as a nurse. She consented, and Ali-Bey thus became my foster-brother and Iskhender-Khan my foster-father. Suata, as the nurse was called, did not last it out very long among us and returned to the mountains. But Ali-Bey visited us annually in the summer and stayed at our house in the village of Mardakyany near Baku. It is a village without peasantry in which there are only villas, and around the villas gardens are laid out. Just beyond it the oil desert ceases and the green plain begins.

I was only allowed to visit Mardakyany occasionally. It was said that malaria was rampant there among the melon and peach plantations, and, every spring when the asphalt began to get soft, I went north to Germany, France, and Switzerland, and the house in Mardakyany remained empty but for my father, who would sometimes recuperate there from the fatigues of the oil business. Then came the war, and the trips abroad ceased.

In the summer of 1916 I came to Mardakyany for a prolonged stay, saw my foster-brother Ali-Bey, ate of the melons and peaches, listened to an old servant telling fairy tales, and—fell sick of the treacherous malaria. The house at Mardakyany broke into a panic at my illness. Doctors, experienced men from the oil office, and my ever-present aunts gave their opinions. Everyone regarded himself as partially at fault, and no one seemed quite sure how to be of any assistance against the malaria. The real cure for the disease was discovered by the old servant, the inexhaustible teller of tales.

This servant was a eunuch; he had lost his manhood somewhere or other in Persia in the days of his youth and acquired therewith a taste for wise tales, profound meditation, and sweetmeats. My father had dug him up somewhere fifteen years before, since when he had lived with us half as manservant, half as maidservant, and was fully and proudly aware of his versatility.

»When God, the Almighty«—so spake the eunuch— »created the earth, it was flat and level like the surface of the sea. Upon the level earth dwelt creatures: Men, Beasts, Spirits, Troubles, and Pestilences. Not until after the creation did the Merciful One bethink himself that he had conceived the earth too flat and level, and he therefore decided, in his bounty, to give to every land some hills and little mountains. So he packed a mass of mountains into a sack and began to distribute them justly upon the earth. But the Evil One, the master of Troubles and of Pestilences, did not wish this gift to be granted to mankind. And as Allah hovered between the Caspian and the Black Sea, the Evil One slipped up beside his sack, slit open the cloth, and all the mountains fell down into the plain between the two seas. Thus began the Caucasus, the Land of Mountains. But the Lord of the World was very wroth.

'Thou Evil One,' said he, 'thou corruptest my creation and makest the first unrighteousness. Therefore, as a punishment, shall the mountainous land that is here created be forbidden thee. Man and Beast shall dwell in the mountains, but thou and thy servants, thy Troubles and thy Pestilences, shall not set foot upon the mountain land. Life among the crags will be hard enough without thee.'

»So spake Allah, the Righteous One, and so it came to pass. Trouble and Sickness dwell in the plain amid the gardens where life is easy. But the heroes and the noblemen stay up in the mountains where there is no pestilence and no trouble.«

The eunuch was a wise man. All of those about me listened to him attentively. I arose from my pillow and said: »I want to go to Ali-Bey in the Land of Mountains.«

My father cleared his throat. »In the mountains dwell wild men whose speech we none of us know. Idolaters and brigands dwell there; what do you want with the mountains?«

My foster-brother Ali-Bey arose and began to defend his home. »In the hills,« said he, »live my father, my mother, and my brothers and sisters; they will protect my sick foster-brother. In our aul [mountain village] there are no robbers. No one in the whole of Daghestan will attack my brother. My father has many friends all over the land, and the air in the mountains is better than that of the plains. My brother will get well there.«

It took several days before my foster-brother, the wise eunuch, and myself finally succeeded in talking my father into allowing my journey to the village of Iskender-Khan. I was to be permitted to stay a whole summer in Daghestan and later to journey through the mountains to Besh-Tau, the luxurious Caucasian watering-place. My father was not able to accompany me. Only my foster-brother went with me, and the wise eunuch—who played the part of nurse—as well as two reliable men from the oil office. Accompanied by this escort I was at last permitted to visit my Caucasian foster-kinsmen. Before my departure my father gave me a golden Caucasian dagger and taught me under what circumstances it was used in the mountains and how to behave there so as to rank as a decent and well-brought-up person. He himself knew the wild mountainous country, and he was aware that the laws and conventions there are far more complicated than in the drawing-rooms of an oil town.

»The wild men of Daghestan,« said he, »are different from all men in the world, wild or otherwise. It is difficult to travel in Daghestan without making mistakes. Above all, you must respect old people, submit yourself to the customs of the district, and always remember that money has no power in the mountains. In case of doubt do as the servant does.«

These words of advice were fully adequate, for the eunuch was a man of particularly wide experience. So off we went, well armed, and even better equipped with good counsel, together with foster-brother Ali-Bey into the wild land of many tribes, of idolaters, knights, robbers, and heroes.

2.

THE IDYLLIC ROBBERS' DEN

WE TRAVELLED AS FAR AS Gunib, to the west of the township Temir-Khan-Shura, in the heart of Daghestan. Behind Gunib, near the ruins of an old castle of the Shamkhals, lay the aul of Iskender-Khan, clinging to a terrace of the cliff. Our journey had lasted five days; at first we travelled along the shores of the Caspian Sea, on the famous nomad route by which, for centuries, the people that dwelt to the north used to overflow the plains of Transcaucasia in the spring of every year, until a wise ruler blocked the passage with an iron wall from the mountain edge to the sea.

»Here begins Azerbaijan,« the ruler chiselled in the iron, and thus, to the confusion of the nomads, he diverted the road to the plain. Beyond Temir-Khan-Shura—the town that was founded by Tamerlane and destroyed by Russian generals—began the mountains. The green forest of the Caspian shore ceased. The hills looked grey, aloof, and threatening. Here still the wild boar and the leopard dwell; here immemorial ruins fall into decay, while the wild Lesghians sit at the doorways of their houses and shoot into the air when strangers venture near, by way of threat or welcome, as the case may be; and here men stare appraisingly after the passer-by and laugh at him if he should not be dressed according to the latest style of Daghestan.

At the very first village I had to change my suit. My white Circassian clothes wounded the aesthetic sensibilities of the mountain people, especially as I wore a golden dagger. I was looked upon as a barbarian. White and gold might be worn in a town or in that sink of luxury, Besh-Tau, where nobody with good taste is ever about. But in the mountains it is prescribed that the clothes must suit the dagger. With gold, only dark or entirely black clothes are suitable. In my case, black and yellow was the right combination for a well-dressed man. And at that, only the dagger ought to be of gold. It would have been a serious mistake to have carried a revolver inlaid with gold or a sword, or even to ride through the villages with one's decorations on. This last was considered rank bad taste. The humblest shepherd would undoubtedly turn his bade in contempt on a man in such a get-up, even if the decorations had been conferred personally by the Shah of Persia or by the hand of the Tsar of Russia himself.

Beyond Makhach-Kala came the end of the modest Daghestan railway. We were to accomplish the rest of the way on donkeys along the mountain path from village to village. And in every one of these sat a friend of Iskender-Khan who received us royally and gave us news of the latest heroic deeds of his master, my foster-father.

Beyond Gunib we stopped where a wide gorge lay before us, and on the terrace, not far from the cliff, I perceived the goal of our journey. One glance at the inaccessible position of the place was enough; one knew that here the master of the aul could really feel security from every foe.

»Let us first stop here,« said the eunuch. »Ali-Bey shall go ahead of us to announce our visit and prepare the reception.« For this last we had not long to wait. The veiled figure of a woman appeared in broad, coloured trousers, with a child on her back. She stepped towards us in her gold-embroidered slippers, followed by a few armed men. »Assya,« she cried, »Assya,« and for the first time I heard the name which my nurse had given me as I lay at her breast.

The woman then said something in the Lesghian tongue, and the guard turned away so as not to see her face, from which she now removed the veil. Only the eunuch and I were allowed to see her dark features with their great wild eyes. As she inclined herself before me, I expected a kiss, but instead of that my foster-mother began to smell me, lifting up my arms and smelling under them, and all around my breast and mouth. Finally she did kiss me and said contentedly: »Almost hast thou the smell of a man; it is good.« Then she sat down upon the ground and, bidding me sit by her, she continued: »Assya—my son— they say that thou art ill. But I say unto thee that thou art not ill, thou art but hungry. I calmed thy hunger when thou didst lie in the cradle, and I will do it again now.« And suddenly she bared her body to the waist, leant over towards me, and presented one of her breasts to my mouth. Terrified, I glanced at the eunuch. »Drink,« said he in Russian, »it is thus that people greet each other in the mountains.« So I set to bravely and drank for the last time from the breast of my nurse. I drank until the infant, her youngest child, which she bore upon her back, began to scream in protest. With relief I let go of the breast and got up from the ground. »Most worthy mother,« said I, »let the little one have the rest.«

A man stood beside me all the while; it was Iskender-Khan, whom I had not yet recognized, and he laughed now and picked me up in his arms and carried me like a small child into the village. The nurse, the eunuch, and the rest followed after us. And thus was completed my arrival among my foster-relatives.

The little *saklya*—a sort of villa with a balcony and flat roof—which I now inhabited with the eunuch, boasted no other furniture than silk cushions. Meals were laid on silk cushions, one slept on cushions and covered oneself with cushions in the night. Each evening Iskender-Khan came up to see us and brought me *busa*. Busa is milk with a strong admixture of alcohol which the mountain people consider helpful in every kind of illness. In addition, my nurse appeared punctually every morning and read remarkable Lesghian incantations which were supposed to have an extraordinary effect when administered with busa. All day long I lay idle on the roof and gazed dreaming at the mountains.

To this hour, I do not know what it was that cured me, the mountain air, the milk and alcohol, or the Lesghian incantations. One thing is certain: within a single week the last traces of my malaria had disappeared, and I left the silk cushions and the roof to gain a closer acquaintance with the country of the last remaining knights-at-arms. The excursions which Ali-Bey, the eunuch, and I made together took us through the villages, mountains, and valleys of the polyglot, variegated land of Daghestan, a sombre, a rough, a mysterious, and yet a hospitable land, that is known, and wishes to remain known, only to the few.

3.

THE LAND OF MOUNTAINS

SOMBRE, MYSTERIOUS, AND INSCRUTABLE the mountains are. Grey peaks in Daghestan, green jungles in Ichkaria, white glaciers in the Chechen country. In Daghestan, in the auls, in the courtyards of the grey mosques, pale emaciated men sit for ten years, twenty years, bent over the incontrovertible wisdom of the Koran, set down in minute and graceful writing. Where the jungle begins the Koran ceases; no one there knows the great teaching.

In the midst of the jungles, between hills and streams, stand small tents which none but the initiated can find. Within the tents, upon stone pillars, are set small wooden figures, the gods of the forest folk. Before them burns the pyre, and priests with white beards kill sacrificial animals, eating the raw meat and smearing the gods and themselves with the sacrificial blood. The warriors too are smeared with it, as they arm for the fight, for some campaign of rapine against the Cossacks who conquered the valleys and put the people to flight. Then comes a burning of Cossack villages, a screaming of cattle, and a cracking of rifles. And then the imperial power throning in Tiflis, in the palace with the hundred windows, is the recipient of long reports and writes on them in the margin with a red pencil: »Punitive expedition.«

Five times a day in Daghestan there resounds from the top of the minarets the cry »Allahu Akbar.« »Allah is great.« And five times the people of the mountains hear the cry and pray »Allahu Akbar.« Everyone in the mountains understands that. It is Arabic, the language of the graceful Koran writing, the only language that is known apart from the mother-tongue, the speech of the native village. Five or six villages (the ten to twenty thousand people who together may speak a common language of this kind) constitute a small nation. But beyond the next

18

mountain from them lives another nation, speaking yet another language utterly different from their own in every word and sound.

The languages of the people who live next each other in neighbouring valleys are as different as Chinese and German. The mountains of the Caucasus are without number, and equally numerous are the valleys and the peoples who speak unrelated languages, and have different-shaped skulls, and belong to races that are foreign to each other. A hundred, two hundred, or perhaps even three hundred languages are spoken in the mountains, and it is only rarely that anybody can understand his neighbour's speech. Nor does he need to, for it is both difficult and dangerous to leave one's native village and trust oneself to the mountains of the outland. Only the Abrek does it, the warrior and robber, he and the pious scribe, the mullah, who travels throughout the land and preaches Islam. The speech of the scribe is Arabic. He can find people in every aul who understand Arabic and interpret his preaching.

The language of the Koran is difficult to learn; the worthy scholar must remain bowed over his books for some ten or twenty years to absorb its wisdom. Warriors, peasants, and women are not capable of it. But the peasant and his wife do learn Azerbaijani. It is easy, and anybody, however stupid, can understand and use it.

But this language does not befit the prince and the robber. There are too many people in the mountains who understand it. The very women could overhear what one knight-at-arms was discussing with another, and such affairs are not the business of women, peasants, or serfs. So the princes have a special language of their own, a language that is understood only by the prince and his peers. This is the famous hunting language. It was contrived by the inhabitants of the knights' citadels, the princely palaces, and the robbers' strongholds. The secret of it is strictly guarded, and no outsider has hitherto succeeded in becoming familiar with it though it is current throughout the whole of the mountains and among all the members of the caste. It is said to be the language of an extinct line of knights; but only within the last few decades has it come to be known about at all, so secretive were the princes. All important business is discussed in this language, secrets that no man must hear, and enterprises which affect the fate of the mountain people. Only five words of it are known to science, and they resemble no single word of any other known language. *Shapaka*– a horse, *amafa*–blood, *ami*–water, *asaz*–a gun, and *ashopshka*–a coward. The name of the language itself is Chakobsa.

All of the many languages referred to are without a written form, for there is nothing that hill people need to write down. The scribes look after all that in Arabic. The larger mountain races–and the word »large« must here be understood in a very limited sense–possess only a very modest literature, and the smaller ones have none whatever. They all live according to their complicated mountain law, the *adat*, which differs with each race and is known by heart by the elders. According to it, child-murder and fratricide, to take examples, are not punishable. Only the murder of people of foreign blood or of another clan is punishable, and then by the laws of blood feud.

Sometimes on a trip through the mountains, rifle barrels can be seen, beside the road, near the villages, glistening between bushes or behind rocks. There is no need to be afraid; these weapons are not directed against the travellers. They belong to men engaged in a feud, waiting for their victims, for some member or other of the enemy tribe who is expected along that road. Only a large family can attain its end or successfully protect itself in a blood feud. Smaller clans are pitilessly exposed to the almost never-ending persecution of a numerically superior enemy family. It is not so much wealth, wisdom, power, and courage that are esteemed in the hills as the number of male relatives, of protectors and avengers, who belong to a great clan. Hence comes also the prayer of the mountain folk: »God grant above all that the numbers of my relatives may find increase and that those of my enemies may diminish.« A large number of relatives–that is the aim of peasant and knight alike.

In every aul, upon the summit of every mountain and at every spring, citadels arise. Not all of them are the citadels of knights; most of them are simple stone towers with a gatevay and a few tiny windows. Everybody knows what it means when the gates of these towers are barred. Languishing, anxious faces gaze from out the windows; men and women hold out their hands beseechingly and beg for alms. These are the »lifers,« persons who have shut themselves in for life because, in the critical moment of a blood feud, they were found »poor«; poor, that is, in family. If a member of a family, whether innocently or with guilt (this question never arises), has committed a murder, then he exposes that family to reprisals. If it is small and weak, then the murderer cannot protect himself but must fly. He closes his house, says good-bye to his friends, abandons his fields and his flocks, and betakes himself with his family for ever into one of the secure stone towers. He never leaves it again. At the entrance, his enemies, the avengers, lurk behind rocks, taking turns at hiding in the bushes and the grass. They wait patiently, year in, year out, until all those within the tower are dead or until, by a process of attrition, they open the doors and step out of their own free will to face the rifles of the enemy. No one may visit them; once a day only their friends bring them food and drink.

It is obviously a terrible thing, when one is »poor,« to call down upon oneself the enmity of a powerful tribe. I know of a case in which the avenging party besieged a tower of this kind for thirty years, and such periods are not in the least unusual in the execution of a blood feud.

Not every race has princes or an aristocracy. The Chechens, for example, are a numerous people, but they have no aristocracy. »We are all princes« is the proud contention of the Chechen. They are a people who have no superiority of rank, and never have had, and into whose language the word »command« cannot be rendered. The word is unknown to them and must be translated by »request,« as, for example, it might be said: »The Tsar requests Mr. X to spend ten years in jail« (for the tribe is under Russian law).

In the neighbourhood of the Chechens, not far from their villages, are the Kabardians who are the most resolutely feudal race of people in the whole world. They have carried through the uttermost medieval principles of feudalism with an unprecedented logic, and it is impossible even today to imagine them without their king, princes, counts, barons, feudal lords, courtiers, knights, burghers, craftsmen, peasants, and slaves. Perhaps for this reason they are considered by many scholars to be a relic of the Crusades. Yet even in this instance a prince without family connexions is poverty-stricken in comparison with a peasant of a numerous family. A prince who has nobody left at all is driven out of the country, for without relatives even he is a man without power and respect.

Knights and scribes travel through the mountains. They are honoured and feared, for they go »the way of the righteous.« They are not loved, however; only the ashuk is loved, the universal artist, the singer and teller of tales, the frivolous gossip, the bringer of news, the troubadour. The ashuk represents public opinion in the hills; he can organize movements, form parties, call forth bloody battles with his dark insinuations, his subtle jokes and symbolic fables; he can stir things up, or he can quiet them down again. When the ashuk has sung his song in a man's home, he stands up and takes the carpet from the wall, or seizes his host's dagger or anything which takes his fancy, and appropriates it. It belongs to him, it is his fee, which he himself decides upon, and which no one disputes him. In former times, if the ashuk, the journalist of the hills, came of a line of princes, then the wife and daughter of his host also belonged to him. For the ashuk is the man who—as they say in the mountains—broods upon the affairs of the people, and for this reason the love of the people also belongs to him.

These innumerable fragments of races are remarkable, mysterious, and unexplored; no one knows where they came from or what part they once played amid the dark desolate mountains. Long treatises have been written about them, in Latin and Greek, Arabic and Russian, as well as in the western languages. But in the last analysis these treatises contain nothing; they are unable to penetrate the secrets of the hills. If you ask the mountain people about it, they shake their heads and stroke their beards, and send you with a smile to their wise-men.

The wise-man doesn't smile; he proclaims instead that »When God, the Almighty, was planning the flood, he saved two of every kind of animal in Noah's ark. But when the flood began, the Merciful One decided that he would also save two from every nation. And these people were hidden upon the peaks of the Caucasus, which are higher than Mount Ararat. It is from them that the mountain races are descended. But they are not allowed to increase too much, since the valleys are destined for other men who did not come to be until after the flood. The Caucasians have to stay in the mountains in everlasting memory of God's mercy and God's vengeance.« If you ask the wise-man where he obtained this knowledge, he replies: »It is written thus in a book.«

This is the reply one always gets in talking to the wise-men of the hills. Even from the lips of the wild mountain men-at-arms strange words are sometimes heard: apothegms and illusions which could not possibly originate in the brain of a primitive man. They emerge as the precious remains of a forgotten culture; they come unexpectedly into sight as if the veil of the past had suddenly been torn asunder. These things then are all reported to originate in »a book,« and one which apparently nobody has read for himself. This book of wisdom is accessible only to a few. Once every ten years the wise-men of the tribes gather upon the bank of the mountain lake Esan. By night the book appears to them and itself speaks to the assembled men in all languages. It speaks for half an hour only, but that is sufficient for ten years of silence. The Caucasians are still terra incognita to science. Of the dozen languages that have been investigated only a few resemble the other languages of man. The rest stand there isolated. Even the origin of the population is difficult to explain. Moreover, not every race or every language even possesses a name. Many of them, that is, have no word designating »our people,« »our language,« or else they have forgotten that designation or are keeping it concealed. Thus there are some eighty thousand people in one district of Daghestan, who speak a uniform language and have no name. They had to be arbitrarily named Avars by the scholars, though they have nothing in common with the old Avars.

The origin of all these people is not known. Thousands of years ago they must have lived in the steppes of Europe and Asia, and were then perhaps conquered and annihilated by new immigrants, all, that is, but a small residue who were forced back into the mountains. It is probable also that, in the course of the innumerable migrations of peoples which passed over the Caucasus throughout the ages, there remained frag-ments of wanderers here and there in the mountains. And even within the memory of history, certain of the tribes settled themselves in the mountains by force.

In other and far distant parts of the world such as Spain, North Africa, Italy, and the frontierland of China, disappearing tribes are to be found which bear a relationship to the Caucasian mountain folk. And in Syria and Egypt there are remains of an architecture which resembles that of the Caucasus, and in India and Burma too there are customs which are otherwise known only in the mountains between the Black Sea and the Caspian. If the people of the Caucasus, or the mountains and the stones, could speak, a new history of the world would have to be written. Thousands of years of human existence, of extinct culture, and forgotten campaigns repose in the silent features of the mountain folk. They cannot recount nor transmit the things which were seen by the eyes of their ancestors and which were done by the hands of their fore-fathers. The history of man is incomplete. Some of its most mysterious secrets lie buried in this forgotten lumber-room of the past. Just occa-sionally antiquity shines forth in an adage, in an unexplained custom, or an habitual action; incomprehensible this past certainly is to the stranger from without, but none the less alluring and ripe with promise. For there is one thing certain: these illiterates who go about armed to the teeth, these brutish barbarians, are by no means savages, by no means virgin wax upon which Europe can set its imprint. An ancient cul-ture has held sway over many of these races, and it rules over them still.

Thus quite near the primitive and really savage Khevsurs live the Ingushes, whose etiquette and social intercourse are more fully stereo-typed and defined than the ceremonies of the most authentic court of Europe. And the spiritual culture of the Kabardians, for example, shows itself in their every movement, in every step they make, in their fine degree of tactfulness, the composed pride of their ancient princes, and the mild contempt with which they treat their less civilized neigh-bours. It is not easy to discover this culture for, besides knowledge of the languages, connexions within the country, and a general knowledge of Oriental relationships, one must possess above all else good recommendations, without which one can never win the confidence of the hill people. Actually, the lack of recommendations is never felt because everywhere, even to the most remote aul, one is received in the friendliest manner on no other ground but that one is a foreigner. All doors stand open to the guest, everyone puts himself out to serve him. But, nevertheless, he will never perceive the real aspect of his hosts, he will never learn to know their life, their opinions and customs, if he is not recommended beforehand by a prince or a kunak (friend). The mountain people are distrustful and secretive towards Europeans. They have nothing good to expect from that quarter. Yet even to the travellers from the West they will open their doors in welcome, though at the same time they shut up their hearts in suspicion.

It is not often that an illiterate Lesghian is met with in Daghestan, and equally seldom does one meet a literate Nogai Tatar. In the East a literate person is a curiosity—all the more remarkable, therefore, is the eagerness for knowledge of the Lesghians, who, moreover, do not even have a writing of their own. They are Mohammedans, pious Sunnites, and supply the most scholarly mullahs for the entire Caucasus. Wherever ten Lesghians are gathered together, an Arabic school is opened, but for all that they are the most warlike, most piratical, and bravest tribe in the country.

Since these tribes all live in the Caucasus and must organize their method of existence accordingly, it is only to be expected that there should be a certain amount of uniformity. Hospitality and a chivalrous honour are sacred laws everywhere, as are also piety and the warlike spirit. Dress, also, is almost universally similar. All bear weapons of the same form, and all without exception despise people who are not of mountain stock. Common to all, too, is an ineradicable love of liberty and the ability—everywhere and in every phase of life, be it at a European court, an American bank, or the African desert—to hold their own in their own peculiar way and thus win sympathy and friendship.

But their speech, their past, and their customs differ. Their gods and their temples vary, and so do the types of their calm, distinguished features. Ages ago these people were shut out for ever from their first homes, from the scope of some elaborate culture into the dark grey stone walls of the Caucasus, into the land of high mountains, of obscure gorges, and white glaciers, into the land which they defend with proverbial bravery against every invader.

4.

INACCESSIBLE TREASURES

ALI-BEY, MY FOSTER-BROTHER, needed no money; instead he used sheep, and daggers, and horses. It was otherwise with his father, Iskender-Khan; what he wanted were ringing pieces of gold, strings of pearls, and precious stones.

Iskender-Khan was incapable of making money easily. He went at it too simply, made things too hard for himself, and gained far too little by it. Perhaps he did roam the valleys with his companions and fall on the wealthy men who dwelt there, taking away their money, and turning homeward through the villages boasting to his friends, the princes: »See how great a knight I am!« Perhaps he did, or again perhaps he did not. My servant at any rate used to scoff: »Iskender roves about on expeditions starving and hiding, all for two handfuls of gold. By God, thy father in the valley is better off than that. He neither rides nor lies in ambush, nor plunders people; he robs nothing but the earth, and even so he makes more in a day than Iskender-Khan does in a month.« That was what the eunuch said.

We rode through gorges, and through the villages of neighbours. And everywhere the eunuch would say: »Heroes live here; and they are heroes because they are without knowledge. The old wise-men are dead, only Sheikh Jafer is still alive, and even he is silent and will not betray his secret.«

I began slowly to understand what the eunuch meant. The Caucasus is enormously rich. There is really no need to plunder in order to make money. Nobody except a very few people know anything about this wealth, and the people who know can make no use of it.

Once, as I was sitting at the edge of a dried-up stream, I felt something sticky slip through my fingers, something that was like clay and ran from the edge of the little weather-beaten rock into my hand. I played with this bit of clay and squeezed it between my fingers and made a figure out of it. A long-familar, sweet scent greeted my nostrils. At first I paid no attention to it. The scent was only too well known to me; it was the smell of crude oil mixed with clay. But suddenly I started to my feet. I had entirely forgotten that I was not in Baku, not in the oil town where every piece of earth is soaked in oil. I was in Daghestan. Giant mountains lay between me and the nearest oil fields. I examined the spot, and in truth, a small streak of ground oil flowed beneath the stone. I knew the significance of a streak like that. Many a European bank has not money enough to pay for just such a tiny unpretentious trickle. I grew up with oil men, men who live for little trickles like these, and I saw at once that the oil which was flowing out here was genuine crude oil of the most valuable kind, undoubtedly coming up free out of deep layers. This was not the kind of ornamental stuff which is exhausted in a month, but the dead-certain evidence of an inexhaustible permanent spring. I sprang up in excitement, not knowing what was to be done about it. At my feet lay wealth greater than all that Iskender-Khan could loot in his whole life.

»Ali-Bey,« I cried. »Look, Ali-Bey, what I have found.« My foster-brother, who had been in Baku often enough to know what oil meant, came up, but his face remained unmoved. »Oh, that's nothing. Two years ago, when we were digging for water in the next village, an absolute fountain of oil shot up from the earth, it went on for three days, and then the mullah cursed the spot, and the fountain stopped. No one dares go there any more. The hole has been filled up.«

I was dumbfounded. Oil, which I used to think in those days was the most sacred thing in the world, was here being nonchalantly shut off. The eunuch also came over. But he lost no whit of his composure. »There is oil everywhere around here,« he said, »only the people don't know how to exploit it. We must tell the Bey [my father] about it.«

It was indeed not the only place in which I noticed that homely oil smell during my stay in the mountains. By degrees I even became accustomed to smelling oil without getting excited about it. When I told my father at home some months later he only laughed. In his youth he had discovered a great deal of oil in the mountains and had even sent geologists in to make a closer examination of it. The country conceals enormous quantities of ground oil, more perhaps than Baku. But what use is it? The people who live in the mountains will have none of it and stick to their plundering expeditions. And even if one could master them, it would not be of much help. Oil towns could be built and oil could be made to flow out over the rocks to one's heart's content, but there is no way of laying oil pipes through the hills or of building railways, and without these things the richest well is worthless. Oil requires above all else adequate transportation facilities. Railways or pipes, the only things which can make the oil accessible, will presumably not be built in a hurry. It is possible that, when there is no more oil in Baku, it will be necessary to reconquer the Caucasus with this idea in mind. Meanwhile, Caucasian oil is only prospected for along the coast, and the wild Circassians at Grosny on the Caspian Sea have turned out to be model oil operators, the very image of other oil operators the world over.

These oil fields of the future run from the Caspian to the Black Sea through the heart of the mountains. At present the Kabardian princes and the Kumyk petty aristocracy stand guard over them because they hate everything unconnected with the true spirit of chivalry. How long will they keep this up? The smell of oil that is wafted from the hills is all too strong. It is redolent of the richest fields in the world.

Once as we were approaching our aul after a long ride, Ali-Bey suddenly said: »Shall we visit Jafer-Sheikh? He is old and will soon be dead. It is always good to visit old people.« The eunuch agreed eagerly. He too, it seemed, was a friend of old people. We branched off, rode down the glen, and knocked humbly at the Sheikh's saklya. He admitted us. Jafer was no ordinary wise-man; he was a saint in the eyes of the people, and a great sinner, as he himself maintained. His life was an enigma. Years before, when the great Imams ruled the mountains, Jafer fought in the front ranks of the Murids, the holy warriors. After every battle he returned home with a sack full of hands severed from his enemies, and these hands were nailed to the walls of his house. For every hand Jafer received a gold coin from his sovereign. It was the law of the times. Later the Sheikh became Naib-Governor of a province, with power to deal death to tobacco-smokers and the rack to anyone who did not pray five times a day. But at this point the army of the Tsar came into the mountains for the first time, and it was all over with the glory of the Sheikh.

As the Russians pressed victoriously through the mountains, Jafer-Sheikh lay hidden with his men behind some rocks. In the forefront, on a white horse, came His Excellency the General, the new ruler. The Sheikh, perfect marksman that he was, could not miss. The General's minutes were numbered. The rifle shot rang sharply out, and he sank from his saddle without a sound. Off flew the Sheikh to the remotest mountains and valleys, bragging everywhere and saying: »Ten thousand women have I made widows, and as many children are become orphans. Fair is the wife of the General, young are his children, and now they and their Tsar are weeping together. All this have I done.«

Such is the customary boasting of the mountains. But the Russians who came out of the valleys were severe.

»The days when a man can kill a general with impunity are passed,« they said, and set about punishing the mountains. The five villages in which the Sheikh had ruled were surrounded; a new general came and proclaimed that »All five villages shall be razed to the ground, if the people will not pay five hundred thousand roubles within a month.«

The General knew perfectly well that even a hundred Caucasian villages could not possibly raise this sum, and he knew perfectly well that he was going to destroy them. Their population, which now became responsible for its erstwhile master, had to resign itself to its fate. News of the impending calamity was spread everywhere, but the sole cause of it, the Naib, who could save his people by his appearance, was not to be found. Day after day passed. Fuel was on its way from the town to be poured on the houses, and the inhabitants were just about to give up all hope, when suddenly the unexpected happened. A horseman arrived from a great distance with a letter to the General saying: »Your Excellency, the people shall not be permitted to submit to your cruelty because of me. My emissary will satisfy your rapacity.«

The words of the letter sounded improbable, but they were true for all that. The messenger brought three sacks with him. One was filled with uncut diamonds, and the two others with crude placer gold dust. They could not have been looted riches, as they would then have been polished, minted, or moulded. The treasures clearly came direct from the mines. But where the mines lay, no one knew, not even the natives of the district.

Incessant prospecting for diamonds followed this incident. Russians and natives clambered up the trackless heights and struggled against other treasure hunters. The General himself and his whole staff joined the gold-diggers. A veritable gold fever attacked the Russians. But all in vain. Not the slightest trace of gold or jewels was to be found, nothing but worthless mountain crystal, while the diamonds which the Sheikh had sent proved to be genuine precious stones.

The Sheikh then withdrew from the fray, settled in a small saklya in the neighbourhood of our aul, and immersed himself in prayers of repentance. Once he was arrested by the Russians and tortured, but he never betrayed the locality of the fields. All that could be learned from him was that unlimited quantities of diamonds lay in the mountains, but that they were inaccessible. Finally he was left in peace.

And now the Sheikh stood before me. A tall old man, with a beard dyed red, red-stained nails, a brown skin, and large grey eyes. We greeted him and he led us into the guest chamber. Ali-Bey introduced us. When the Sheikh learned that I was the foster-brother of his countryman, he arose and spoke a form of greeting in the Azerbaijan language, concluding it with the strange question: »Hast thou already slain unbelievers?« »No, not yet,« I answered, ashamed. The Sheikh shook his head reproachfully, recited a warlike Arabic verse, and ended up with: »When I was as old as thou art, I had already killed two unbelievers and one blood enemy. It seems to me that the children of today develop very slowly.«

The eunuch now tried to guide the conversation into more peaceful channels. »Most honourable Sheikh,« said he, »we came to thee because of thy fame which is spread through all the mountainland, and we would willingly take home with us a drop of thy wisdom.« This pleased the Sheikh. He spoke about the grim sect of Sikra to which he belonged, about the Tarikat, the holy law of the ancient Murids, about the path of the righteous, which must be strewn with the corpses of enemies and which leads to the heavenly castles where fair boys and maidens, according to one's taste, surround the faithful.

Heavenly castles and fair maidens held absolutely no interest for the eunuch. »Amongst our people at home,« he began, »thou art renowned as the saviour of the five villages which the Russians wanted to burn.« At this the Sheikh's face darkened, and he refused to utter a word on the subject. »It was the one sin of my life, for which I shall do penance.« Then he fell silent. I was told later in the aul that the unknown diamond fields of the old Murids were said to have been found. But the lord of the Murids, Imam Kasi-Mullah, recognized in this wealth a danger to the freedom of the people and above all to the piety of his subjects. He therefore forbade that the fields be disturbed, cursed the treasure, and commanded the few people who knew the position of it to forget it for ever. Jafer-Sheikh was apparently one of the Murids who were initiated into the secret and who had violated the command of the Imam and obtained diamonds and gold but of sympathy for his countrymen who were threatened on his account. This deed gave him qualms of conscience. And for this reason he settled in the valley, offered up prayers, and accepted charity.

A man who has millions at his disposal and lives upon charity is possible nowadays only in Daghestan. It is the firm conviction of the Caucasians that the diamond fields do exist. And in point of fact there are some families that have in their possession rough diamonds and nuggets of gold that bear out the belief. I had, at that time, received a stone, as a gift from a friend, which was seamed with gold, but none of us could trace its history to the source. It faded out into the mountains.

At the present moment the Soviet Government is at pains to discover these treasures. These attempts are certainly not hopeless, since more than half the Caucasus is as yet unexplored by foreigners. The geology of their country is of no interest to the natives, but expeditions into the unknown regions of the mountains are beset with very grave dangers for the Europeans. It is none the less interesting that, when there is great need among the people, there are always persons who crop up suddenly and assist them with sacks full of gold and jewels. The thing also happened once in the middle of the last century when the Circassians wanted to migrate to Turkey and their people had no money for it. It was also the case during the last revolution when the whole of the Caucasus was drenched with blood.

No one likes to talk about these treasures in the hills. It is even considered a slight indiscretion to inquire about it. But still there are people, both Russians and natives, who are in the grip of gold-delirium or diamond-fever and who clamber about in the mountains all their lives, hunting for the treasure. From time to time their corpses are to be found at the bottom of mountain gorges.

I do not know whether there are still men alive in the mountains who know the secret. At least they keep quiet about it and trust nobody. They know what happens if the fields are discovered. The freedom of the mountains is gone for ever, and freedom is more precious to them than diamonds.

Next to gold, jewels, and the oil, the other riches of the hills seem of secondary importance. But, on the other hand, they are simpler to exploit, are protected by no one, and are easy to promote and transport. They would be enough in themselves to make of the Caucasus one of the richest countries in the world. In Darial, on the bank of the Terek, where Queen Tamar built twenty castles to match the number of her generals, there is silver in the soil. The mines have been exploited from ancient times and are not exhausted yet. Sulphur and copper are also obtained from the mountains. When the mountain tribes go to war, they manufacture their own powder and cast their own copper cannon. They thus require no help from unbelievers. Iron and coal come to light in thick veins, as also zinc and valuable medicinal salts. On the summits of the mountains and the bottoms of the dried-up lakes, iodine is to be obtained, quantities of iodine for which the world is still thirsty. Health-giving springs flow from the mountain's edge near Besh-Tau and Zkhra-Zharo where every sickness can be cured, even including love-sickness.

The Caucasian sets no store by wealth; the number of his relatives is of far greater concern to him. No money can protect him from blood vengeance, nor can it avenge a murder. When the Caucasian needs money or jewels, he simply rides down the mountains and plunders the cowardly people of the valley.

There is also buried treasure in the Caucasus, the treasure of the old Sultans. It is mentioned in legends, and for that reason I refrain from reporting about it. In talking of the wealth of the mountains, there is no need to quote legendary tales. In this connexion facts are more convincing than stories. I will only repeat one which is more than a legend and upon which official material is extant. That is the story of the treasure in the Lake of Esan.

The Caucasus—unlike other mountainous places—is poor in lakes. For this reason they are much revered. The holiest is the Lake of Esan, on whose shore the wise-men of the tribes foregather.

Many years ago when Shamil the saint was fighting against the Russians, his treasure house stood by the Lake of Esan. For thirty years Shamil fought and for thirty years he was sole ruler in Daghestan. His treasures grew to be immeasurable. Then he noticed suddenly that men served him not for Allah's sake but for the sake of money. So he assembled his chamberlains and governors and generals and courtiers on the border of the lake and spoke to them of God and his eternal laws. When he had finished, Russian prisoners were made to bring forth the great chests from the treasure house. One chest after another was thrown into the lake, a hundred of gold and polished stones, and three hundred of silver. The Imam and his generals looked on, praying and cursing the riches. Shamil became absolutely poor. Poor and confident, for he knew now that his people would not serve him for the sake of money. Later on, when he was conquered by the Russians, the Tsar had to pay him a pension; otherwise he would have starved—he, Shamil, the saint and wealthy autocrat. To this day, his treasure lies on the bed of the lake. The natives cannot lift it up, and they admit no foreigner to the lake-side.

5.

THE NAKED CITY

EVERY EVENING, when the sun went down and the cattle came back into the aul, I went into the mosque. Not merely to pray—though I never failed to do that also— but because the court of the mosque is the substitute of the clubroom throughout Daghestan in all the villages and towns, and constitutes the centre of the life of the mind. If you come to a village and know nobody, you simply go to the mosque courtyard and introduce yourself to the oldest person present. At once people flock around you offering unlimited hospitality. In any case, it is worth while strolling round the court. The Abreks come there after successful raids to tell all about their latest deeds, and it is also the place where one may soonest learn the news of the country, the towns, and the whole Orient generally. But it is most interesting when the courtyard begins to get empty, when the circle of those who remain becomes more intimate, and problems are openly discussed over which the government in the town may perhaps be cudgelling its brains. In these quiet evening hours the maddest adventures and the craftiest tricks are picturesquely gone over, so that the young men may learn something useful, and the old men may die in peace in the knowledge that they leave worthy successors behind them.

The most famous story that was current throughout the mountains in my day, and which was most admired, was the surprise attack on Kislar, a modern city with banks and post-offices, three-story houses, wealthy businesses, and with police and an entire regiment of soldiers as a permanent garrison. To the Government in Makhach-Kala, the capital of Daghestan, the whole trick was a mystery; treachery was assumed, but no one knew where to look for the guilty parties. Even in the hills nothing precise was known about the circumstances of the case; people were just pleased about the »great event.« Not till weeks later, when the adventurers reappeared in the mountains, was it possible, in the courtyard of the mosque, to hear the whole course of the affair from them under pledge of secrecy. Fate was especially kind to us in that the ringleader of the adventure was from our village and one of the most intimate friends of Iskender-Khan. He gave us a straightforward account of the details of his undertaking without all the usual boasting (which was superfluous in the nature of things). I shall try to repeat the story here as I heard it.

One day the news reached Kislar that the year's budget for Daghestan would be brought from Russia under a strong convoy. The money was to lie for some days in Kislar and then be transported on to Makhach-Kala with a reinforced guard. The protection of the money—certainly no easy task in Daghestan—was entrusted to the commander of the native and governmental troops garrisoned in Kislar. Its actual transportation was therefore assured, and even an unexpected attack on the part of the mountain tribes would scarcely have discountenanced troops several hundred strong. The money arrived in Kislar according to schedule and was turned over to the military authorities, who at once began to prepare for the expedition to Makhach-Kala. Money transports of this nature are not unusual in the Caucasus. It is generally understood that transport between towns which are not connected by rail is undertaken by the military. Usually a small protecting patrol is enough to cover the distance in complete safety. Moreover, all this was taking place in a period of the profoundest peace, when for years the matter of convoys for the transport of money had been purely formal. There was consequently not the slightest occasion for uneasiness. Private money transports had long discarded special protection, without ever being attacked. Both towns—Makhach-Kala as well as Kislar— were almost completely European, and the inhabitants smiled pleasantly when visitors from Europe asked about the wild bands of robbers. For hundreds of years Kislar had not even heard a shot fired, except for the shots at the monthly military balls. It is only in the Orient that such contrasts are to be found—a European town, peaceful and modern, and within a bare six hours' journey the twilight of medieval-ism, the untouched Orient, ignored and apparently forgotten by every-one. Just such a pleasant town was Kislar in the neighbourhood of the mountains, indeed almost a town of luxury, and the pride of the Euro-peans who lived there.

Shortly before the arrival of the money the Colonel received an anonymous letter by mail, in which it was written that a numerous and newly formed band had determined to attack the transport. Every detail of the proposed attack was set down in the letter with a minute-ness which precluded all idea of a practical joke. Two days after the arrival of the letter, a distinguished native prince visited the Colonel and informed him excitedly that his friends in the mountains had also heard about the coming venture and reported preparations on a grand scale. The Colonel became thoughtful. But when on the next day there again arrived an anonymous letter, he telegraphed to Makhach-Kala for instructions. They arrived immediately.

It happened that similar rumours were being circulated there, and the Government ordered the strictest measures to be adopted for the safety of the money. Disquieting news arrived every two hours from the hills, and pretty soon suspicious-looking horsemen were to be seen watching the road, and before long it was being said that the robber band constituted a complete army with machine guns, cannon, and so forth. The excitement grew. Bets were made in the town as to whether the money would be stolen or not, and the Colonel got more and more anxious every hour. Finally, for the sake of greater security on the road, he decided to undertake the journey to Mackhach-Kala, not merely with a reinforced escort, but with the entire soldiery at his disposal, Russians, natives, police, militia, and voluntary cavalry. A crowd of enterprising inhabitants also offered themselves as volunteers. Thus the peaceful money transport took on the proportions of an impressive military expedition.

Before the departure the Colonel made a pompous speech: »We shall show the bandits,« he thundered, »that we are up to any danger! Any hold-up is now a lunatic undertaking. Woe to him who has still failed to grasp this fact!« The audience shouted their huzzahs and drank champagne as the dangerous expedition started.

The journey, which normally took twenty-four hours, lasted four days. The several thousand men, who all had to be provided for, called a halt in every town, in order to parade their uncommon military strength before the eyes of the peaceful citizenry, so that the news might reach the mountains and the raiding party be frightened away by their determination. As it happened, the intimidated band did not show itself; the expedition passed off peacefully and uneventfully. »They are afraid, the scoundrels,« murmured the Colonel, for in his heart of hearts he had rather hoped to march victoriously over the hills and into Makhach-Kala after a small and successful skirmish. But unfortunately nothing of the sort occurred. The army rode into Makhach-Kala after four days, where it was royally received, and the Colonel, in all seriousness, permitted a celebration in his honour as the mighty victor. He telegraphed his arrival to Kislar and received a telegram of congratulation in reply. He was as radiant at this juncture as a child on its birthday. The dangerous expedition had thus drawn to a successful close; the army remained a few days more in Makhach-Kala; to recover from the fatigue of the journey; the commander-in-chief held a review; and the mountains were entirely forgotten for a while.

But in the meantime the following had occurred: When the army left Kislar with the money, the population turned back to its daily work and tensely awaited news from the scene of war. It was not long in coming. On the evening of the same day small clouds were to be seen on the horizon. They soon became bigger, and the people living on the edge of the town perceived dozens of peasant wagons harnessed to oxen approaching the town at an easy pace. On the wagons were seated ragged-looking figures who resembled from a distance market trades-men, or mountain peasants. The carts came calmly in, drove as far as the big town square, and made a halt. The drivers answered no questions; they got out of their conveyances with deliberation and set genially to work cleaning up the big shops in the square and loading their contents into the wagons. The astonished citizens, who supposed there was a misunderstanding of some kind, attempted to restrain them, but they soon gave it up. The ringleader of the intruders climbed onto a cart and explained, briefly and pointedly: »The town belongs to us! We shall take whatever we please away with us!«

And that was that. The ten policemen, who had remained in the town, were disarmed with lightning speed, the post-office occupied, and the great raid was thoroughly and systematically continued. Unhurryingly the new masters of the situation went nosing through one house after another, broke into the banks, and emptied the tills. Every inhabitant of the town was seized, seen to his home, and forced to give up everything he possessed in the way of money and valuables. Finally he was undressed and left stark naked between his own four walls to prevent him from interfering with the work elsewhere. Every scrap of clothing was sedulously removed, and the new arrivals were thus able to celebrate an entirely bloodless victory. Four days were time enough in which to carry off everything that seemed desirable in the town, by means of the wagons which kept going back and forth. The inhabitants, who were frightened to death, made no attempt to offer any sort of resistance, or even to escape from the town, notwithstanding their complete nakedness, and bring help. The customary methods of the hill people in such matters were only too well known to them. The mere sight of the raiders, armed to the teeth, made it clear that they were dealing with genuine Abreks, and the inhabitants had every reason to be glad that they had at least got out of it alive. Furthermore, the robbers behaved relatively decently: none of the women was violated or abducted and not one single Russian was shot. As for rape, there was a lot of violent discussion about that afterwards. Nobody would believe the women, who had also been robbed of their clothes, when they declared that they were still un-smirched, although the robbers had fixed a poster to that effect on the town hall. When finally the telegram from the Colonel in Makhach-Kala came through on the fourth day, announcing his fortunate arrival, the raiders wired him, in the name of the inhabitants, conveying with supreme humour their most heartfelt and grateful congratulations. Upon which they began to withdraw with the rest of their booty in as leisurely a manner as they had come. The naked city breathed again. But when the Colonel marched into the town again with his army, he found the city fathers »gone native,« sitting in the post-office wrapped up in straw, trying in vain to substitute some kind of device for the stolen telegraphic apparatus.

The scandal which this story occasioned was terrific. The Colonel was cashiered on the spot, as well as all the disarmed policemen. The Government blustered; the papers were forbidden to write about the incident; and numerous punitive expeditions were sent out to roam about the mountains long and fruitlessly. Of the stolen goods and money not the slightest sign was ever discovered. The people in the mountains had experienced advisers this time, and they knew how to cover up every vestige of evidence.

Who these advisers were nobody in the town had any idea, and nobody in the mountains had any very exact knowledge either. The full truth was probably known at that time only by the ringleader, who told us the story in the courtyard of the mosque. But not until years afterwards did it become universally known.

Some months after this raid, there was an outbreak of bomb-throwing in Russia; hundreds of secret presses printed appeals to the workers; and the Tsarist police were suddenly overcrowded with work. The reason for the activity of the »criminal element« could not be fathomed by anyone. The seal that the mountain leader had put under the poster in Kislar was known only to a few people. The leader himself did not know what it meant. He could not even read.

In the courtyard of the mosque, under the pale light of the moon, he handed me a small round object, and I bent over its engraved surface and deciphered the words: »The Caucasian Communist Activist-Terrorist Group, Mountain District.« »The man who gave me this thing,« said the leader, »received half the booty; the idea was his and many other things—he is a great man.« At that time I was not interested in the »great man« and I did not even know what the term »Activist-Terrorist« meant. I gave the seal back to the leader and listened to the deep-chested robber song which he began to sing. The song was the leader's own and was dedicated to the great man who had given him the seal as a talisman against the Russians.

I know now, indeed many people know, who the man was. His name was Kamo, and he was an Armenian from Tiflis, a reserved wild animal of a man, who could barely read, hated everybody and everything, and had spent most of his life in prisons. Kamo only called one man friend, a Georgian who travelled about from place to place, and conducted conspiracies even when he was in jail. Kamo dedicated his life to this Georgian, just as the Georgian dedicated his life to another great man who lived at the world's end, but also in the mountains, to wit at Zürich. The latter was seldom heard from and merely sent laconic letters from time to time with the dry device, »Instruction.«

For some little time this Georgian had been worried, for the great man in Zurich sat there penniless, and his mighty work faltered. Kamo could not watch his friend suffer.

»Kamo will help,« said he, and set forth into the mountains. The Georgian also was not inactive; the great plan, which the man in Zurich had to accept, originated with him. Only the leaders of the plan were looked after by Kamo. And these leaders were honest to the core; they shared the booty like brothers; and for a while the faces of the men in Georgia and Zürich were free from care. The presses could set to work again; pyroxylin could again be brought across the frontier to prepare for the Day of Days. Kamo, the Armenian, is dead now; he died a ridiculous death, for he was run over by a street-car in Tiflis as he was hurrying over the square into the Palace to congratulate his friend the Georgian who was in possession as ruler. The great man from Zürich is dead also. Only the Georgian is alive and rules now over one-sixth of the world. Stalin is the Georgian's name, and Lenin was the name of the man in Zürich who accepted the plan.

That is just one of those stories that one comes to hear on moonlight nights in the courtyard of the mosque, as a model for the future guidance of young men. The people of the hills knew nothing at that time of the two great men, and indeed they know little enough about

41

them now. And they know still less what a significant part they played in the antecedent history of the greatest of all revolutions, by making it possible for the great men to continue their work. The hill folk are simple folk, upright and warlike.

In the mountains the girls sing: »If thou comest back, craven, from a raid, I will drive thee out.«

»If thou diest like a hero in the raid, then I am glad,« sing the mothers. And the heroes themselves sing: »What honour and understanding have we if our loved ones drive us out?« Thus they sing and become Abreks, mountain robbers, the most honoured caste of the Caucasus.

»The Abrek lives like an animal, and is exalted like an angel,« runs a proverb of the hills. Many families even look upon it as a kind of deficiency if there is no Abrek among their number. I have seen many of these Abreks. There are princes and peasants among them from every district of the Caucasus. They are all of them lovable and boastful. They are enthusiastic about their profession and hate all authority. They are knights, real knights, and, even if they are robber knights, they still remain the last that are left in the world.

And they are withal cheerful, and laugh and joke in the thick of the fray, betwixt death and flight. They seek danger for danger's sake and they steal to give to their wives. They are proud, and no one may compare himself with them, except possibly the priest, to whom God is made manifest. An Abrek never feels himself lost; he knows how to look after himself in any situation; he may never despair; and he never will.

Sami-Aga was the name of the greatest Abrek I knew. He was of gigantic stature, had a black pointed beard, and hands which any pianist might have envied.

6.

THE CAUCASIAN SCIMITAR

THE STORY OF THE KNIGHT SAMI-AGA, the great warrior and the still greater robber, deserves to be told here. He is a characteristic figure of the mountain country, a magnificent example of the disappearing breed of »Jighit,« an adventurer and feudalist. When I saw him for the first time, he was lying on his stomach at the entrance to his citadel drinking red Kakhetian wine out of a sheepskin sack. He could drink this wine by the hour, without getting drunk. He despised the base custom which prescribes the use of glasses for drinking. At the outside he would so far lower himself as to use a gigantic horn.

Whenever he happened not to be drinking or dancing, he was hatching one of his notorious raids, at which he was superior to everybody. Or else he was yearning for the gold-embroidered uniform of an aide-de-camp to His Majesty, the bestowal of which seemed to him the natural climax to his career. Only the winter and a part of the summer was spent by him in his medieval citadel in the neighbourhood of Kasbek; the rest of the time he devoted to his »work,« which consisted in plundering the Russian mails to Georgia every now and then and imposing a tribute on the merchants and caravans on the far side of the mountains.

He was kindly disposed to me from the outset, because I always exhibited a profound respect for him, which he for his part considered perfectly natural and only his due. He often used to tell me of the various heroic deeds which other warriors had achieved, but he wrapped himself in silence when I asked him about his own. His fame and the legends which surrounded him were enough for him. But his deeds of heroism and his victories availed him little when the fiery glow of the revolution lighted up the mountains three years later. He had the ill-luck to kill a Communist Commissar somewhere or other, without

43

meaning any harm, and was therefore raised by the Bolsheviks to the rank of »Shark of the Daghestan Stock Exchange« and as such honoured with a special campaign. Yes, indeed, the Daghestan stock exchange! There was no such thing, of course, but the indictment was so worded, and it sounded quite marvellous.

For the sake of peace, and by way of re-establishing the political equilibrium, Sami killed a general of the White Army, upon which the Whites in their turn decried him as »the Red Executioner of Daghestan« and also treated him to a punitive expedition.

Completely compromised, Sami-Aga now tried to organize a movement for liberty in the mountains and to found a republic, but was forced to the conclusion that all the tribes were disposed to be either Red or White and had very little use for the green flag of the prophet. So there was nothing left for Sami to do but to leave his citadel, which had become insecure, and migrate to Constantinople in all haste, where he scented a suitable sphere of operations for his talents. But unfortunately he also arrived a little late here, because, when he reached the city of the Caliph, the English occupation had already begun, and everyone professing loyalty to the Caliph seemed especially under suspicion, particularly when this loyalty was incorporated in the ill-famed figure of the »Red Executioner« and notorious Communist agent, as the emigre newspapers put it.

I met Sami in Constantinople on the Galata Bridge, in his sumptuous Circassian clothes, with a magnificent gold-sheathed scimitar, enthusiastically clamant, in his capacity as newspaperboy, over the emigre newspaper which calumniated him. I bought a copy. He recognized me at once. »Why don't you sell your sword?« I asked. »It is surely better to have a full stomach and no sword, than to have a sword and sell newspapers!«

Sami only smiled. No, he didn't want to sell the scimitar. The money was too quickly spent; he would be in low water again too soon afterwards. He had decided to turn his back on the Orient, where people couldn't appreciate him, and emigrate to South America. And it was for that very reason that he needed his sword.

»What will you do in South America?« I asked in astonishment.

»I shall sell the sword there, acquire some land, and teach the true principles of knighthood to the savages.«

And that was just what did happen. One night, in a quiet and dark harbour street, Sami assaulted the editor of the emigre paper, robbed him, and the next day took passage on a huge ocean liner. And the vanishing horizons of the sea swallowed him up.

For years I heard nothing more from him. Even his countrymen— who were starving on the streets of Stamboul, armed with sword and dagger, striving to foster among the timid inhabitants memories of past glories and the blue ranges of the Caucasus with their nappy robber tribes—even they knew nothing of his fate.

Ten years later I met him again. In a café this time on the Potsdamer Platz in Berlin. To be sure, he was no longer in Circassian dress, and he had no scimitar either, but was equipped with an elegant, brightly checked lounge suit, a mathematically exact hair parting, and a fourseater Mercedes car. His chauffeur bore one of the proudest names in old Russia. He waved to me joyfully with his canary-yellow gloves, embraced me effusively, and recounted without much ado the fantastic story of his career, or, as he expressed himself, »of his recognition in the Wild West.« His ascent, only possible to a wild Caucasian among equally wild South Americans, took place as follows:

At the custom-house of the South American Republic which he had chosen, Sami was held up. His scimitar caused a sensation, first, because the introduction of weapons into the Republic was forbidden, and, secondly, because there was a specially high duty to pay on gold objects. Sami put the sword to one side, sat himself down in the official's seat, and began arguing with the South Americans over various questions of international customs laws. After half an hour he suddenly discovered that his sword has disappeared during the discussion. And with it, of course, the future hacienda and the leading part in the political life of South America. Daghestan warriors are apt to be temperamental under such circumstances and inclined to fits of temper. Sami got up in a fury, banged the table with his fist, and yelled with the full force of his Caucasian throat: »You scoundrels, I am Sami, the hero of Daghestan. The people of my home commissioned me to give this scimitar to your renowned President in recognition of his deeds of heroism. In my country warriors are esteemed, but here the gifts of honour are stolen. If I do not get the scimitar back immediately, I will inform the Prime Minister and you are all of you lost men!«

These words were effective. The sword was found, and an hour later Sami was travelling in the Pullman car of an express train to the residence of the South American hero. There was now nothing for it but to hand over his invaluable and beloved scimitar to the President (who was deeply moved by this high honour) and to postpone for the present the acquisition of the much longed-for hacienda.

The President knew what he owed to the emissary of the knighthood of the Caucasus. For two months Sami lived as a guest in the President's palace; he made a dignified appearance at balls which were given in his honour; and he talked a lot about the glory which the President (who was cordially hated in his own country) enjoyed in Daghestan. Then, after two months, Sami was unexpectedly, and in spite of all the President's enemies, appointed General of the National Guard, and was shortly afterwards entrusted with the personal protection of the President himself. Today Sami-Aga is chief of the general staff and the military right-hand man of the President.

He was staying in Germany to study the latest achievements of the Prussian police, so as to introduce such of them as were useful into his country.

The knight of the Caucasus had won back his place in the sun. The singular part about this story is that to the honest Sami himself this career seemed the most natural thing in the world. For a Daghestan warrior it is after all not such a far cry from a baronial stronghold in the Caucasus, via newsvending in Constantinople, to the palace of a South American President. The people of the mountains have done far more wonderful things than that.

»Was the sword an heirloom?« I inquired, after Sami had concluded his story. »Heirloom?« he asked in astonishment. »No, I found it in a house.« »What sort of a house?« »Oh! we were raiding a village, and there in a house sat some fellow or other whom I killed and from whom I took the sword. It's hanging in a museum now.« And with a happy grin Sami offered me a cigarette from a gold case.

That is the story of Sami-Aga, the great hero. It is not the only one of its kind. After the great change at the end of the war, thousands of warriors fled from the Caucasus. Unlike their Russian colleagues they became neither waiters nor dancing partners. An ineradicable feeling for palaces and staffs is in their blood. In Europe, Asia, and Africa, wherever palaces, soldiers and battles still exist, brown Caucasians are to be found, tall figures, with flashing eyes, aristocratic features, and elastic movements. They flatter those who are in power, make love to their daughters, and shed their own blood recklessly in desert, mountain, or fortress, wherever there is need of a brave warrior.

Why do they do it? »It is shame for a warrior to die in bed,« so runs a proverb in the hills. And again: »It is a joy to shed blood.« Men who are still able to say such things have not yet heard of the word, »inhibition.«

7.

THE MASTER OF FRAGRANCE

NOT EVERYONE IN DAGHESTAN is a robber or a warrior. On the peaks of inaccessible mountains, in the auls and in the still existing strongholds of the knights, live priests, scribes, exorcists, and even artists, who are here, as in the East generally, regarded as the especial favourites of Allah. Not merely the poet, the painter, and the singer are artists in the mountains; in forgotten waste regions, in dirty little hovels, there is to be found another special variety of artists, who would scarcely even be recognized as such in Europe, which knows nothing of them, though theirs is nevertheless the last survival of a very ancient human craft.

The last remaining masters of this disappearing art neither write books, make music, nor fear critics. They live withdrawn in their secret workrooms and pursue their practices in Daghestan, Constantinople, and Persia. Theirs is the noble task of making mankind smell beautifully. And it is not an easy one, so at least I was assured by one of the greatest masters of perfumery in Daghestan, who was thinking sadly of the days when there were still people with a nice understanding of his art. This expert, who was now out of work, and living as the guest of a Lesghian Maecenas, told me (because I was modest, polite, and eager for knowledge) all about the basic rules of his craft as they were ultimately observed only at the court of the bloody Abdul-Hamid, in his palace of Ildis-Kösk at Stamboul on the Bosphorus.

It is the business of the Master of Fragrance to discover and manufacture the right perfume for everybody, and above all for every woman. The hairdresser looks after this in Europe or Monsieur Coty in Paris. Still these people are mere cobblers and sellers of factory-made articles, who allow thousands of women to go about, rightly or wrongly,

48

smelling the same way. The Master of Fragrance thought this was a piece of colossal barbarism. No woman was like the next one; consequently her particular personality had to be marked by a scent which belonged only to her.

Whenever a new girl was brought to the harem of Abdul-Hamid, to the Flower Palace of the Shah, or to the mountain stronghold of the Shamkhal of Daghestan, she must first, before even she was seen by the ruler, appear before the Master of Fragrance, who was the only man allowed to confer alone with her. The Master asked the girl about her origin, her habits and upbringing; made her dance, eat, and sing; looked her over from all sides; asked a thousand other questions, and then retired, with heavily knitted brows, into his laboratory.

He then set to work, frequently for weeks at a time, to produce a few drops of sweet-smelling essence, which should distinguish the girl from all other women for ever after. The object of this perfume was to bring out the hidden characteristics of the woman and either complete or conceal her physical peculiarities, just as the inspiration of the Master, or the laws of the perfumer's art, dictated. A wild Lesghian girl would be given a coarse, sharp-smelling scent, while an over-cultured princess would receive a soft, sweet scent, or else, by way of contrast to her gentleness, a markedly strong perfume. The determining quality was the general impression given by the girl, her figure, her walk, her movements, all of which inspired the creative spirit of the Master. Often, if the lady possessed any special characteristics, experienced eunuchs would be called in for their opinion, and in particularly difficult cases, such as for instance that of a European woman, the ruler himself would be roused from his exalted calm. The girl is thus always distinguished first of all by a perfume, and then sent on to the hair and cosmetic artists, whence she goes to receive the last touch from the eunuchs in charge of jewellery and dresses. A pretty girl, in the eyes of the Master of Fragrance, is the raw material of the harem lady, supplied to him by nature, a valuable material, in the refinement of which he plays the decisive role. Clothes, jewellery, and even cosmetics are merely details to his way of thinking, especially clothes, which he may be said to regard as temporary wrappings for his work of art. The only thing that matters to him is the correct scent which the lord shall perceive in his hours of pleasure. If he has done his task well, the lord in his joy will stuff his pockets heavy with gold on the next day.

The use of scent, which originates in the East, is an established custom of cultured mankind. Nowhere was it better looked after than in the laboratories of the old masters.

Another branch of the same art is the perfuming of men. In this case other rules are observed. The warrior has to possess a perfume which makes him courageous and confuses his enemies, and for this purpose perfumes made of garlic and other strong-smelling substances were manufactured by the general staff of the mountain warriors and handed out to each fighter individually. They smeared their bodies and faces with this stuff just before the battle, and the Master maintained that this narcotic acted as a drug to fear upon those who carried it and confused the senses of their opponents. But, nevertheless, the manufacture of war scent was a less respected activity of the Master. Women were much more important to him; it was to them that his real creative genius was of first importance.

Women and soldiers are mortal. They are easily forgotten. After their swift death there is nothing to proclaim the high skill of the artist. But a true genius creates for all eternity, and it is for this reason that the Master of Fragrance dedicates his most exalted hours to books, which have to be treated like women. A book must also carry a scent, for its contents are not always enough by themselves to intoxicate the reader. The author, the illustrator, the calligrapher, and the Master of Fragrance, all play an equal part in its development. It is by no means an easy task to find the right scent for a book. The Master looks through a new publication devoutly, meditates, searches the works of old masters, confers with the author and illustrator, and demands occasionally that corrections be made.

A book is far more important than a woman. It proclaims the art of the author and of the perfumer to all eternity. Its scent belongs to it and must harmonize with the contents, the binding, and the writing. It must not have a distracting effect but should rather interpret the contents in its own way.

»A book must have a scent,« a master of perfumery once said to me. »Old, finely written theses must exhale an enlivening aroma, so that the exhausted reader shall not fall asleep at his work, but give thanks to the memory of the Master.«

Today this art has died out; women and books no longer distil a perfume of their inner selves. Their conservative possessors dream only occasionally of the glorious times of the wise calligraphers and eunuchs and master perfumers.

And where are these masters now? The last of them live scattered about Turkey, in Persia, or in the strongholds of Daghestan. They tell fairy tales, which no one any longer really believes, and they despise the manufacturer Coty for having annihilated an exalted art.

8.

LOVE

THE LOVE OF AN ORIENTAL is timid and unobtrusive. The European says: »He knows nothing about love. He can buy his woman; she is nothing but a beast of burden to him, an animal that he doesn't even see before his marriage. How can he possibly love her? There is no love in the East.«

The European is quite justified: he comes East in padded luxury and visits the kind of pleasure haunt in which the women carry a price card round their necks; he sees veiled wives who were won in financial transactions by the men; he never hears a word about love-making or love-sickness; he never sees men looking to their wives, or wives solicitous of their husbands. Never a love scene does he witness, nor fond caresses and tender protestations, nor tears nor kisses. The women all appear veiled, and, if you ask a man about his wife's health, he replies curtly and briefly with a »What can you expect? She's tough enough, the brute.« So the Westerner thinks that love is unknown to the Oriental, and that at best he is merely capable of a sort of debased sensuality.

He is much mistaken. There is such a thing as love in the Orient. Its manifestations are more manifold and subtler than that of the European and are as completely concealed from the Occidental as the Kaaba is at Mecca. The Westerner cannot come to grips with it, and therefore he does not believe in it. Or does he perhaps not wish to believe in it? Perhaps he is also unaware that every Oriental who comes to the West in the padded luxury of an express train likewise affirms that »there is no love in the Occident, but only a sort of sensuality.« The gulf that separates the love of the East from that of the West is too wide, the burning of the flame is too conspicuously different.

In the East there is a universal love ritual whose symbols are understood by everybody. From Morocco to the gates of China people fall in love in the same way, make love in the same way, and even declare their ardour with the same uniformity; everywhere it is so done, on the street, on a visit, in a garden, or at a festival. Everyone observes the signs of love and understands them. Only to the stranger who may happen to be present are they incomprehensible.

Actually this old way of doing things is slowly dying out. The West is beginning to obtain an ascendancy. The complete observance of the old customs, and the old love scenes, are only to be met with nowadays in a few districts. But they live yet in North Africa, in Turkestan, in the oases of Persia, and most especially in the Caucasian hills, where everything is preserved, and the adoption of the slightest thing from the West is avoided.

The Oriental love affair begins at the well, the small village well or the great splashing city fountain. It begins quite unromantically. The girls go to the well every evening with pitchers on their shoulders, alone and unaccompanied by eunuchs or older women. Their elders are fully aware that it is at the well that a love affair begins. Not far off, the young men sit in a circle and ignore the girls completely as they pass by. They discuss war and rapine or tell comic stories or the gossip of the day. The girls fill their pitchers slowly, and go slowly back, for they have good cause to linger. The pitcher is heavy and filled to the brim with water. In order not to stumble, they throw back their veils and cast down their eyes modestly. Every evening they do this, and every evening the young men sit at the end of the square and chat of war and peace. Accidentally perhaps, quite accidentally, one of the girls may lift up her eyes and cast a glance in the direction of the men. They pay no attention whatever. But when the girls come back again one of the men turns round and looks up at the sky. Often his glance meets that of the girl, or equally often it does not, in which case another man takes his place on the next day and tries his luck also. After glances have passed between two persons several times, everybody knows what it means, and what is coming.

Three courses are now open to the man. Either he sends old and respectable people to see the girl's father and to hand over her price, or else he goes off on a thieving expedition to acquire a lot of money. But if he does not want to do either of these things and his love is unbridled, then he kidnaps the girl, escapes at top speed before he can be caught by her father, and places himself under the protection of the prince of the land.

This accordance of protection is regarded by the prince as an honour to himself; he is under an obligation to protect the refugees, to house them, and to go to the house of the parents as soon as their wrath has died down a little, to plead for the man as he would for his own son.

There is also a fourth method, which he uses if the girl refuses to exchange glances with him. But that I shall leave until later.

A young man does not put his decision to the test immediately. A purely ocular understanding between lovers, even if it lasts for months, is not enough to justify the opening of negotiations. It merely establishes the first slender link—a mute agreement which must be carefully advanced.

On visits, at festivals and weddings, the young people of the village (men and unveiled girls) sit separated in different corners of the room. Yet, even here they do not talk except with their eyes. But presently the dancing starts. First of all the men perform a war dance, and later the girls get up and show their graces.

Then all at once a young man will step out and have the mountain dance played. He advances towards the row of girls, dances past them for a while, and then stops and bows before the lady of his choice, with whom he has previously come to an understanding in the silent language of lovers. And now the famous Caucasian love dance begins; it is erotic, fiery, subtle, and warlike, indescribably wild and expressive. Only one couple may dance at a time, the others must wait until their turn comes.

At dances, on visits, or at the well, and indeed on all festive occasions, the pair may never speak to each other. They don't need to; what is there to say to a lover when a hundred ears are listening? It is better to keep quiet. There are quite enough silent ways of agreement.

On hot days, when the village is dead, the couple meets upon the street, or in the evening in the garden when all is asleep. For weeks on end at the same time of night the lover seeks out a quiet and lonely spot where he sits hour after hour, waiting for his lady. Sometime or other she will find out where he is waiting for her and will steal forth to meet him. When at last she does come, she sits down at some distance from him, and their talk begins. It has to be figurative in form; the man has to tell a fable or any kind of a story which expresses his desires by innuendo. But his words must sound completely harmless in order that nobody who may be eavesdropping can possibly spread any unkind gossip about them afterwards.

This conversation is the last stage of courtship. After it comes the proposal of marriage and the complicated, prolonged ceremonies of an Oriental wedding.

In the Caucasus a wedding takes place as follows. First of all the *kalym*, or bridal money, must be settled, that is to say, the price which the man has to pay the parents of his bride. It is this practice which gives Europeans the idea that the woman is being auctioned off like a domestic animal, but one may observe without impertinence that the habit is more easily defensible than the merchandising of the man in Europe, which is the way the Oriental would describe the practice of the bridal dowry.

To the Oriental way of thinking the child is the property of the father, so that when he gives away his property he must be correspondingly rewarded. The height of the prices has always varied very considerably and is in direct proportion to the wealth of the man and the beauty of the woman. It is only recently that the due was finally standardized by the government of the Republic of Daghestan. The law which deals with it is very long, involves a myriad small points, and was completed by a special commission of experts and clergy after exhaustive study. According to this law, girls were divided into several groups, ugly, average, beautiful, very beautiful, and exceptionally beautiful. And also into virgin, semi-virgin, and no longer virgin. The classification of a girl is decided upon by the committee of experts and endorsed by the authorities. The price varies from one hundred and twenty-five to five hundred dollars for virgins to a few cents, nominal charge for those no longer virgin. The lowest price for a virgin is a hundred and twenty-five dollars, that being the amount that is needed in the opinion of special-ists to educate and look after a girl until she is old enough to get mar-ried. Everything above that is considered as an extra bonus for beauty; the former bonus for girls of good family has now been done away with by the democratic government. Payment by instalments has always been permitted. The negotiations about the price are carried on by rep-resentatives of the bridegroom, and the refusal of an official offer of marriage is regarded as an unheard-of insult; though the father is at lib-erty to demand a fabulously high and exorbitant kalym, thus refusing the offer without social indiscretion.

When the kalym has been decided upon, the wedding celebrations begin, and the whole village takes part in them. The feast lasts for weeks together, but neither the bride nor the bridegroom are present at it. Shortly before the wedding, the bridegroom withdraws to the house of some friend, lives there in seclusion, receives nobody, and abandons him-self to dreams of love. At night, when there is none to see (though every-body knows about it), the bride visits him and passes a few hours with him. The elders allow this in order that both of them may be sure, before they even get married, that they can get along all right together, and that they are not making a mistake. At these meetings a third person is always in the next room watching them and ready, in case of need, to break up the meeting. Companionate marriage is unknown in the mountains.

A few days before the wedding these meetings cease. The woman has much to do, and the dowry must be made ready. This consists of gold, apparel, and jewels, which she presents to the relatives of the man on the day of the wedding. Every relative receives a present and must respond in the same way. The presents given by the relatives belong to the woman, but the most expensive of them all is the one the man must give her. The value of it is fixed beforehand, is payable after the wedding, and may also be made by instalments. The woman may, a few days after the wedding is over and in the presence of the wedding witnesses, renounce the payment of this present. This is considered as a special mark of affection for the man, since the gift is supposed to be a recompense for the pains which await the woman during the first few nights. Widows, and women who are no longer virgins, are not entitled to it.

On the day before the wedding, that is to say, the day before the bridal night, the couple do not see each other. The Oriental thinks that it is harmful to the man to see his bride on the day of the wedding. It is said that his virility may desert him at the decisive instant. The bride, heavily veiled, is fetched by the armed friends of the bridegroom and waits for him in the festal chamber. Here they are separated only by a thin curtain, hanging from the ceiling, and their little fingers are linked together while the mullah asks the required questions. The last question to the man is as follows: »Are you capable of being the husband of a woman?« After the response »Yes,« one of the old women generally murmurs an incantation against evil spirits, directed against the man's enemies, because it is thought that if in the instant in which the man says »Yes« somebody draws his dagger half-way from the sheath and whispers, »It is a lie, he cannot,« then the bridegroom will be impotent for one whole year. Injury to virility is a popular form of revenge in the mountains. There are a number of secret charms and means whereby this result is supposed to be obtainable, and there are also people whose business is the composition and sale of such incantations. The anxiety of the bridegroom's friends is therefore entirely justified.

Immediately after the marriage, the newly wedded couple parts; the woman goes to her friends and the man to his; and both of them celebrate separately. After the celebration, the woman returns to the room next to the bridegroom's apartment, where she must await her husband.

It is not easy for the man to reach his wife's room on the bridal night; at every door a veiled figure awaits him and blocks his way. It is not until he has pressed gold into its hand that he is allowed to continue; and even in the bedroom the surprises that await him are various. Perhaps an old grandmother is discovered lying on the divan and refusing to leave until she has received her mite; or it may be a dozen cats or a dozen chickens put there by the young man's friends, and many things of the same order. After all these disturbers of the peace have been discovered and ejected, the bride enters the chamber, and the most involved and longest part of the wedding ceremony begins, to wit, the undressing of the bride.

This custom requires some explanation. From immemorial times the Caucasian has had a fixed and unchanging ideal of beauty. This ideal is slenderness (adopted by Europeans within recent years). Everything which the European woman uses to maintain a slimness of line has been known and used in the Caucasus since the beginning of time. The Caucasian girl does physical exercises, drinks no water for weeks on end, and avoids sweets, all for the sake of keeping her figure down. In contrast to all other Orientals, whose women are often prized almost according to their weight, the Caucasian loves a narrow waistline, breasts that can be covered with the palm of the hand, and a breadth of shoulder equal to that of the hips.

The body of a Caucasian girl is laced up from childhood, from her neck right down to her knees, in thin morocco leather, and she never removes this corset except to take a bath. Otherwise she only removes it upon her bridal night. The morocco leather device plays the same part as the binding of the feet among Chinese women: it forms the body. The Caucasian remains slim and narrow, and the highest praise that has been paid her all through the centuries is the phrase, »Thou art like unto a board,« thus proving in its entirety the wise proverb of Ben Akiba, for even the slender figure is no new thing under the sun.

The leather corset is held together by strings, which are knotted in front. The knots are of a complicated sort, and require endless care in the undoing. More often than not the women do it themselves, but on the bridal night it is the duty of the man. The woman is not allowed to help him. Nor is he allowed to cut the knots with a knife, for it would be considered a shameful thing that he should show so little control on the bridal night. All his friends come in on the next day and ask to see how the knots have been undone.

But the undressing of the bride is by no means the end of the wedding ceremony. All around outside the bridal room at walls and windows there is a guard of honour consisting of the man's friends. And if the bridal pair are very young, the friends sometimes go so far as to creep on to the roof of the house and throw cats, dogs, pieces of money, and food into the room. Then the man has to open the window, throw the objects out again, and make cheerful conversation with his friends for a while. Only after repeated requests is he finally left in peace.

Here the most important moment of the ceremony occurs. At the instant when the man has convinced himself of his wife's virginity, he seizes a revolver and fires a shot into the air, and immediately his guard of honour begins shooting too, and then the guests and neighbours and all who may be near do the same. And so it continues until early morning. On the next day the festival goes on, but the couple retreats to the house of a friend to celebrate their honeymoon. No one may disturb them there, and they themselves may not leave the house. The guard of honour will not permit it.

It is still a custom in many parts of the country for the woman to go back to her parents' home for two years after the honeymoon, and only receive her husband from time to time. At the end of this period, during which the man has to get a home of his own going, the real married life begins.

This life is entirely different from that of the European and is very seldom unhappy; it is built upon traditions which, in the opinion of Oriental specialists in the matter, anticipate everything within human experience that can possibly upset the marriage. Thus these marriages are some of the happiest in the world. Moreover, the Orientals are born family men.

The first principle of married life in the mountains is that »the problem of the mother-in-law does not exist.« According to an old tradition, which still prevails in many places, the man may not see the mother of his wife during the first twenty years of his marriage. The mother-in-law is forbidden to set foot in the house of her son-in-law, and must disappear at once whenever she meets him anywhere.

Even her meetings with her daughter are rendered excessively difficult. Only the men of the woman's family are given free access to the newly wedded couple, and they are responsible to the husband for his wife's fidelity. If a woman is untrue to her husband she does not injure him so much as her father or her brother, whose fault it obviously is for not having brought her up properly, and they are therefore obliged to appear as blood avengers.

In any case adultery very seldom occurs. Just as seldom do quarrels or disagreements, although it is the correct thing to be always complaining about one's husband or wife, to placate the envy of evil spirits. Once married, the Oriental remains the same as he was at the time of his courtship at the well, when for the first time his glance met that of his bride. His love is tender, modest, and warm; he is kind to his wife and his happiness is all turned inward, with none left over for the world at large. Thus he does not boast about his wife, never speaks about her, and considers it a gross lack of taste on the part of anyone who asks about her welfare. He answers in a deprecatory manner so as not to be asked again. Only when he is alone with her, in the »harem,« where none is allowed but himself, does his inner being show itself. He then sits at her feet, strokes her hands, looks up at her with tenderness, listens to her songs, and himself tells her stories. He does not dare to kiss her, or to embrace her, for she knows for herself that the man desires her. It is she who must first lean towards him. In the night he does not go to her whenever he likes, but must stand in front of her door or her window and sing songs or whisper his affection, till she lets him know with a soft whistle that she is inclined on that day to fulfil his wish. The man never dares to insist upon his rights, and months will often go by without his hearing his wife's soft whistle. But he is always ready for her signal.

The man knows that his wife is not there for the night alone; during the day, when she sings songs, allows her hands to be stroked, and smiles upon her husband, she is performing an even greater duty. But it is when the woman brings a son into the world that she obtains her full power over him. He is not allowed to have any part in the education of the children at this time but must fulfil his wife's every wish and wait silently for the time when the children are grown up and finally become his own property.

Letting other people see his love for his wife and children the Oriental considers a foolish form of showing off, and unworthy of a man. Love is not a public exhibition. He is even cool towards them, if strangers happen to be present, not from arrogance, but from embarrassment, shame, and fear, lest the outsider should smile at his feelings. If you come accidentally upon an Oriental as he is playing with his children, or helping his wife at her work, you must behave as if you had noticed nothing; otherwise he feels himself disgraced, as if he had been seen naked on the street. The most savage warrior will blush violently if the working of his innermost feelings is noticed by an outsider. It makes him awkward, he doesn't know what to do next, and casts his eyes to the ground like a small boy caught in a forbidden action.

Consequently, love in the West is incomprehensible to the Oriental. He can never understand how a man can appear in public with his wife. Even to receive visitors with her is equally impossible to him. In the East a visitor comes to see the woman or the man, but not both. Married people never go out together. Under any circumstances they dislike being seen together. Love is an excessively private and delicate matter to the Easterner, which must be tacitly ignored by his fellow-men.

However, the course of love is not always undisturbed; even in the East there are rivals, unhappy affairs, obstacles to marriage, hate and deception. At the well itself occurs the first grief, if the girl obstinately refuses to respond to the man's looks of love. In this case, there is only one course open to the man if he is a real man: he must abduct the girl by force (abduction with the girl's consent has already been mentioned above), take her to another village, and violate her. Then, according to mountain law, the girl and the man must be married. Abduction by force is one of the most romantic things that can happen in hill life; it is subject to special laws and traditions, has an established course of its own, and is followed by the whole country with great excitement.

The suitor carries out the abduction in the evening at the well. Surrounded by friends, he attacks the girl, throws a sack over her head, and snatches her up into the saddle. Shots resound—even, so the tradition exacts, if no one means to interfere—and the noise of hoofs rings out. Sometimes one short scream from the girl is heard.

The relatives of the kidnapped girl at once give chase to her abductor. If they get him, they are permitted to kill him and all his companions without incurring any penalty. But usually the man manages to reach some mountain nook or other in time, and there the friends of the man protect the house against all attack, while the unhappily smitten kidnapper completes the job like a man.

But the family of the girl is not to be placated in a hurry. It is at least a year before her people make peace officially with their impetuous new relation, and before he is allowed to go home with the wife whom he has married while in hiding. Both parties are bound to enter into matrimony after the girl's forced surrender, but in this case divorce is made specially easy for the girl. In any case divorce is not difficult, though fairly uncommon. It is always at the expense of the man, who is obliged to settle lavishly with his wife, even if the divorce is on her account.

Adultery is no ground for divorce, but it is very strong ground for a blood feud. First of all the lover is killed. This the man does as his bounden duty. His wife, however, he returns to her people, who generally stab her on the spot, unless she was innocent of the adultery, or, in other words, if she was violated, when she is exempt from all penalty. In the latter case, the criminal is led in bonds before her, and she is obliged to stab him in the presence of her husband.

But the execution of the lover is not the worst revenge taken for this misdeed. The following method (it is also used under other circumstances) is much more terrible in effect. The offended man has to attack his enemy in the night, tie him up, and pull his trousers off his legs. He then hangs the trousers on the door of his house where everybody can see them. This is considered the most dreadful insult which can be offered to a man. It is impossible to wipe it out, even with blood. The man whose trousers have been stolen must either commit suicide, or immediately leave his home country, never to return. And even abroad he must adopt another name, and keep away from his fellow-countrymen. Usually he will choose suicide in preference to exile.

The greatest obstacle to lovers is a more or less close kinship between them. On an average the Caucasian has five hundred blood relations, who all live in his village or in his immediate neighbourhood. Thus most of the girls that a young man sees around him are related to him in some way or other. But marriage, according to Caucasian law, is forbidden between even the most distant of relations. There is usually no other course open to the young couple, in this case, but to escape from their country and settle anywhere where their degree of relationship is unknown. Such cases are frequent, but they always arouse terrific consternation when they occur.

Poverty is no obstacle to marriage. Nobody weds a woman for money, for she brings no dowry to the man by marriage, and he is never allowed to touch her private property. Any woman who should hand over her personal fortune to her husband would be a universal laughingstock. If the bridegroom is too poor to pay the price of his bride, and for any reason is unable to go off on raids, then hundreds of his relatives club together to raise the required sum. If this is also unsuccessful, the bridegroom goes to the prince, and the latter is obliged to make the necessary outlay. But the relatives, and the prince too, only pay up if the kalym does not exceed what is due and correct, because, otherwise, as has already been said, it is assumed that the father of the girl wishes to reject the offer discreetly.

Lastly—a small disappointment for the reader—there are no harems in the Caucasus. Polygamy is allowed by law, it is true, but does not occur in practice. Even if a man does have several legitimate wives, they always live in different houses, usually in different villages. In most cases, the marriage contract contains a clause obliging the man to have only one wife. Only very wealthy and elderly people can afford more than one wife, and then only with the express approval, or even at the express request, of the first wife.

So all in all one can scarcely conceive of the Caucasian woman as a downtrodden, pitiable harem slave. She is free, independent in her decisions, mistress over her husband and her children, perhaps the happiest wife in the world. But it must be conceded that beauty and love carry certain disadvantages along with them. But of that I will speak in another place.

9.

THE SLAVE TRADE

FOR MANY REASONS the Caucasus became the centre of the slave trade in olden times. The threads which connect the mountains with the slave markets (and this includes slave markets other than those of the East) are innumerable. The trade has a thousand-year-old history and tradition behind it, and can hide behind a myriad disguises or avoid the most experienced of European police officials with the greatest of ease. Slaves are now handled in secret, and not only the traveller from Europe has nothing to report about it, but neither has the Oriental. Outwardly, it simply does not exist. And yet it flourishes more than ever, scorns all attempts at suppression, possesses widespread organizations and contacts, is organized into secret societies, and has even been able to influence public opinion to such an extent that nowadays, when people hear the words »slave traffic,« they merely laugh and say it no longer exists. Let me give the following information regarding this »non-existent« traffic.

The Caucasians are beautiful, beautiful and poor as they always have been. That has been their misfortune. From the East and from the West pressed the armies of two mighty monarchs, the Sultan and the Shah, and later on these were allied on the North with the Russians and on the South with the Azerbaijan armies. They overflowed the valleys of the Caucasus, penetrated into the auls, and laid waste the cities. Wherever the armies of the East and West had passed, there remained nothing but a waste land, for the enemy spared nothing, having no intention of stopping in this land. The mountains seemed too poor a place to set up a Wali for any length of time.

The princes and kings of the land defended their own territories and played off the Shah and the Sultan against each other until finally they were forced to recognize the authority of one or the other of these lords and become his tributaries.

What could they pay as tribute? Money was practically unknown to most of them, and cattle, which they used as currency, was not acceptable to the great monarch. There was only one form of wealth left to the mountains, to wit, beautiful children, and logically these becams their tribute.

Every year a messenger came from Stamboul to the countries which were tributary to Turkey, bringing a long, exact, detailed list of requirements with him. It was compiled by imaginative dignitaries and contained the exact description of the type of girl that was needed that year on the Bosporus. Every part of the girl's body was described. Thereupon the princes of the Caucasus had to prepare a campaign against their subjects and neighbours, for the purpose of obtaining hundreds of girls to be sent to Turkish harems. They were likewise obliged to collect the same number of good-looking boys as a freewill offering to the other ruler, the Shah of Persia.

The latter was not a lover of girls, he required boys, or *tuksusi*, as they were called. They were not to be paid as tribute but as a voluntary gift in honour of the Shah. If this were not done, the Persian fell upon the land and took his present for himself. And the same thing took place in all the countries of the Caucasus which were tributary to the Shah. Every year a messenger would come to them from Teheran with a note describing the boys in as much detail as the Sultan had described the girls. The princes received the letter of the Shah, kissed it, and fulfilled his wishes as already described, sending in addition the same number of girls to the banks of the Bosporus. Every year the same thing. It is no wonder then that there is scarcely a noble family in the East in whose veins no Caucasian blood flows.

These are not mere bogy tales from the dim past. In times when Europe was already closely threaded with railway tracks, and steamers were plying between continents, even then messengers continued to arrive from Stamboul and Teheran to collect their tribute of pretty girls and small boys.

It is just eighty years ago that the last contract for the delivery of these living goods was annulled. Up till then the old customs had been harmoniously carried out. But after that, the real slave trade began. Under Russian dominion, the payment of human tribute ceased, but the demand for women and boys from the Caucasus persisted in the harems of the East. These wishes had to be gratified. From the East and from the West, from Turkey and Persia, came cunning eunuchs to the courts of the Caucasian princes. And when the Russian general, who was appointed adviser to each of these princes, had his back turned, the emissaries quickly drew out their purses, and the eyes of the princes were intoxicated with greed.

And then the Nukri, the prince's horsemen, would ride out over the land and bring back the merchandise which the prince now sold to the Shah and the Sultan out of friendship. The export trade in human flesh flourished, and the wealth of the princes piled higher and higher. The last ruling prince of Mingrelia sold live merchandise to Turkey for one million pounds—which was a fantastic amount for those days. But even that didn't satisfy him. He established a stud for the production of young girls, in which this type of goods could be cultivated just as horses are bred in Europe.*

Good-looking men were coupled with beautiful women and received a commission on the proceeds of their cooperation. Princes of the frontier districts also followed this example and were not ashamed to take part as simple workmen in the activities of their factory. The princes were better off now under the new secret form of slave traffic than they were before, for now they received money for a commodity which they had been obliged previously to supply for nothing. Of course, this good fortune of the princes could not last for ever, for the Russian generals discovered in the course of time where it was that their proteges gained all their wealth. They dared not inform the Tsar

---

* In this connexion, cf. the Memoirs of Beresius, the Russian adviser in Mingrelia.

because he was a friend of most of the princes, who were potentates like himself and therefore first cousins to him.

But it could be managed without the Tsar. There came a sudden tendency towards deposing the princes; they were showered with decorations, stuffed into gorgeous uniforms, accorded large pensions, and sent away permanently to the court of the Tsar. No scandal was to be allowed to occur, nor anyone in Europe know, that men standing under the protection of Russia, most of them actually Christians, were carrying on a slave traffic with their subjects.

Of course, it was not altogether the fault of the princes. How could they help it if their subjects possessed the fairest daughters in the world, and that they themselves knew of no other export commodity in the country. Neither could they understand why anyone wanted to stop the slave traffic; on the contrary, they were naively and frankly astounded that hard-bitten, old Russian generals should tear their hair and betray so much moral indignation over so natural a matter.

Forty years before the revolution, the last Caucasian prince renounced the right to his crown. But those who hoped that with this occurrence the slave traffic would finally come to an end were gravely disappointed. It now began really to find its stride. Where the Sultan, the Shah, and the native princes had failed, the initiative of private capital was successful. The slave trade was organized, built up as a serious undertaking, and conscientiously cultivated. The capitalists did not merely kill the goose that laid the golden egg; they invested money in the enterprise and saw to it that the market was properly exploited.

The control of the Russian Colonial Government in the newly conquered Caucasus was confined solely to the towns. Nobody concerned themselves with what went on in the villages. At stated periods Russian officials went through the land to collect taxes and then returned to the towns. If in any given place the taxes were not forthcoming, then a punitive expedition would be sent out. So just in advance of the tax collectors, the employees of the slave traders would go through the land, seek out the prettiest children, make a lump sum of the price (which was usually about the same as the amount of the taxes), and then close a deal whereby the girls went into the employ of their purchasers. Each village was visited once only in the course of several years, so that the coming generation might gradually be allowed to develop. Once a year on the shores of the Black Sea, the traders would gather with their girls, while on the shores of the Caspian Sea assembled the traders with the newly purchased boys.

The ships were boarded in all secrecy and the well-prepared smuggling trip would begin. Siberia was the penalty for slave trading, so the traffickers were very careful, although as a rule the undertaking was not dangerous because the slaves knew well enough that a better fate awaited them in distant countries than in their native villages. But, as a precaution, the few girls who did protest (most of them were too young to do so) were simply given their freedom, which meant that the price of the others went up accordingly.

The treatment of the Caucasian girls in the Turkish harems was always very good, so that it was only rarely that there was any scandal. But in these cases the punishment was very high, for the Russian Colonial Government was pitiless in its treatment of the slave traders and bribery lost its ordinary powers at this point. Every slave trader was beaten and imprisoned for life.*

The people who were really injured by this suppression were the buyers, who had to keep paying higher prices. The actual trade did not suffer at all, nor did the population, since what was formerly appropriated by the princes and sultans in any case was now being honestly paid for to its rightful owner. Moreover, not all the tribes of the Caucasus were involved in the traffic to the same extent. The determining factor was the beauty of the girls and the character of the inhabitants. Some of the tribes never sold their offspring. Others, the traders didn't even dare approach.

The state of the market was best in the peaceful countries on the shores of the Black Sea, in Mingrelia, Abkhasia, and Ajaristan. It is there

---

* Cf. in this respect, the criminal records published by the office of H. I. M.'s Viceroy in the Caucasus, as also Turkish sources.

that the most beautiful girls in the Caucasus live, and the population, which is mostly Christian, has been so educated up to it, first by the princes and then by the slave traders, that they regard their daughters as their most certain insurance against need and danger.

It is said, and it sounds quite plausible, that, when German troops approached this territory in the year 1918, every village on the frontier sent all its most beautiful women, accompanied by a delegation of village elders, to call on the German staff. The elders made a speech in which they assured the Germans that they had long been aware of what they owed a conqueror and begged with tears in their eyes that their customs be accepted and that no other tax be levied on them than the ancient woman-tax. The Germans were at a loss what to reply—probably for the first time in their colonial history. Should they respect the customs of the land even in this? They did not do it, but sent the girls back. At least, so the story goes in the Caucasus.

Later on, when the Caucasus became Communist, the people again did not fail to offer their girls to the new wielders of power with at least this much success, that the girls who were offered were all taken into the propaganda schools of the Third International. But the slave traffic is by no means done for even now. It was only with the abolition of the harem that conditions were materially changed. It is only in those parts of the hills where girls were not sold even in the old days, but merely seduced or abducted, that its existence has ceased in practice.

Apart from the export slave, the Caucasus also has house slaves, and they are the fairest of the fair. But aside from this, they are responsible for one of the most comic chapters in the already humorous history of the Russian colonization of the Caucasus.

When the Russians came into final occupation of the Caucasus a few decades ago, they declared that slavery was irreconcilable with their cultural mission. But in order not to injure the rights of the Caucasian princes who were the owners of house slaves, the Russian Viceroy held a meeting of the princes in his palace and informed them that the Tsar in person requested them to give up slavery. Every one of the owners agreed on the spot, but they made the remarkable request that the personal wishes of the Tsar should be ratified officially so that they should be legally compelled to dismiss their house slaves. Somewhat surprised, the Viceroy gave his consent, and in a month the emancipation law was ready.

When the law was about to be proclaimed, a deputation of slaves appeared in the Viceroy's palace and pled with him not to disturb their age-long rights and privileges by annulment. The Viceroy, who had pictured slavery in quite a different light, asked in surprise what reasons they had for this unexpected request. »Slavery is our sacred right,« the liberated men solemnly protested. »In what respect?« the dignitary insisted. »Many of us,« the slaves replied, »are of the hereditary nobility, and some of us are priests. The Tsar should have a respect for the rights of the native nobility.«

At first the Viceroy took the whole thing to be nothing more than a bad practical joke, so he summoned the owners, and they affirmed with embarrassment that it was really true that many slaves were members of a very old aristocracy, and that some of them were also priests. Noble slaves? That was beyond the understanding of the Viceroy. It seemed to him still more important that these nobles and priests should be freed from their unworthy bonds.

The slaves, who had all appeared in sumptuous uniforms, protested violently. But their owners knelt before the Viceroy and declared that they were absolutely determined to respect the law of the Tsar and to regard all slaves as free men from then on. This statement caused such a tumult among the subjects of the discussion, that the Viceroy thought it better not to put the law into operation just yet, and so he set up a special commission to look into the case.

The material which this commission assembled brought some amazing facts to light. The house slaves were indeed members of the oldest aristocratic families in the land. Centuries ago, an impoverished member of the family had sold his freedom to some prince or other, whereby the rights and duties of the new slave and his descendants were exactly prescribed. The slaves were only obliged to do the work which had been done by the first of their line. And for this they were maintained by their masters all their lives and in certain circumstances they were rewarded with presents.

In the course of time, it was the princes who became impoverished and the aristocratic slaves who increased in the most devastating fashion. It thus came about that many a slave owner had to expend his whole income in supporting the descendants of his original slave. If the first of them had been a cook or a groom, all his descendants—and their number increased with the passage of time to dozens—could be nothing else but cooks or grooms. One slave owner with three horses had to maintain thirty grooms, who lived in his own home and demanded presents from him. Another, who was living from hand to mouth himself, had at his disposal twenty cooks, and it never occurred to a single one of them to do anything but lounge about in the kitchen. All the slaves had valid documents in their hands, which protected their position, and they regarded this attempt to free them as a brutal injustice and violation of their ancient privileges, whereas for most of the owners the riddance of their slaves meant bliss unheard of.

As both contending parties were not only of the aristocracy but also Christians, the Colonial Government was tolerant enough to do justice to them both. The slaves were set free, but received from the government maintenance for one year in order that they might accustom themselves to their new family and living conditions.

And the Viceroy was able to report to the Tsar: »Thanks to the complaisance of the local aristocracy, slavery has also been abolished in this part of Your Majesty's territory.« Upon which the Tsar conveyed his express and affectionate thanks to the entire Christian aristocracy of the Caucasus, but to whom this gratitude was really due, whether to the noble slaves or the noble slave owners, was never made quite clear.

This story applies only to the Christian portion of the Caucasus and to the nobility. The liberation of the bond-serving peasant is another chapter of mountain history altogether.

As against Christian practice, house slavery was all but unknown among the Mohammedans. They were also innocent of slave exportation. Latterly, according to the official statistics, there were only thirty-four slaves left in Daghestan, and these were freed without further ado.

10.

HOW TO BECOME A PRINCE

IN THIS SELFSAME BLESSED LAND OF MINGRELIA, where priests and nobles

may be slaves, where once upon a time institutions for breeding beautiful girls flourished, and where out of the two hundred thousand inhabitants the number of high-born hereditary princes was one thousand five hundred, in this place a delightful incident occurred some twenty years or so ago.

It happened in the reign of the last Mingrelian Queen Dedopali, who had all her life bitterly hated her neighbour, the last King of Abkhasia. This enmity had the following grounds: In the days when he was still a bachelor, the King of Abkhasia came to the court of the King of Mingrelia to request the hand of the Queen's beautiful cousin, Princess Menika. As both kings were neighbours, Christians, and of equal rank by birth, nothing stood in the way of the marriage. Court officials agreed upon the dowry which the King of Mingrelia was to pay to the King of Abkhasia and also upon the dates of payment, and the two monarchs signed the marriage contract. The wedding was solemnly celebrated, and the most handsome couple in the country were duly married by the archbishop. On the next day the King crowned his wife Queen of Abkhasia in the presence of the court and the entire diplomatic corps. The newly wedded King remained for a few weeks at the court of Mingrelia and then set forth for his own country, in order to prepare the ancestral castle for the reception of the young Queen. The caravans with the first instalments were to arrive in a few weeks, and the Queen was to follow them after some months.

The dowry arrived, and the King examined it closely— to his entire dissatisfaction. The horses were not well enough bred, the gold was of too low a carat, and the jewels were full of flaws. His Majesty felt that his honour had been betrayed.

»This is no royal dowry; the wedding contract provided for something very different,« said he, and wrote an angry letter to Mingrelia demanding further payment. The ruler of Mingrelia took offence in his turn. »Our money isn't good enough for him; protest his claims,« said he to his Foreign Minister. And a diplomatic conflict began.

In vain did the Russian adviser attempt to placate the two disputing princes. The only result was that the Abkhasian curtly announced that he would only receive the Queen if the dowry were fully paid according to his wishes. The exchange of notes between the monarchs lasted for two years, and became more and more bitter, while all this time the lonely young Queen waited for a settlement of the quarrel. But it never was settled. One day the King of Mingrelia received a letter to approximately the following effect:

»We, by God's grace, Michael I, King of Abkhasia, Lord of Samusarkan, Zebelda, etc., etc., do not give a rap for your dowry and have no wish to have any further correspondence with your Majesty. Our Archbishop married us yesterday to the Heiress of the Svanetian throne, whose royal father is less miserly than you. As far as the first instalment is concerned, we are keeping it as recompense for the period we have been kept waiting. Signed, Michael Rex.«

Not a word about divorcing his first wife! The insulted King's first thought was to declare war on Abkhasia. But the Russian adviser, who had more power than both kings put together, forbade it. There was nothing left for the Mingrelian ruler to do but to die of rage. Which he did, exactly one week after receiving the letter. His wife, Dedopali, ascended the throne, and, in order to annoy the King of Abkhasia, handed the frontier territory between the two countries over to the rule of the deserted Queen. The fair Menika retained the title of Queen of Abkhasia and remained all her life the sole ruler of the frontier land with all the rights which pertain to a crowned head. She organized small raids into the country of her husband, hanged all his subjects who set foot in her territory, and surrounded herself with princes and nobles who were ready enough to call her »Your Majesty.« It was in her territory that the piece of princely rascality occurred which I am now about to relate.

One day, Queen Menika was sitting in the court of her palace drinking tea. She was just emptying her third cup when a notorious pickpocket by the name of Temurkva, who had long been wanted by the police, entered the court, leading a cow on a rope in his right hand. The courtiers were about to fall upon this ragged scoundrel, now at last discovered, and clap him into jail, when he fell upon his knees and begged that he might first be allowed to say a few words to the Queen. The latter having given her consent, Temurkva began his confession:

He said that he—Temurkva—had up to now been a common pickpocket, and all decent people had avoided his society.

He was in rags, and things went ill with him.

But now he had decided to reform and seek refuge with the great, the exalted, and the world-renowned Queen Menika. As a sign of his repentance he was bringing with him his modest gift to the Queen, a cow which was his only possession on earth, and he begged her to offer him any kind of employment. The Queen was touched. This man, she thought, must be assisted, and she summoned her minister. At the end of half an hour help was at hand. The Queen accepted the cow and presented the pickpocket with a small property in the neighbourhood of her Residence which would enable him to lead a decent life. Temurkva came of a respected middle-class family and had sufficient ability to manage an estate. The new landowner withdrew joyfully amid a profusion of thanks. The cow was killed on the same day and served up to the Queen and her court.

But still there was a catch in the story. When Temurkva set foot upon his property, he discovered it to be barely an acre large. That was the dark side of it. But, on the other hand, he discovered from competent officials that the possession of this particular acre of ground historically carried with it the hereditary title of prince.

Neither the Queen nor her ministers, least of all the new landowner himself, had ever dreamt of such a thing. But since the property had now been legally handed over to Temurkva, he had his title ratified on the same day by the authorities and began to keep house as a prince.

Three days went by in this way. Then there appeared unexpectedly before the Queen a Russian priest from Mingrelia tearfully demanding justice. The thief Temurkva had stolen a cow from him a week ago, and he now heard that Temurkva had given the cow to the Queen and that it had been eaten by the court. The priest threatened, if the Queen would not reimburse him, to go to the Russian adviser, who would undoubtedly hold the Queen responsible since she had eaten of the cow. Queen Menika had had some unfortunate experience of diplomatic controversies, so she paid damages to the priest and gave orders for the arrest of the thief Temurkva. But he was nowhere to be found. He had already escaped over the Russian frontier, and the Queen could only take possession of his »estate.«

This suited Temurkva down to the ground. He went to Tiflis to the Tsar's Viceroy, introduced himself as a prince, showed his papers, and explained that Queen Menika was persecuting him on account of his pro-Russian tendencies and had even expelled him from the country. Now it was the Viceroy's turn to be touched; at the request of this true friend of the Motherland, he granted him the passport of a Russian prince; and, since for the moment a quarrel with Mingrelia was inadvisable, he gave orders that Temurkva be indemnified by the Russian exchequer for his enormous losses. Temurkva was satisfied. He even returned later to Mingrelia, and, when the Queen wanted to call him to account, he reminded her that she was merely a certain Menika, some sort of Mingrelio-Abkhasian queen, whereas he was an hereditary Russian prince, and refused to stand any nonsense.

Temurkva ended up as an industrial magnate, but his son was driven out by the Bolsheviks. He is doing very well in spite of it, however, as his title of »Prince« serves him equally well abroad. He married a wealthy American girl, and I myself read an interview he had in the papers. »Yes,« he told the reporter, »my family dates back to the eighth century, and my father was a high dignitary at the court of the Mingrelian Queen. But now my hereditary estates belong to the Bolsheviks.«

Tears, the reporter concluded, shone in the eyes of His Serene Highness, as he spoke of his most honourable and politically influential father.

That is the tale of the swindler Temurkva, and it is not one of the most outlandish of its kind. The Caucasus swarms with inimitable adventurous heroes of his sort, some of them harmless, some less so. This story came to pass, as I have said, some twenty years or so ago, when kings and feudalists still existed. Today times have changed, but not the people. Even now, the same light-hearted swindles and tragic encounters occur in the Caucasus, sometimes with less peaceful conclusions than the quarrel about the throne of Abkhasia. Nowadays the Russian adviser does not always suppress the disturbance, and it is not always an intimidated king who has forgotten the customs of his land that has to be dealt with. In the hills which border on Christian territories, the old customs hold good in all their pristine strength, and there the story which has just been related would end, not with a newspaper interview, but with a blood feud.

11.

THE BLOOD FEUD

THE NUMBERS OF THOSE who have conquered and ruled in these mountains are great, and great is the number of the kings and priests who have brought to the mountain folk the wishes and the laws of their many gods.

Greeks and Romans, Arabs and Persians, Turks and Russians, and finally the Bolsheviks have conquered the Caucasus and introduced their laws. The people submitted to everything, promised to obey all laws, and to meet all taxes. One thing only they insisted should be left to them—their customs. Every conqueror and ruler has had to give in to this request; otherwise the land rose up and the mountains flowed with blood, and the resultant quarrel often lasted for centuries. In the end the conqueror always said to them: »Live together as you please.«

Thus the customs and laws of the fathers remained unaltered, and among them the sacred obligation of the blood feud. Every conqueror tried to abolish it but always without success. The Caucasian can give up many things, but not revenge, even if it cost him his own head to attain it. Year after year the Tsar visited every avenger with a life sentence in Siberia, only to be compelled to tolerate the practice in the end in order to prevent depopulation of the land. Two million men left the mountains at that period and settled abroad, preferably in Syria, where blood vengeance was allowed by the Turks. The Bolsheviks too had to put up with it. It was the only way to win the people over to the doctrines of Marx.

What is this blood feud, which is superior to the laws of the Tsar, the Sultan, the Shah, and even of the Koran? Non-Caucasians always think they know what blood vengeance means; to them it is a bestial law of brutal retaliation, a primitive justice, the product of a bloodthirsty and savage mind. Possibly it is with other races, with Africans perhaps, or South Sea Islanders. I can't say. But in the Caucasus the vendetta is a complicated science, an exacting discipline, miles removed from primitive vengeance.

The law of the *kanly*, the avenger's law, is perhaps more complicated than many European laws and harder to understand than any other paragraph of human jurisprudence.

Blood vengeance is not carried out in sudden excitement; it is subjected to innumerable rules, endless limitations and customs, which constitute the cultural inheritance of every Caucasian, a common knowledge which is nevertheless submitted to the decision of the wisemen in especially complicated cases. Not every blood relative may put these rules into practice. And not every outsider is exempt from them. Murder is not the only thing which involves a man in blood feud, nor does every murder require retribution. Actions which are harmless in the eyes of a non-Caucasian often call forth a feud, and real crimes are frequently not punishable by this law.

The Caucasian resists any attempt at abolishing the blood feud because he knows that as a law it is the most certain protection against universal anarchy. It is only because blood vengeance hangs like a threat over these hundreds of disintegrated tribes that there is occasionally peace in the mountains. Otherwise, a free-for-all war would flare up, and there would be no reconciliation possible such as there is after retribution has been exacted according to the iron ruling of the vendetta, that law against which all other laws of humanity are powerless. For example, everybody now knows why it was that the extensively planned revolt of 1912 against the Tsar– brilliantly prepared as it was–turned out a failure. The leader of the rising was a famous Chechen warrior, most of whose soldiers were from Daghestan. Shortly before the revolt they happened to hear that in his youth their leader had accidentally killed a man of Daghestan while at play. The soldiers of that land at once questioned the leader, who was unable to deny the fact.

»Then,« said they, »you are our kanly«; and with that they left him and fought against him until he was forced to give in and expose himself voluntarily to their guns, and be shot. As a consequence, the revolt never took place. If the leader's action had been discovered one day after the outbreak of the rising, all would have been well, because in war-time »kanly« does not exist. But in this case, the killing was heard of before the rising, and the Daghestan soldiers had no alternative but to act as they did.

The same people also played a decisive part at the outbreak of the Russian civil war. When General Kornilov was advancing against the Kerensky faction, his army consisted for the most part of Daghestan soldiery. Kerensky therefore quickly assembled the most distinguished people in the Caucasus and sent them into the camp of the rebels to establish peace. In the Caucasus a proposal of peace from the wise-men was never ignored. But on this occasion there happened quite by chance to be a prince in the delegation whose grandfather had killed a famous man of Daghestan and had got off scathless. The story goes that, when the Daghestan troops learnt about this, they dismissed the delegation of which their kanly was a member and swore to destroy Kerensky, who was manifestly supporting the enemy. Civil war blazed forth.

These are only single examples to give some idea of the effects of the blood feud. Its origin and its development, as the most important law in the mountains, require further explanation.

The whole world over, people are split up into nations. Outsiders have tried to carry this classification into the Caucasus also, but they have failed. For most Caucasians the word »nation« is incomprehensible, and at best meaningless. Families and circles of friends take the place of nations, and they are together styled »societies.« One does not say, such and such a man is an Ingush; that means very little. One says, he belongs to the Galgaish or the Berkinish Society. This instantly conveys as exact a conception of the man as if one had known him for years. The members of a society or a family are answerable for one another and bound to afford each other every protection and every assistance. Degrees of relationship have nothing to do with it. The family or the society is run on a communal basis, and the greater the number of members in the family the greater is its importance in the mountains.

The loss of a member, of a warrior, weakens the family and leaves a gap in the ranks. It also strengthens the enemy family, which must unconditionally be made to suffer the same loss in order to restore the balance. Whether the adversary really meant any harm or not, or whether or not the unfortunate occurrence happened by accident, is completely beside the point. The loss is there and must be compensated. Consequently, it is also entirely logical that any murder within the family, even the murder of a brother, of children, or of a father, should go unpersecuted. It is not the murder, but the loss which it involves, which is punishable. In the case of a murder within the family, the murderer himself is the loser—is in fact one relation the poorer. And if they were now to punish the murderer, they would only weaken their own family by still another member. Blood vengeance between relatives is therefore nonsense. Whosoever kills his father, his brother, or his son would at the most only be laughed at for a fool. In such a case they say: »The dog has lapped up his own milk,« and bother no more about him.

Blood vengeance follows not only upon murder, but also upon any other form of loss. Thus, for example, a substantial theft is a ground for it, or a love-affair with a girl by which her moral value is diminished. Intercourse with animals—an abuse which is very widely practised in the mountains—also demands blood vengeance. The animal in question is considered polluted, and the miscreant must pay the owner the whole price of the animal if he wants to escape blood vengeance. In this respect, the price of a cow, for example, which has not yet calved, is reckoned much higher than that of a mother animal.

The causes which lead to a blood feud are innumerable, but they always rest on the same basis, to wit, the violation of some material or moral value. Of primary import is the avenging of murder, for, as already stated, the loss of a member of a family is reckoned irredeemable, and the blood of the other family must be substituted for it. Vengeance is taken in the following way:

Immediately after the murder, the injured family arms for the campaign, and the house of the enemy family is besieged. No member may leave the inner rooms. During the siege the besiegers support them-

selves at the expense of the enemy, until the intermediaries are successful in concluding a treaty between the parties according to which the
murderers are permitted to move freely about their own house and
courtyard upon payment of certain damages. At this the beleaguerers
withdraw, and only the closer relatives of the murderer are watched.
The moment the latter leaves the house, the hunt begins. He cannot be
at peace anywhere. On the street, at his prayers, in the fields, everywhere, the daggers and bullets of the enemy await him. His life is a burden to him, and only at night does he dare to sneak out of the house.
Every month the avenger fetches the price which guarantees non-inter-
ference within the home, and often a family will remain a tributary in
this way for ever. The avenger then lives for a long time upon his victim
until the revenge has been finally fulfilled and the beleaguered family
can breathe freely again.

A considerable number of families have become wealthy because
they had blood enemies who were obliged to pay them tribute every
year. But the ultimate end of a blood feud for murder is invariably the
blood of the enemy or of his relations. As soon as blood has been spilled
for blood, the feud is at an end, the balance has been restored, and any
further persecution is forbidden. The avengers are not in turn punished
by the enemy for their revenge because that would mean carrying on the
feud indefinitely. It is only if several of the enemy have been killed during the process of vengeance that the opposing family declares a feud on
their side and the whole business begins all over again.

Almost every tenth Caucasian is involved in some affair that has to
do with a blood feud; he is either seeking the blood of an opponent or
hiding from an enemy himself. One should never introduce two Caucasians before finding out in what feuds they are involved. Killing in
self-defence, manslaughter, and accidental homicide are unrecognized
by the justice of the mountains. When, for example, a thief sneaks into
a house and falls into a hole on his way in and breaks his neck, then the
owner of the house is responsible for this death, is considered a murderer, and is exposed to revenge by the thief's family. Even when a thief
meets his death falling off a stolen horse on which he is escaping, the

aggrieved owner is guilty. In the same way one has to be careful of lending one's weapons to anyone in the Caucasus. Because, not merely the murderer, but above all the possessor of the weapon—even if the weapon were stolen—is declared a blood enemy. In short, a murderer is anyone who willingly or unwillingly, personally or through the medium of his property, has caused a death to take place. The Caucasians are very proud of this theory and they maintain that nowhere in the world is human life rated higher than in the regions which are under the laws of the blood feud.

Only in very rare cases, and then only if the »murder« was obviously and indisputably involuntary, is it possible to persuade the avengers to keep the peace. The peace negotiations generally go on for ever, and consist in a blend of reconciliation and blood costs. Often the avengers require that the murderer shall have an ear or a finger cut off, and that the grave of the dead man shall be sprinkled with the blood of the delinquent. Generally the blood price constitutes a fortune. But even after it has been paid, the family of the murderer always remains in an inferior position to that of the avenger. As a general rule, it is not considered fair play to forgive a murder and conclude a peace.

Cases have also been known in which poor families have killed one of their own members, put the blame of the murder on to a wealthy family, and in this way, after receiving the blood price, built themselves up slowly to a position of greater esteem.

Since all members of an enemy family rank as blood foes, it often happens that, in remote places in the Caucasus, sanguinary wars will start between hitherto peaceful neighbours who have received news of a killing at the other end of the mountains; the murderer being the relative of one neighbour and the man killed, of the other. Often, too, someone who is not a relative is obliged to join in a feud as, for instance, if the murdered man was his guest or his travelling companion. The honour of the revenge is then divided between him and the blood relations.

For every cause of blood feud, except that of murder, a forfeit may be paid, and it is extremely comic to see old, experienced people meeting together in council in order to decide how high a polluted cow, or an old stolen shoe, is to be rated. I once saw, with my own eyes, seven cows and twenty sheep extorted for a rusty nail which had been stolen. In point of fact, the nail lay in the chimney, and thefts from the chimney are considered especially insulting and punishable.

The law of the blood feud renders any peaceful government of the mountains an impossibility. No policeman dares arrest anybody, no judge dares punish anybody, because they would instantly be declared blood enemies of the damaged family.

It is only in cases of universal danger, as, for example, the descent of an enemy against whom the country must be defended, that the wisemen announce: »Till the end of the war there shall be no more blood feuds.« Then the mountain people come together, enemy and avenger are joined in friendship, and both fight shoulder to shoulder for the freedom of the mountains. But scarcely is the war at an end, scarcely is the enemy driven out, than the avenger falls upon his foe again, the very man by whom he has stood through thick and thin until that moment. On the day when peace is declared, a panic breaks out in the Caucasian army. Officers fly from their men, men hide from officers, and generals ride off at top speed to all points of the compass, to reach the stronghold of their nearest relative. Blood feud, that eternal law of the hills, prevails again from that very day.

It is by no means on the decrease; on the contrary, it becomes more deeply rooted in the consciousness of the Caucasian every year. No veto and no punishment has any effect against it. Even if the blood enemy is sometimes hailed before a court of justice, that is no reason why the avengers should consider themselves satisfied. They are much more liable to feel insulted that their enemy has been snatched from them and to start a feud against his whole family.

It was only within quite recent years that a serviceable cure was found for blood vengeance in a small Caucasian country, in the Republic of Ingushia. The discoverer of this cure was the Soviet Government of Ingushia. The country is Soviet but it retains its own laws and customs. Communism is purely a nominal power and is scarcely known even by name to the majority of Ingushes. The President of the Republic, who had much to fear from his own blood enemies, founded one day a »Commission for the Abolition of the Blood Feud.« Among the members of the commission there was not one single Communist. The Soviet Government of Ingushia knows its subjects. Princes from the most respected families, priests, dervishes, and the oldest Ingushes of the land constituted the Commission. They travelled across the country, visited every settlement, every village, and every valley. »Who is kanly here?« inquired the princes, priests, and elders as they went slowly from hut to hut among the blood avengers with the dignity which became their station. Were he a simple shepherd or even a slave, they knelt before each man they found, kissed his feet, and said: »Forgive thine enemy, we beseech thee!«

The princes' task was a difficult one. The custom being so deeply rooted, nobody was willing to forgive. But the members of the Commission knelt persistently, kissed the hands and the feet of the slaves, and spoke for so long and to such good effect that each avenger finally sprang up weeping, flung himself to the earth, and forgave his enemies.

If nothing else had any effect, the princes said: »If thou dost not forgive, we shall hang ourselves upon thy threshold, and the blame shall be upon thee!« This terrible threat was rarely necessary, for the respect for the elders is great, and the honour which they conferred upon the avenger by their request was entirely out of the ordinary. Everybody tried to remain implacable, but no one finally succeeded in doing so. When the best of the race go down upon their knees, then it is time to renounce the customs of one's fathers. In every village, the reconciliation was celebrated, and the princes would not rest until the enemies had drunk together from a glass of milk and had sawn a silver coin in two, of which each of them tied a half round his neck, thus becoming brothers. In some villages it happened that people who had heard of the approach of the Commission and did not want to forgive left their houses hastily and withdrew into the mountains. But the elders were stubborn and pursued the avenger to the topmost snow-covered peaks, reached him, and made him concur with their wishes. They left no single blood enemy behind them. That which the Tsar was unable to accomplish with death penalties, nor the Koran with hell-fire, was accomplished by the salt of the land by humility, and pleading, and bending of knee. But for how long, I wonder, will the peace last which they have created?

I have the law of the blood feud to thank for my very sudden departure from the aul of Iskender-Khan. He too had blood enemies who were governed by a single wish– to destroy him and his village as quickly as possible. This feud had had a long previous history. Many years before, a relative of Iskender-Khan killed a man of a poor family. The circumstances of Iskender-Khan's life at that time required peace and friendship with all his neighbours. He therefore paid the blood money, and the murderer took the place of the murdered man in the neighbouring family, as a sort of substitute for the loss—a custom that is met with among many Caucasian peoples. This relative had now in his turn been killed during a thieving expedition, and the neighbouring family required a second substitute from Iskender. This seemed to Iskender to be pure extortion, and he proclaimed that, if the neighbours wanted a substitute, they could come and get him for themselves. This news at once threw my eunuch and my three outriders, who were idling around the town, into a state of gloom.

»Now blood will flow,« observed the eunuch. »We shall do well to be on our way.« The horsemen held the same view. But to get out seemed hardly as easy as all that. We were guests in the village and had no right, from the point of view of decorum, to consider ourselves in any way endangered or threatened. The assumption that Iskender was at all unable to protect his guests sufficiently would have been an insult that could never be made good. My eunuch was clever enough to avoid such a thing at any cost. But how were we to find a proper excuse for our departure?

After a good deal of hesitation, we informed him of my complete recovery and asked him for recommendations to his friends, so that I might get to know more of the hill country before returning to my father, who was so eagerly awaiting my arrival. Iskender understood the grounds of our departure at once, but, since the amenities had been observed, and he himself knew only too well that we were quite right to be anxious, he agreed and began preparing the farewell celebrations on the selfsame day. They lasted a week. When we were finally able to leave the place, there was a further celebration on the frontier of the village, until finally the eunuch explained that, as untrained valley dwellers, we were really coming to the end of our endurance. So much mutton fat, wine, and busa could really only be supported by a hill dweller. So off we went, down the mountains, and reached the Daghestan railway again, but, as I still wished to remain in the hills, we left it once more when we had reached the gates of Georgia and the great Georgian military road.

The district around this road, the home of the Ossetes, Ingushes, Chechens, Khevsurs, and dozens of other tribes, is just as wild as Daghestan, but is, for some unknown reason, considered more civilized. My father agreed, after a considerable exchange of telegrams, that, as it was the height of summer and the temperature in the valley stood at 122° F., I might travel farther and visit his own and Iskender-Khan's friends; in short, I was to make myself better acquainted with the mountains.

Many people send their children to the hills for several years, because the polish that is acquired there is considered the best social education in the Orient. »He looks« or »he behaves as if he had grown up in the mountains« is the highest praise that an Oriental ever can hear said of himself. In the mountains live the knights, and knighthood still holds a highly honoured position in the East. Just as the young people were sent to court in the Middle Ages, so the Georgian or the man of Azerbaijan sends his son to the mountains first, and only afterwards to the cities of Europe. »The good qualities of the soul are formed in the mountains and only cleverness in the West,« they say in the Orient; and indeed the proverb is not without truth.

My father didn't think much of the polish acquired in the mountains. He would have preferred to keep me away from them. But as I was already there, there was nothing left for him to do but put a good face on it and give his blessing to what he chose to call my predilection for barbarity. I was therefore at leisure to travel about in the hills for as long as I chose; I could pass the period of my convalescence on the mountain of Besh-Tau, in the company of Caucasian knights from whose polished manners I could derive much profit.

12.

ALAMUT – THE GARDEN OF HEAVEN

WE RODE THROUGH GLENS, and our path was crossed by stormy mountain torrents as it bore us steeply down. There are no bridges over the streams here. Two or three felled tree trunks are thrown over the precipice and tied together with a rope. Shut your eyes as the horse steps onto them and you are safe; horses are never giddy. On steep cliffs over the river's edge crumbling ruins rise sheer above the precipice, remains of old walls which each Caucasian potentate erected round his property of yore.

These ruins were formerly castles, are still to some extent castles even today, though they are falling apart with time; the inhabitants move to some other cliff, where they build a new citadel and forget all too soon the heroic deeds which haunt the old one. Men are quickly forgotten, and nowhere quicker than in the mountains where one hero follows another overnight. You practically have to have been a world-ruler to be remembered in Caucasian legend. I stopped before every ruin and asked as I gazed at the crumbling walls: »Is this Alamut?« But no, it was not Alamut, nor was the next mountain, nor the one after that. The ruins of Alamut are not easy to reach; they are half forgotten and avoided, because the spot where the stronghold stood is cursed by all the gods. Why should men care any more for such a place? The word Alamut is taboo; the Caucasians take no one to the ruins.

For centuries the Orient was ruled from this citadel. Everybody from Morocco to China trembled when its name was heard. The Caliphs, Sultans, Crusaders, and Bedouin chieftains, the Christians and Mohammedans, fulfilled blindly every command which emanated from the hills. War and peace, want and plenty, were dispensed from the citadel of Alamut. The Emperor of the East could thank the Master of this castle for his crown, and Baldwin, the Nordic King of Jerusalem, lost his crown and his life to boot because he braved the biddings of the citadel. Good and evil both came out of Alamut, the heart of the Caucasus, the dark stronghold, the ruin that is shunned to this very day.

The Lord of Alamut was no Emperor, and no Sultan; he had no army fighting for him and no subjects to pay him taxes. He was simply Hassan-ibn-Sabbah, the Lord of Alamut, the famous »Old Man of the Mountains,« the first terrorist of world history. He was a Persian, in his younger days a friend of Omar Khayyam, and of the mathematician Nizam-ul-Mulk, whom he later caused to be stabbed to death. He passed his life in the company of dervishes and poets, in mosques and palaces, until the great revelation came to him and he left the poets and dervishes and founded the first great mystic sect of Islam, known as the Ismailites, the worshippers of Ali. He himself, Hassan-ibn-Sabbah, was the incarnation of the holy Ali. To him, therefore, the people owed obedience. He built his citadel of Alamut in the mountains of the Caucasus, in order to exert his tyranny from there. His instruments were terror and hashish, terror for his enemies and hashish for his friends who carried out the terror.

On the walls of the stronghold a garden was laid out, the fairest garden in the world, to which the disciples of the Master were brought, their wits having been previously obscured with a bowl of hashish. There the Master appeared to them and, pressing a dagger into their hand, he bade them: »Go forth, slay, and die.« On the dagger was graven the name of the victim. The disciples were not allowed to return alive, even if they had fulfilled their task and successfully evaded pursuit. They had to die in order to stay for ever in the Garden of Alamut, for the Alamut which they saw in their hashish dreams was the eternal garden of heaven, and the Master was the Lord of Creation himself. After his revelation, Hassan-ibn-Sabbah passed his life shut up within the walls of his citadel. His face was always covered with a veil, and none of his pupils ever was allowed to see him. From time to time the great men of the world received a curt command from him. If they did not at once obey him, it was repeated, but at the third time the command was pinned with the dagger of the Ismailite into the breast of the rebellious man. For it was the Lord of the Ismailites who must rule the world and not the kings, sultans, and caliphs. Many great men tried to destroy the citadel. They undertook campaigns with gigantic armies against Alamut, but their generals were stabbed by the Ismailites within sight of the citadel, and the armies scattered like dust in wild panic. Hassan-ibn-Sabbah and his successors continued their world power for centuries; their word was law in all the Orient. Their power was limitless. The Crusaders even trembled before them and fulfilled their every wish.

It was the Crusaders who brought to Europe the news of this Eastern sect of Assassins and handed it down to history. The servants of Hassan were commonly called Hashishites, and it is from this that the French word »assassin,« a murderer, is derived. But when the star of the Mongolian conqueror Jenghiz-Khan appeared, the hour of the Assassins' rule had struck. Jenghiz-Khan had no need to fear Alamut. His warriors, and only they, could approach the citadel without becoming assassins. They were all true Shamanists, worshipping only the horse's tail, the sword of the Khan, and the blue god Teb-Tengri. Khulagu, the nephew of the great Khan, besieged the Assassins' nest with his mighty army. The citadel was conquered, put to flames, and demolished. All the holy books were destroyed, and the Assassins themselves were torn in pieces by the Mongols. Their very remains were burnt up, so great was the hatred of the world against this sect of slaughterers. The last of the Ismailites fled into the desert.

Even today, there are a few peaceful nomad tribes in Pamir, in the north of India and the south of Turkestan, who are the last to worship the dread Hassan-ibn-Sabbah and his descendants. But the citadel in the Caucasus is an accursed spot, and no Caucasian will even listen to any mention of their legends.

13.

CHRISTIANS WHO DO NOT KNOW THE NAME OF CHRIST

IN PRE-REVOLUTIONARY TIMES IN TIFLIS, the capital of Georgia, it was customary, whenever His Highness the Viceroy's police discovered a Bolshevik conspiracy or a secret printing press, or when the minister urgently demanded the arrest of Bolsheviks after some successful political assassination, to distribute leaflets with pictures of the criminals and the size of the reward to all corners of the town.

Thousands of police agents would chase through the city and search all the suspicious houses. But when they had searched for three days in vain, they would inform the chief that any further investigations were useless. For they knew then that the criminals had fled to Khevsuria, the political Switzerland of the Caucasus. There a man could at last be safe.

Khevsuria is quite near Tiflis, and yet the land is free, independent, and no policeman dares to follow his victim there. A gigantic wall of rock surrounds Khevsuria and separates it from the rest of the world. After surmounting this wall, a precipice confronts you. Far below in the valley are to be seen the free villages of the Khevsurs. From the cliff wall down into the void there hangs a long rope.

Whoever has the courage can catch hold of the rope and let himself down to the Khevsurs. The police never follow; what could a couple of men accomplish in the free land of Khevsuria? The valley folk protect the refugee. For eleven months in the year the rope is the only communication between Khevsuria and the outside world. For one month only you can cross the mountains' dangerous pass. Through it the first immigrants must have entered the land. Only the refugee dares use the rope, to be accepted if he is so inclined into the society of the Khevsurs and protected for ever from all dangers.

The Khevsurs maintain neutrality on all political questions. When the Bolsheviks got the upper hand and began to search the houses in Tiflis in their hunt for the enemy, the latter also flew to the Khevsurs. Even the last of the Georgian White Guard, Prince Chelokashvili and all his staff had to make use of the Khevsur rope when his army and his glory were forfeited in battle to the Reds.

Down in the Khevsur valley an eternal peace prevails and you can walk for days through the country without meeting a soul. Throughout the entire land, which in actual area is not one of the smallest states, there are strongholds which are widely separated from each other, and around every stronghold stand a few four-cornered towers built of stone. That is all. Nothing more has ever been built there. In these thirty castles the Khevsurs live, a strange and mysterious mountain race. Who they are and whence they originate nobody knows. They are surrounded by a secret which it is now impossible to unveil. The race, which is utterly different from its neighbours in its ways of life, its customs and usages, has been too little investigated.

To start with externals: it is only occasionally, when strangers visit their villages, that the Khevsurs wear their Circassian clothes, which is the customary apparel in the Caucasus. Otherwise, they wear curious habiliments: a short, low-cut shirt beneath a long, enveloping overgarment, on the front of which a large Maltese cross made out of strips of yellow cloth is sewn in the middle of the chest. Unlike all other people of the East, the men and women of the Khevsurs do not wear wide silk trousers, but only tight stockings which reach over the knee joint. As a headdress they wear a four-cornered cap, with a coloured cloth wound round it. Head and beard are shaven clean, but the moustache is left. The yellow Maltese cross is not only sewn on to the shirt, but it is worn in a smaller form everywhere it can possibly be applied.

This is the peace-time dress of the Khevsur. In war-time he looks entirely different. His harness, which he has inherited from generation to generation, is neither European nor Asiatic. It is medieval. A helmet covers the head, a steel shirt protects the shoulders and buttocks, and the arms and legs are protected with heavy brass plates. In his left hand

91

the Khevsur carries a round shield with a Maltese cross on it, and in his right a lance or, of latter years, a rifle. At his belt hangs a straight sword. The whole appearance of the man is more that of a Crusader than a wild mountaineer, and the impression is strengthened when one takes a closer look at the swords and shields. Knights, eagles, and old coats-of-arms are engraved in the steel, with Latin inscriptions. These read: »Genua Vivat Stephan,« »Vivat Husar, Souvenir,« and even »Solingen.« On an old shield, the letters A.M.D. may be deciphered, signifying »Ave Mater Dei,« the motto of the Crusaders.

Thus equipped, the Khevsurs go forth to battle, usually to a duel, which is carried out in the following way: The opponents kneel upon the right knee, draw daggers, and start fencing with them. After a while they spring up, singing a regular war song as they strike out furiously at each other, and then again they defend themselves in the crouching position. Anyone who comes between them is struck down. There is only one way of stopping them. A woman, preferably a young girl, may throw her kerchief between the two fighters. At this, both opponents must sheathe their swords at once, bend the right knee before the woman, and then withdraw from the field of honour. Often the warriors tear the kerchief in two pieces, each appropriating one of them to use as a sign upon his shield of a fight which was stopped by a girl.

The inscriptions, the armour, and the type of duelling are sufficiently remarkable to justify the strangest suppositions. Who can the Khevsurs be, the proud wearers of the Maltese cross, the cavaliers arrayed in steel? Crusaders, perhaps, driven from Palestine and forced back into the mountains, where they have gone wild, as the legends of the Caucasus will obstinately testify? Or just an unknown race that has come under the influence of Europe and once assimilated as bearers of a higher culture some fugitive or exiled knights of the Middle Ages? Any answer to these questions is, as I have said, still impossible. Investigators have not yet said their last say about the Khevsurs. The country has been too little observed and too seldom visited. Only persecuted Bolsheviks, emigres, and escaping White Guardsmen (who often spent months among the Khevsurs) could contribute anything of importance

about the people. But they never do; they are as secretive as all politicians, and they have no interest in investigating relics of Crusaders.

But echoes of Crusading days are not by any means the only interesting things to be mentioned about the Khevsurs; no less strange and
grotesque is the religion of these free settlers, which is calculated to
bewilder all learned theologians and turn their ideas upside down.

The Khevsurs are, if you like, Christians. They worship the Cross
and the Mother of God and, above all, Saint George and the apostles
Peter and Paul. At prescribed moments they cross themselves piously
and, when a sheep is slaughtered, they never omit to dip their fingers
in the blood, and sign themselves with a cross upon their foreheads.
Outside of this sign, they know nothing of Christianity. Jesus is
unknown to them, as are all the characteristic attitudes and com-
mands of Christianity. It is true, they do celebrate Sunday; yet not only
Sunday, but Friday, Saturday, and Monday are also their official feastdays. If you ask them for the reason of these holidays, they reply that
Sunday is celebrated because of the Georgians who are Christians, Friday because their Mohammedan neighbours in the mountains celebrate this day, Saturday because of the Mountain Jews, and Monday to
show that the Khevsurs are a free race who can do just as they please,
and may therefore celebrate on Monday also to prove that their religion is different from all others. Resting on Sunday cannot, of course,
rank as proof that they are pious Christians. They also eat no pork, are
polygamists, and practise levirate marriage, and, just to be different
from everybody else, they never spend the night in one room with
their wives. They visit their wives very seldom in any case and obtain a
divorce if the woman becomes pregnant within the first three years,
because that is considered shameful. Apart from the Cross, the Mother of God, and Saint George, the Khevsurs also worship other gods,
the small and the great Pirkushi, Adghilis-Deda, the god of the East,
and the god of the West, the last two of which enjoy especial respect.
Nevertheless, all these gods play a negligible role in the basic life of the
populace.

Which god he prefers is, so to speak, entirely the business of the individual. The official religious life takes place in the temples, the Khati, which are consecrated to the chief godhead of the Khevsurs.

These temples are surrounded by stone walls and consist of four-cornered buildings with steep roofs and some wooden palings, upon which, according to ecclesiastical custom, bells are hung. The greater the number of bells, the more highly esteemed the temple. Access to the innermost part of the temple, the holy of holies, is only permitted to the priests, and even to them only on feastdays. These temples house the religious effects of the Khevsurs, which are like no others in the world. They consist of huge barrels and copper pails. There is nothing else in the temple whatever. In the holy barrels beer is kept, and it is prepared in the holy pails. Beer is the chief god of the Khevsurs, and the brewers are their high priests. At every festival there is a service. The priest prophesies the events of the next year; then he has a beer barrel brought in and pours a glass of beer to all four quarters of the heavens to the health of the spirits. He then intoxicates himself and resigns the drink to the pious congregation. Besides beer and Saint George, the Khevsurs worship a host of other gods, who inhabit all sorts of objects, which must naturally not be disturbed. And thus it comes to pass that the Khevsurs are not only forced to renounce the use of innumerable articles, but they are not allowed to eat fish or game, although the rivers of Khevsuria are the richest fishing streams in the Caucasus and their, forests are swarming with game.

Some of the burial ceremonies of this tribe are quite ghastly. In the old days, if a man died far from home, his corpse was cut into two pieces and stuffed into a couple of sacks full of salt, which were laid on the back of a horse and carried home. The Khevsurs are not buried; their corpses are generally laid out in special houses. The doors of these houses are smeared with lime and are provided with a small flag; it is also customary for all the dwellers in the community to pass the house in turn and hold converse with the dead person, assuring him of how they loved him and of how painful his loss is to them.

Even the sacrificing of animals is still very widespread. At every opportunity they are offered to the gods. The sacrificial animal's throat is cut after wearisome prayers and supplications to the Virgin. After the sacrifice a specially chosen priest falls into a trance and utters sooth to the sacrificer about his future.

In conversation with foreigners the Khevsurs always seriously maintain that they are Christians. But at the same time they flatly reject any teaching about Christ, Christian morality, etc. Christian priests who were sent to them in the valley were laughed at and driven out. »We need no instruction,« they said. »We have our beer and that is enough. In any case you cannot give us anything new.«

The pride of the Khevsur is great. If he condescends to hold converse with anyone (which he doesn't always do), he first gives his tribe's name and then his own. He is then proudly silent, making a long dignified pause, in the sincere conviction that he must give the stranger time to recover and collect himself after the shock of being confronted by such a distinguished person as a Khevsur.

At the edge of every Khevsur village there stands a long low building, which looks just exactly like a large kennel. This building is called Samrevlo, i.e., the Stable. It is not meant for domestic animals, however, but for women. If a woman is unwell, she has to go to this stable, which she must never leave during the whole period of her sickness. Nobody may visit her there, neither man nor woman; at the most, she may receive small girls who have not yet attained to puberty, or old grandmothers whose womanhood is behind them. To this same place a woman must come when she brings a child into the world. This too she must accomplish without any assistance, and she must herself bite off the umbilical cord. If the birth is a particularly difficult one, a man must be found who has murdered somebody, and he is requested to go to the stable and shoot into the air with a gun. That usually helps. The presence of the murderer keeps away the evil spirits, and the shots frighten the woman.

The Khevsur woman has to wash her hands and feet every day with cow urine, and her face and hair every month. If she does not, she is pronounced unclean. Even women who are not Khevsurs, but who happen to be staying in a Khevsur village, are obliged to submit to these customs, otherwise they are driven out of the village, and the house in which they were staying is burnt down. The Khevsur woman is by no means a slave, however; on the contrary she possesses innumerable prerogatives which set her far above the men. Not only is her word sufficient to put an end to a duel, but she can also leave her husband at any moment and get a divorce. Moreover, she may never under any circumstances be married by force and without her consent, and she may without penalty mock her husband and cause him to appear ridiculous in the presence of everybody.

Marriage is usually concluded between members of different villages. A wedding between persons of the same village is considered a misalliance. A wife does not call her husband by his name, but must give him the name of an animal, such as Pig, Ox, or Dog. Whenever she catches him lying, she can demand from him three cows or nine sheep as damages. The Khevsurs cannot reckon in money; they settle their accounts with cows and sheep.

It is not known to what race the Khevsurs belong. They have no uniform type. Fair and dark, big men and small men, can be found intermingled among them. Their speech is related to the Georgian, but it also contains innumerable other linguistic traces. Perhaps the most correct assumption is that this people simply consists of refugees from many lands, who have fled at various times to the sanctuary of the Khevsur wilderness and have bequeathed a fragment of their customs to their descendants and therefore also to the whole community. The extraordinary mixture of Christianity and idolatry, of medieval chivalry and the darkest barbarism support this theory. The Maltese cross and the practice of washing with cow urine are things which could not possibly originate from one and the same people. The same applies to the strongholds, and the beer worship, and the dissection of corpses. If the Khevsurs really began as refugees from all the nations, then the part which the country still plays in the Caucasus to this day is easily comprehensible, for its function as a political sanctuary is then hallowed by an age-long tradition.

Statements as to the population figures of Khevsuria vary between fifteen and twenty thousand. As has been said already, people very rarely dare to use the Khevsur rope, and whoever does so usually has something more important to do than to take a census or study the customs of his extraordinary hosts who are chivalrously protecting him. Besides, the Khevsurs are very reticent and do not say much about their customs. Perhaps they have already existed for thousands of years in their mountain cauldron, or perhaps, amid the guests who used the rope, there were also some Crusaders and pious warriors. Then the old Caucasian tale of the Crusading company which vanished in the mountains would thus find confirmation here within the free vale of Khevsuria. There is something too exceptionally odd about the armour and the crosses of the Khevsurs, about their fighting posture and their respect for their women, who are obliged virtually to pollute themselves before they can be considered clean.

14.

GERMANY IN THE MOUNTAINS

OVER THE CAUCASUS, be it in the ruins of the castles that are so strangely like those of the Rhine, or in the company of the wise-men, as they relate the history of their people to the children, or at the courts of the wild noblemen or the temples of the sinister gods, everywhere in fact, if one enjoys the confidence of the people, one may hear the same obscure legend. »Many hundreds of years ago,« the wise-men say, »our fathers came into the mountains of the Caucasus from the land of the half-moon, from Syria. Our fathers were great warriors, all sheathed in iron, and they fought in the land of the half-moon against their enemies. They were Christians and carried the cross upon their breast and had fair hair and blue eyes. Whence they came to Syria, no man knows; but they were driven out by the great Egyptian Eyub-ibn-Yussuf (Saladin).

»In the mountains they met with wild races, whom they subjugated, and set up strongholds like the strongholds of their home and built churches. Gradually they left off their own customs and married the women of the mountain people. When their Lord in the land of war (Europe) heard of it, he sent pious priests to admonish them in the commandments of their belief and to bring them back to their home. But the conquerors drove the priests away, remained in their fortresses, closed up their churches, and in the course of time forgot their origin.« At the end of the story, every relater affirms with a look of pride: »And from these knights am I descended,« and he names his name.

This tradition, which has, as I say, been maintained among several of the Caucasian peoples, is especially widespread among the race of the Ossetes, who have built their modest castles upon the eternal snow-line in the vicinity of the highest peak of the range. There are few people in the whole world who live at a higher altitude than the Ossetes.

Close behind their settlements is the everlasting snow. What persuaded them to hunt out such an inhospitable region, it is hard to conceive. The very places which were least suitable for human occupation were the ones the Ossetes chose. Any gorge to which the light of day never penetrated, or any rock hard upon the edge of a precipice, surrounded on three sides by the eternal snow, was their preferred abode. These gorges and cliffs they never left again, though there were fruitful valleys in plenty, into which the Ingushes, their neighbours, had withdrawn together with the so-called Valley Ossetes; the true Ossetes, however, remained in the hills. There they pastured their half-starved tiny sheep, and planted a miserable field, which throve but badly under the most exceptional care, and conducted their lives in a perpetual state of undernourishment. Their pastures and fields were surrounded by unfruitful land. The Ossetes knew to a fraction that the land belonging to each village could support only a certain clearly defined number of persons. And for that reason the population of the place was never allowed to exceed the number which it had been permanently established could be given the bare means of subsistence.

They found a terrible solution for the problem of population. All new-born children in excess of a fixed norm were pitilessly strangled. Life was granted to a number equal to twice that of the inhabitants who had died in the same year. The number was doubled because it was found by experience that half the children died in their first years anyway. In spite of this, the Ossetes did not descend into the valleys. They remained high up because, as they said, they wanted to stay in the strongholds which their fathers had built. These crumbling citadels do not house all of the Ossetes, but only their nobility, though the other Mountain Ossetes live under the same conditions and are looked up to in the same way as the nobility. The latter, who are known as »Irun,« are distinguished by insignia which are infinitely less deceptive than hereditary rights, coats-of-arms, and titles, to wit, their personal appearance: they are different from all other Ossetes in that they are fair, and have long blond hair and large blue eyes, which are otherwise almost never met with in the mountains.

If you ask one of these blue-eyed Ossetes about his origin, he tells—
if he is one of their wise-men and is capable of giving information—the
usual boastful story cited above, about the great knights from the land
of the half-moon, and then adds a very remarkable statement which is
much more interesting than his other explanations: he gives the name
of the knights who were his forefathers. »They were called Alleman,«
says he, and raises his glance proudly after the manner of every Caucasian when he gives the name of his family.

»Alleman?« one is startled at the sound of this word, for it is not an
Ossetian word. In all Eastern languages Alleman means German. »Were
the knights from the land of the half-moon Allemans?« I asked a distinguished Mountain Ossete. »Yes, and no ordinary Allemans but the
princes and warriors of their people. The ordinary Allemans stayed at
home.« »Where—at home?« At that my friend was silent. He did not
know precisely. He could not say where the Allemans had their home.
He merely observed: »It is very far from the land of the half-moon.«

If, at this point, one observes to the Ossete that other races in the
Caucasus claim descent from the blond knights, he merely laughs contemptuously. »The others would like it only too well, but it is we who
are the descendants. For we have the proofs.«

The people of the East love to set up claims, but they are less willing
to bring out proofs. In this case proof was important to me, and I asked,
according to the form of the land: »Honourable Lord, quench thy servant's thirst for knowledge, and favour him with the proof.« Politeness
is the best road to success in the Caucasus. The proudest Ossete cannot
resist it but will instantly unfold the proofs which he has to hand. They
are not exactly overpowering: a pair of old daggers and arms which are
undoubtedly of Nordic origin, together with a few old coats-of-arms
such as were current among the Crusaders, but also among Oriental
princes. The Ossetes, however, also possess what is much more important, old documents. Rolls of parchment which they have to show are
genuinely of Syrian origin, are written in complicated Syrian script, and
contain the names of princes of Crusading times.

These proofs are, of course, not conclusive, for they might have got into the hands of the Ossetes by a roundabout way. Even the strong belief which these blond mountain folk accord the tradition about their origin is not by itself of much account. Still, how could the information about the Allemans have reached the citadels of the Ossetes? Are they really only old legends which have been retailed to them by wanderers who stayed with them? However that may be, the blond type, the fortresses, the armour and the legends, together suggest the definite possibility that in olden times bands of German Crusaders did really conquer the gorges of the Ossetes and the savage people that dwelt there, and that later on, cut off from the world, they intermingled with their subjects. On the other hand, the latest scientific investigations show that the Ossetes are descended not from Allemani but from Allani. But this old legend remains, in any case, remarkable.

Other tribes of the mountains were occasionally taken for descendants of the German knights. Many customs and habits of the Caucasians have quite an extraordinary similarity to those of the old Germans. Perhaps these suppositions are untenable, perhaps it is all nothing but legend, which will not support the critical scrutiny of science. But in any event, the following points remain worthy of note. The Orient has sufficient knightly peoples of its own; why should the German Crusaders be the ones especially selected, from whom the proudest of the Caucasians derive their origin? What are the mysterious threads which link (to speak for the moment architecturally) the strongholds of the hills with the castles on the Rhine? Nothing but the most exact investigation of the Caucasus can fully and finally clear up these questions. In other places, however, in the Caucasus there are indubitable Allemans among the mountain tribes. For instance, in all the most fruitful valleys and by all the best-stocked rivers of Kabardia, small groups of houses are often to be met with which are not built in the Caucasian style. These settlements are surrounded by an ample palisade-fence, through which no outsider can see. The courtyard is protected by spring-guns and pitfalls. Uninvited persons (and every stranger or non-dweller within the court is considered as such) fall into one of the traps and are then put out of harm's way by the inhabitants, or at least beaten and driven away. These people are the only undeniably genuine »Allemans« of the Caucasus, even if they did have very little to do with the Crusades. They are Württemberg peasants, sectarians who many years ago attempted to make the pilgrimage from Württemberg to Jerusalem on foot under the guidance of a prophet, in order to wait there for the advent in the near future of the Millennium. One thousand five hundred families wandered from Württemberg, but, when they came to the fertile valleys of the northern Caucasus, only three hundred and sixty-eight people were willing to continue the journey under the leadership of the prophetess Barbara Spann. The rest stayed in the Caucasus, built their huts at distant intervals—so as not to see the smoke of their neighbours—and were regularly plundered by the greedy Kabardians. Finally these Germans surrounded their courtyards with palisades, started a courageous, efficiently equipped home guard, surrounded themselves with covered pitfalls, and in the course of their fight with the »savages« forgot all about the dread prophecies of a threatened Millennium.

In this way the number of the mountain tribes has increased by one. And yet this youngest of the Caucasian peoples refuses to take over anything from its neighbours and has no use for cultural propaganda. The little tribe follows its agricultural pursuits, speaks its Württemberger dialect, wears the clothes that were worn in Germany a hundred years ago, and refuses stubbornly and persistently to allow any native to step across the threshold of its gates.

Once a year these peasants are visited by the tax officials, but otherwise they are molested by nobody. They themselves never leave their settlement, because every man who is absent weakens the guard and thereby incites their dear neighbours to an attack.

This only applies to the Germans living in North Caucasus, especially in Kabardia. To those living in the south, i.e., in Transcaucasia, other conditions apply. The Kabardian Germans practically never come into contact with the natives, and therefore there can be no discussion as to the Caucasian influence upon them. An influence of this kind makes itself felt only when a German lives amongst the natives continuously.

The story of Adolf Peschke, a front-line soldier, shows how a German living at close quarters with the natives can adopt the Caucasian ideas of good and evil and make them his own.

At home Adolf Peschke was probably an honest young apprentice, or messenger boy, or perhaps even a farmhand. He had no feeling for the exotic and would certainly have developed into a conventional German lower-middle-class person, if the war had not come and turned his life course in an unexpected direction, as it did to so many others.

Adolf Peschke arrived on the Eastern front, topk up his appointed position, fired upon enemy trenches, and dreamed of his native land whenever there was a pause in the fighting. One day the great turning-point of his career occurred. During an attack he was overcome by an absolute savage, who trussed him up and took him back to the trenches of the enemy as a prisoner. The enemy in this case was a division of Caucasian cavalry—led by native officers—who were allowed (even in the World War) to behave in the traditional way towards their enemies. Thus their opponents were not turned over to the prison-camps, but were declared the property of whoever had captured them. For a high ransom they were allowed back to their homes. But if they could not raise the money they had to perform menial tasks for their masters.

Adolf Peschke had no money, and his owner needed no servant at the front. But at home in the native village in the hills he could make good use of the prisoner. The young men were away at war and the women alone could not manage the work in the fields. So the Caucasian quickly made up his mind to adopt his prisoner. The adoption ceremony was carried out according to all the rules of mountain law, and in the twinkling of an eye the astonished Peschke suddenly became a Caucasian and the bearer of a name which during the first few weeks he was not even able to pronounce. He now went to the village of his new father, worked in the fields, and became gradually accustomed to his new country. Finally his father and his brother returned from the war, and Peschke soon became a full-fledged member of the warlike Ingush family. He had in the meantime learnt their language and, as a man of good understanding, mentally alert, he had steeped himself in the study of the traditions and habits of the hill people, which had become his own.

The years passed by, and a miracle occurred. The German became so much of an Ingush that the severest upholder of good Ingush custom had no more to teach him. Adolf Peschke appeared punctually at meetings of the village elders and stood humbly at the door as became a young man of the tribe. He never spoke to one of the elders before he was asked, ate with his hands like his comrades, married a native girl, and was painfully careful that no smallest detail of ceremony should be forgotten at the wedding. He soon knew by heart the names and careers of all his five hundred relatives together with their forefathers and ancestors right back to the namesake and founder of the family. In one word, his father could really wish for no better son than Adolf Peschke, the adopted German prisoner of war.

But it now happened that a distant relative of the family to which the German belonged was attacked by enemies and killed. They declared a feud at once. One of the most zealous was Adolf Peschke, the German soldier. Armed to the teeth he lurked in hiding for the enemy, and fell on them whenever he could. In the evening before eating he never omitted to carry out the old, half-forgotten custom of setting the dead man's portion of food outside the window and weeping aloud. He became gradually graver and older and was therefore soon permitted to speak at the village assemblies. He used this freedom—thereby rejoicing the hearts of all the wise-men—by tediously examining every question to determine how far, if at all, it agreed with the law of the fathers.

At the time, of which I have already spoken, when the Republic of Ingushia sent its »Commission for the Abolition of the Blood Feud« into the mountains, and was reconciling one enemy after another, Adolf Peschke was the first to take to the mountain tops for fear he should be forced to forgive his enemies. The Commission of princes hurried after him in pursuit, but he was very clever at concealing himself. When he was finally caught, and the princes of the people knelt before him and begged him to forgive his enemies, he drew himself up proudly and made a speech in the Ingush language to more or less the following effect:

He considered it an unparalleled presumption that they should consider him capable of betraying an age-old custom. He was the bearer of one of the best Ingush names and knew what he owed to the spirit of his dead relative and to the honour of his family. Never under any circumstances would he betray the laws of his fathers, the holiest heritage of the Ingush nation. Even if all his relatives renounced blood vengeance, he would maintain it alone to the last.

The princes talked to him for days. Even his own relatives, who had long been prepared to conclude a peace pressed him to give in. But nothing could move the German; he remained rigid and immovable. All he would say was: »The law says: Upon murder let there be vengeance. Therefore I cannot agree.« »But all the rest have submitted and forgiven,« the Commission begged. »Then shame upon them!« cried Peschke angrily. And even when the princes finally wanted to kiss his feet, he did not give in, but stood up and said that, as a simple defender of the law, he was unworthy of such an honour, and withdrew.

It was in vain that his relatives declared that they would not support him in the prosecution of the blood feud; he only said that, much against his will, he must set his relatives down as apostates and would therefore leave the village with his wife in order to withdraw to the mountains where he could pursue his duty without hindrance. He was as good as his word. He swept off into the mountains and renounced all intercourse with his relatives. Even his wife could not move him to surrender.

It was not until the oldest and wisest man in the land sought him out and proved to him that, according to an old law, reconciliation between blood enemies was possible under special circumstances, that Peschke returned to his village and ceremoniously forgave his enemies. He was now doubly revered for his stubbornness. To this day he lives in his Ingush village, a strict and literal protector of patriarchal law, as behoves a good Ingush.

15.

CIVIS ROMANUS SUM

AN OLD CAUCASIAN ANECDOTE relates that a detachment of Russian troops was once climbing a wild height in Daghestan. Even the most experienced Caucasians in the troop were deeply impressed with the sheer heights and vertiginous depths. The native guides themselves refused to climb farther and swore that no human being had ever set foot on the summit of the pass they were trying to reach.

This very fact stimulated the ambition of the Russian General who was leading the troops. »We are conquering the mountain tribes; let us conquer the mountains as well,« said he, and gave the command to proceed. He wanted to erect a memorial on the summit of the unknown mountain in honour of the first men, soldiers of His Majesty the Tsar, to climb this peak, thus accomplishing something which had never been done before. And so the ascent continued. The men clung to the sheer cliff-walls with hands and feet, conquered the precipice, cut themselves steps in the snow and ice with picks and axes, fell headlong into the depths below, or fainted and froze to death in the eternal snow.

But in spite of all, the vain wish of the General had to be fulfilled. It succeeded. The summit was reached. The soldiers rested and looked for a suitable stone on which to chisel their deed. They had not long to seek. A smooth rock rose up at the edge of the peak and seemed the foreordained place for an inscription. The General and his officers approached, and chisels were produced. Then suddenly they recoiled, looked at each other in dismay, and hung their heads. What an unlooked-for climax! The General finally turned and gave a dry, brief command to prepare for the return.

Carved deep into the rock he had found a weather-beaten inscription of which a few words could still be deciphered: »Pompeius Imperator—Legio XIV Anno ...« The Russians were therefore not the first to conquer the mountain. Two thousand years previously the Romans had anticipated them.

I do not know whether there is any truth in this story, or whether the great Roman did really perpetuate his name in the rock on the occasion of his famous Caucasian campaign. But in any case the Romans were not infrequent visitors to the Land of Mountains. Innumerable Græco-Roman towns arose there, which later on in some cases fell into the hands of Genoese merchants and played an important part as their colonies right into the heart of the Middle Ages. Still later, the Greek, Roman, and Genoese influences disappeared, leaving no trace except for the fair-haired girls of Mingrelia with their indisputable Genoese characteristics, and for the remarkable and mysterious Kubachi clan, whom I should hardly dare to describe here had not serious scholars (among them the German professors Dorn and Frae) recorded the most unheard-of facts about this extraordinary race.

The Kubachi are not numerous; they inhabit only one village in Daghestan, somewhat to the west of the town of Derbent, and they belong to the so-called »Darghi Society.« The village is also called Kubachi and has three or four thousand inhabitants. These people do not in the slightest degree resemble their neighbours the Darghi into whose community they have been accepted. And, moreover, they have absolutely no desire to be confused with their neighbours, and maintain persistently that they are not Caucasians but Romans. And the people of Daghestan for their part are just as unwilling to recognize any resemblance to themselves in the Kubachi.

»The Kubachi are not Caucasians,« they say with contempt; »they came from Rome, from the West.« They hate and despise the Kubachi and avoid their society as they would that of foreigners.

Many years ago, in the sixth and seventh centuries, thinks Professor Dorn, these Romans were summoned to the country by a ruler of Daghestan, and they settled there as armourers. (The word Kubachi means an armourer in Azerbaijan.) They were granted their autonomy, and as early as the fourteenth century they founded a free republic, whose administration is an exact replica of the administration of the free Italian city-states of the Middle Ages. They led a fairly isolated existence, and to this day there is practically no exact information about them. They are hospitable, like all Caucasians, but they will never conduct a stranger into their mysterious underground passages, which they have constructed underneath their village, and about which fantastic tales are current. Into these gigantic catacombs (of which the access is not known) the entire inhabitants of the village disappear from time to time. It is maintained in Daghestan that they lead the lives of their forefathers, the Roman merchants, within these underground passages, which are supposed to house the remains of their ancient culture. Perhaps they pray to the old gods or meditate silently upon their past glory, or perhaps—as their enemies the Kumyks maintain —they even forge money there. As a matter of fact, the Kubachi are decried all over the Caucasus as arrant counterfeiters, in spite of the fact that the profession of armourer is considered sacred. They maintain a remarkably high level of culture, as exemplified by the fact that they introduced compulsory education for girls some centuries ago.

Further reports say that they possess a magistracy, streets which are well cared for, and can even boast a street-lighting system of their own, which is to this very day a thing unknown in all the rest of the Orient.

The mental gulf separating this race of »Romans« from the other Caucasians is a remarkable one: their women wear no veils and carry their jewellery openly about, and upon marriage no purchase money is given for the women, but a dowry is brought by her to the man, on the European model.

Reliable Arabic scholars, among them Abu Hamid el Andalusi, have told of women's schools and women teachers among the Kubachi, and have even instanced praying temples for women. This alone ought to be enough to mark them as not Oriental, but »Roman« or »Ferengi« (Franks, i.e., Europeans). There is moreover one custom of theirs that one frequently runs across which is now known neither among Europeans nor among Orientals. It is a sort of sacred prostitution which is certainly not Latin. It is customary for widows and women who have been forsaken by their husbands to lie down on the thresholds of their houses in the evening, with their eyes bandaged, and there to await the passers-by, to whom they are allowed to give themselves between the hours of two and three at night. Only they are forbidden to see the face of their chance lover. Any unmarried man may approach these women, and it is considered dishonouring to a woman not to subject herself to this practice. The children who are born of these nights are considered the property of the community, enjoy certain privileges, and are brought up at the expense of the town. The Kubachi are careful, however, not to carry on their customs if a stranger comes anywhere within range of their village. They are far too reticent to betray the very smallest of their customs and intellectual inheritance to a stranger, and are afraid of the outside world because they know that they are decried and disliked.

There is just one of their passions which they like to confide to foreigners; in fact they literally overwhelm him with it. Oddly enough, they are fanatical antique-collectors, and, more remarkable still, really great connoisseurs in the matter. Many of them have quite large museums in their houses, and the Kubachi likes nothing better than to be asked to show his treasures and to tell the history of some individual piece. They are by no means poor as a race, but pass their lives travelling about through all the countries of the Orient, and take the opportunity of buying up any antiques which seem to them to be valuable.

It is not advisable to buy anything from the collections of the Kubachi. They are only too ready to sell and are past masters at foisting off forgeries which they have made themselves. They rarely, if ever, part with a really valuable piece, such as the remarkable old sword which was discovered among them by a scholar and which bore the inscription in Latin »Viou Re Aut Vio Gungard. Vicere Ant Mo Glori Igarni.«

These latter characteristics of the Kubachi seem rather to contradict the possibility of Roman descent. But there still seems no doubt as to their European origin. »Ferengi« they are, beyond question.

But in any case the proud claim of the Kubachi, »Civis Romanus Sum,« is not just fabricated out of air. In the middle of their village, on the little market place, there stands a fairly high stone building without windows and possessing only a small entrance door. This building is more honoured by the Kubachi than their richest collection of antiques. It is the only authentic cultural memorial of late antiquity in the wilds of Daghestan. The outer walls of the building are covered with bas-reliefs representing various animals and horsemen. The style of the sculptor's work is of classical antiquity. No stranger is ever allowed into the interior of the holy place. Only one man has been successful in viewing the interior and that was the German scholar Professor Dorn. He saw the inner walls decorated with similar reliefs, and among them one which represented two women who were celebrating a feast at a table, together with a man in a sort of monk's cowl. When the inhabitants were asked who the man was they replied: »Our lord, the Emperor of Rome,« but by this they may also have meant the Pope. When they are asked who constructed the building, the Kubachi answer solemnly: »Rome,« and at this word they raise their hands fervently to heaven.

Surrounded as they are by a phlegmatic population, these remarkable Romans are well known in the mountains of Daghestan as very active organizers. They are all handicraftsmen and they are organized into a kind of syndicate, which has had branches in all the important towns in the East and even in St. Petersburg, Paris, and London. They all co-operate in their work at their weapons and their gold and silver articles, with a perfect system of division of labour. Each worker prepares one single, and always the same, part of the article and consequently acquires, even artistically speaking, a noticeably high degree of craftsmanship. The taste of the Kubachi is more European than Oriental, though it has been proven that they have never come into contact with Europeans during the last two hundred years.

Whence then does this remarkable people originate, fitting as it does so uneasily into the world of Daghestan? They have taken over the language of their neighbours the Darghi, although it differs in various particulars. And it is precisely in its differences, that is to say in the words which do not tally with the Darghi language, that this tongue sounds so surprisingly European. »I,« for example, is »je,« both in Kubachi and in French; »he« = »il«; »we« = »nussa« (nous); »eye« = »ule« (l'œil); »hat« = »kappa«; »mouth« = »mulle« (German, mewl); and so forth.

All these facts—the legends of Roman origin, the ancient sculpture, and the surprising linguistic relics— awakened at one period the curiosity of certain scholars.

They visited Kubachi and began taking skull measurements, which seemed to them the quickest and surest way of establishing the racial affinities of the Kubachi. The skull measurements established beyond a doubt that the Kubachi were but little related to the other tribes of Daghestan. But the scientists were soon left speechless with astonishment by the fact that, as soon as the anthropo-metric data were scientifically examined, it transpired that the Kubachi must be most closely related to the Parisians and the Savoyards, and that consequently this Caucasian race was of Latin origin.

The unexpected discovery of real Parisians in the mountains of Daghestan—added to the fact that these Parisians called themselves »Romans« or »Franks«—might have become a sensation if the world at large had been sufficiently interested in the Land of Mountains. Only think of this European, Latin, or Roman stem flourishing in the midst of a wild primitive people, in the rude mountains of Asia, cut off from all the rest of the world, disconnected from Europe for perhaps a thousand years. Underground catacombs, Roman inscriptions, a sense of organization and handicraft, and the strange legends of their Roman origin all distinguish these people from their neighbours.

The latter stare in hostility at this intruder with his alien culture, and have often tried to destroy or drive him out. But each time the Kubachi disappear for months on end into their catacombs. One day they emerge suddenly and unexpectedly, drive away their enemies with a surprise attack, and continue to defy their opponents.

Thus have they maintained their customs throughout the centuries, and retained everything from their native land which was dear to them. They kept on unconcernedly trading and travelling and never faltered in their marked preference for organized, rationalized, communal work. This race is apparently indestructible. The ravages of men and of time are powerless against it. It still exists today, at this very hour, as the most remarkable example of the everlasting toughness of a noble race which maintains its individuality even when surrounded by enemies. The Kubachi have forfeited their language and their beliefs. They are officially Mohammedans. But if you ask a Kubachi about his origin, he replies (even if it be in the rough language of the Darghi) with the old proud phrase of his forefathers: »Civis Romanus Sum«: »I am a Roman citizen.«

16.

THE HERO OF THE MOUNTAINS

THE CAUCASUS is not merely a fairyland. Apart from the amazing remnants of nations, the dark legends and grim ruins, it can also boast of occurrences which have played a decisive part in the life of today. Here it was that the political and economic battles began which shook the entire Orient to its foundations, and here, too, conspiracies were enacted of which the informers of the Tsar seemed never to get news quickly enough.

Here, amid the blue mountains and the green valleys, was the meeting-place of the most dangerous of Russian conspirators; here, too, those organizations were founded which trained leaders and terrorists for future battles against the Tsar. Here the proclamations of Lenin were printed, and bold men carried them hence over the mountains and spread them throughout the great empire of the Tsar. Generals were assailed here with bombs; threats were uttered here in the open, which were punishable in Russia by imprisonment in Siberia.

The police, that dread implement of the Tsar, was powerless. The Caucasians laughed at it; they had reliable ways and means of protecting themselves against it, means which even the power of the Viceroy, the first man in rank after the Tsar, was no match against. Every time the police succeeded, after long preparation, in catching a revolutionary and imprisoning him in the fortress of Mtekha, one could be certain that the prisoner would escape after a few months. And if the revolutionaries needed money, arms, and help, they knew where to go for it and who could help them without running any danger of pursuit. It was, therefore, nothing to be wondered at that the Caucasus produced the most feared revolutionaries and bombers in Russia, and that the men who alone accomplished the first and second revolutions, who overthrew the Tsar and carried the five-pointed star to victory, were from the mountains.

The Tsars, it is true, subjugated the Caucasus with fire and the sword, and oppressed the inhabitants, and exercised their tyranny over them for a century of uninterrupted campaigns, but today the people of the hills can be certain that their dead warriors have been avenged with blood. For a Caucasian rules today in the land of the Tsar, and he is surrounded by Caucasians. They make the laws, control the lives of a great people, suppress what they want to suppress, and introduce Caucasian customs into the Kremlin, just as the Tsar once introduced his customs into the palaces of the Georgian princes. Russia, after fighting with the Caucasus for a hundred years, has been forced at last to bow before a band of Caucasians and to turn over the government of the land to them.

The name of the Caucasian, the Georgian, who with his countrymen conquered Russia has already been mentioned in these pages. But Stalin is not his only name; he has called himself Koba, David, Nisheradse, Chichikov, Ivanovich in the course of his career and only latterly Stalin. His real name is Joseph Vissarionovich Djugashvili—the son of a shoemaker in Tiflis.

The rise of this man is remarkable. Stalin began his career as a pious student of the theological seminary in Tiflis. One year before taking his priest's examination he was expelled for »Socialist heresy,« as they said in those days. This fate did not fall upon him alone; several other of his fellow-students were thrown out with him. The seminar was apparently a nest of Socialists, and it was these expelled priests, with Stalin at their head, who became the kernel of the Transcaucasian Activists, the most faithful of Lenin's disciples.

They were a very remarkable race of men, these Transcaucasian Activists. Their members belonged to small national groups and were mostly illiterate, wild warriors who had, God knows how, found their way to Marxism. Fundamentally they had not a thing in common with Socialism. It was a typically Caucasian band of mountaineers, who hated towns and their culture in direct proportion to the revolt which they felt in the depths of their souls against the churches with their golden cupolas, the white-haired priests, and portraits of the Tsar next crucifixes. They came riding into the towns on little horses, plundered the inhabitants, abducted the pretty girls and fat sheep, sent off a couple of shots into the air for the sake of effect, and disappeared again into the blue highlands, where they sang wild songs about their glorious past as they sat around the fire upon some crag.

In former times, when the Caucasians were still fighting against the Tsar, they were called »Defenders of the Fatherland«; later they were Mohammedans enlisted in the holy war against the Christians; now they were named (with their full consent) »Socialists« or »Marxists« or, more important still and more comprehensibly, »Transcaucasian Activists.« They were feared far and wide. So much so that the real Marxian faction in Russia used to conjure with the name Transcaucasian Activists as the surest means of intimidating their adversaries.

Stalin did not immediately become the leader of these Activists. He had first to go through a long hard school of conspiracy, of propaganda work, of coldbloodedness and of revolutionary strategy. The secret work which Stalin devoted to the revolution is still only too little known. It is only certain that for years he manufactured the propaganda material of the revolutionaries in secret underground printing presses. For years he scarcely emerged from his hiding-place into the light of day. Later on, he also undertook the dangerous transportation of revolutionary literature (the Bolshevik presses were situated in the Caucasus) and escaped several times from prison, even from Siberian jails. It was not until after the break between Lenin and the other revolutionaries and the formation of the Bolshevik party that Stalin's real activities began, those activities which earned him the name of the bloodiest man of the party and laid the foundation for the tremendous development of his power in the revolutionary period.

In the years 1906 to 1907, the years in which the post-revolutionary reaction in Russia was at its height, Stalin gained his first laurels.

Lenin and Trotsky were at that time living in Paris and only possessed one pair of shoes between them. The party treasury was absolutely empty. The attempt to manufacture false bank-notes was a failure. The experiment of marrying off young Communists to old and wealthy widows, in order to use the dowry for party purposes, also failed after the first few successful attempts. The latter idea was Lenin's own. The executive committee therefore decided to take steps to carry out »Exes.« An »Ex« signified an expropriation of private property. The activities consisted in Communists penetrating a bank, a private house, or a shop, stealing money, jewels, and other treasures, and adding them to the party funds. It was not easy to find good workers for the »Exes,« for not every Communist was willing or inclined to participate in theft or murder. So gradually »Exes« became the special province of the Transcaucasian Activists, and Stalin was the first to declare himself ready to carry out, at the head of his compatriots, any »Ex« that was required of him. And a series of daredevil raids, which usually involved the taking of human life as well, were actually perpetrated in the Caucasus under the leadership of Stalin in the years 1906, 1907, and 1908.

Even today the older inhabitants of Tiflis are still ready to tell of the greatest of all the »Exes,« the attack upon the cashier of the Russian National Bank. It occurred on June 13, 1907, at twelve o'clock noon. The cashier of the bank, Kurdjukov, had fetched a consignment of money from the post which had just arrived from Russia. It contained a million roubles, in notes of five hundred roubles. On its return to the bank, the conveyance, accompanied as usual by a guard of Cossacks, passed in front of the Viceroy's palace on the most crowded street of Tiflis (which is an entirely Europeanized town).

From the roof of a house adjoining the palace a bomb was suddenly thrown at the truck, and at the same time several of the passers-by began shooting at the Cossacks. A panic resulted into which were swept the Cossacks, the police, everybody. A young man came out of the adjoining house and hurried towards the truck. Several Cossacks observed this and made for him, but the young man quickly threw another bomb, and Cossacks and horses fell lacerated to the ground. By a miracle, the young man himself remained unharmed. Revolver shots rang out. He returned the fire as he gained the burning truck, tore the money bag away from the dead cashier, and disappeared without leaving a trace behind. The whole affair took place within the space of a few minutes. Fifty dead men lay on the main street of Tiflis, and the booty contributed a million roubles to the treasury of the Communist party. The young man who carried out this »Ex« was Stalin.

The whole Russian police set to work, but neither the perpetrator nor a single penny of the money was ever found, for it lay in good custody, half in the divan of His Highness the Viceroy and half in the mattress of a peaceable astronomy professor. No detective could suspect it of being there. Later the money travelled by the usual route to Lenin in Paris and was changed in various Paris banks, before the Paris police had been informed of the numbers of the stolen five-hundred-rouble notes.

Only the very last note was intercepted. The man who presented it was locked up. He was a follower of Lenin, a Communist by the name of Wallach. He is now called Litvinov and is well known as the Minister for Foreign Affairs in the Soviet Union.

Scarcely had the money been shipped over the frontier, than Stalin began to prepare new »Exes.« A few weeks later he attacked a mail coach on the main road between Tiflis and Kachory, the summer residence of the Georgian princes, and again carried off one hundred thousand roubles. Seven men had their throats cut in the process.

Such »Exes« were also brought off throughout the rest of Russia, but it was chiefly owing to the sums brought in by Stalin that existence was made possible for the Communist party. Occasionally, of course, an »Ex« resulted in someone's private enrichment; it was impossible to keep any control over the loot.

But behind the low forehead of Stalin such thoughts found no place. He sent everything to Lenin, down to the last penny. He was banished five times to Siberia, and succeeded five times in breaking out of the prison. It was then that his legend began, and it was then that he acquired the immense number of his followers, men who are not so much intellectually convinced comrades, as the followers of an Oriental chieftain.

I have met this remarkable chieftain, have stood face to face with him and looked into his little dark eyes, in which there is a peculiar and typically Caucasian smile. Oriental despots and diplomats often have such eyes, when they consider themselves possessed of a higher truth, which protects them and for which they are fighting. Abdul Hamid had eyes like that, and he was the only ruler of modern times who could match Stalin in the number of murders he committed. Stalin has a long curved nose, thick, coal-black hair, and a very low—a pathologically low—forehead. In olden times he would have become the founder of a dynasty. He has no programme and no ideas which he need set about realizing or which he could be compelled to deny. His only intellectual furniture is abstract Communism and the unshakable conviction that mankind can only be ruled with the whip. He rarely comes into the open himself. He has also never been an émigré like all other Russian politicians. Even when he was being harried by the police and on the verge of ruin, he never fled the country but stayed in the rude mountains of his home country affording material for new legends. He is modest and pays very little attention to externals. He has never solicited a leading position. Today, when he is at the summit of power as the dictator of Russia, he is outwardly no more than the general secretary of the party.

He is pleasanter in private intercourse than he is in his public life. His Georgian nationality, the friendliest nationality in the world, is not quite extinguished. But even when he is drinking, his inborn monkish severity never quite leaves him. He is still the erstwhile student of the priesthood, and several unfrocked priests can be found in his own immediate circle. Many revolutionaries were furnished by the Caucasian priests' seminaries. The Armenian Mikoyan, Stalin's friend, who is now Minister of Commerce, was also at a priests' school. Stalin likes to surround himself with his own kind; with Caucasians who rave about him; with ecclesiastical students who still know the Gospels by heart from the old days, as he does himself; with simple, wild people who tell stories of the good old days, of the famous, bloody, foolhardy »Exes.«

When he is irritated, he lowers his head and looks up at his opponent from below. There is something of the primitive savage about him at such times. The cynical smile disappears, and he becomes red in the face. You are afraid that something terrible may happen at any moment. It is dangerous to irritate Stalin.

The fact that he has not long ago become a legendary figure is due to his talent for obscurity and to his masterly concealment by means of innumerable names, which he changed incessantly. And lastly it is due to the fact that, at the same time that he was carrying out his »Exes« for Lenin, another Caucasian, another »hero,« was carrying off all the laurels of Oriental fame and capturing the attention of the mountain people, embodying in his own person the romance of Caucasian knighthood.

This Caucasian had nothing to do with any revolution. And he was neither a prince nor a wise-man. He was simply the Abrek Selim-Khan from Kharachoi in the land of the Chechens, the greatest, and most feared and renowned robber in the mountains. The deeds of this Abrek are wonderful. There was no bank in the Caucasus which he had not once plundered, no millionaire whose burden of wealth he had not lightened, no Russian officer or official who had not trembled before him. The Abrek robbed and murdered and divided up the spoils among his poor countrymen; he bowed low before every prince and every priest and wrote grotesque letters to the Russian generals who could not catch him.

One of his letters said: »General, do you know why you can't catch me? Because you are a wicked man! Your father certainly took bribes, and I suppose that you yourself were once the playboy of a priest. Your daughter also is a harlot and sleeps with a Frenchman. How should God help you in a fight against me?«

For many years the Russians had to let these gems of style as well as a great deal more pass without reply. Finally the Government sent a complete army against the facetious Abrek. At the head of the army rode a brutal general, who destroyed entire villages, tore down houses, and killed every armed man, whose family he then turned out of the country or locked up, on the theory that the population as a whole was supporting the Abrek.

When Selim-Khan heard about this, he spread his hands in amazement. »How can he destroy houses? The people have built them!« Then he sat down and wrote to the General: »I, the Abrek Selim-Khan, have been a brigand for ten years and I have caused less damage than you have during the ten days you have been in the mountains. Why do you kill people? You only have to kill me! I suggest the following to you: You leave my people alone and I will leave your soldiers alone. Instead of a universal murder I am naming a place where we two can come together and fight a duel, as befits decent people.«

The General did not care to recognize the challenge, because a brigand was not capable of giving satisfaction to his rank. But soon he realized that he would do better to accept the duel, for the Abrek was distributing his letter in all the villages, and everyone was whispering that the General was a coward! He was afraid of the Abrek! Finally his own people, the Cossacks, who had grown up in the hills themselves, began to grumble and despise their General who would not behave like a gentleman.

So finally he agreed, and they came together in a lonely valley; His Excellency the General, knight of all the orders there were, courtier, diplomat, and cavalier, and the brigand, the peasant's son, the Abrek, who was none the less his equal by birth here in the mountains. The battle, which was conducted according to all the rules of the art of war in the Caucasus, did not last long. The General was carried off the field of honour severely wounded. The Abrek now thought, as any other man from the hills would also have thought, that he had conquered Russia and would henceforward be left in peace. But he was mistaken. The General recovered quickly and persecuted the hill people more than ever. At this the Abrek raged with fury. He, and not the General, had been victorious in the fight. No conquered man should behave so meanly as this.

One night he slipped into the town to the house of the General and drew a home-made bomb out of his belt. Now he was certain that the

General's hour had struck. But by chance a native prince came round the corner, and recognized the Abrek with horror. The Russians would have tormented every mountain dweller they could lay hands on almost to death, if the attempt upon the General took place.

The prince had no time to explain all this to the robber at once. So he went by him quite calmly, stroked his arm, and said: »It is forbidden.« That was enough. The Abrek attached his bomb to his belt again and disappeared from the town. Later on, he did kill the General in open battle in one of the mountain ravines. After that he started plundering banks and rich men again (but not princes), saying the proper prayers as he did so. When he was told that there were people who wanted to overthrow the Tsar, he was most childishly amazed. He, Selim-Khan, whom the legends so often confused with Stalin, was convinced that he was one of the most submissive and devoted servants of the Tsar and the princes. In 1913 he was killed by the bullets of Cossacks and blood avengers.

Songs are sung about him to this very day.

There was never a greater robber in all the Caucasus. Only Stalin could have been a match for him. But Stalin would look down on such fame nowadays; he would prefer to rule in the Kremlin. Stalin, Selim-Khan, and many others—one must know them to understand the Caucasus in the slightest degree. Nowhere in the world are so closely interwoven the threads of past and present, chivalry and Marxism, romance and political economy, secret presses and simple murder and robbery, as in the Caucasus; nowhere does the unbelievable so quickly become the actual, or the actual so quickly become an exuberant legend.

17.

LAMAROI

SEMM-KHAN, THE GREAT ROBBER, was a Chechen and came from the jungles which cover the north-west Caucasus. The inhabitants of this district are split up into a number of independent peoples. I leave it to specialists in the matter to sort them out. The Russians arbitrarily call these people by the collective name »Circassians« although the real Circassians, or Cherkesses, only constitute a small section of them. The rest of the Caucasians call them Lamaroi, that is to say, »dwellers upon the hill-tops.«

These Lamaroi, and above all the Cherkesses, lead a remarkable existence. They have been able to make their way through world history without ever grasping the meaning of the concepts, »government« and »authority.« Every Circassian lives for himself, obeys nobody, and never can understand how people can obediently pay their taxes and still think themselves worthy of respect. Once, for example, in the dim and distant past, the Chechens, who are a division of the Lamaroi, invited a foreign prince to come and defend them against their enemies so that they might be left in peace. The prince was supposed to keep a portion of the loot which he captured for himself. He »ruled« for a few years and then fled from the land and swore never again to accept the invitation of a mountain people. Every Chechen laughed at the prince and treated him—although he was officially supposed to be the ruler—as a sort of employee or domestic servant. Since that time, the Chechens have never had another prince. Everyone is his own prince, makes laws which only he obeys, and despises the man who accepts a master.

It is said that shortly before the war a Russian prince was travelling through the mountains with a brilliant cortege. He visited the hut of a young Chechen and was surprised that he did not even rise at his entry.

»Why don't you stand up? Don't you know who I am?« asked the prince.

»Well, who are you then anyway?«

»I am a prince, a relative of the Tsar.«

»What is a prince?«

The prince felt it was obviously incumbent upon him to make his meaning clear to this savage. »A prince is a great man,« he said; »he has many lands and many servants; his forbears were famous people honoured by the Tsar; a prince is almost the greatest man in the land.«

»Good,« said the Chechen, »tell me one thing, who stands between you and God?«

»Between me and God stands nobody but the Tsar.«

»There you are—now between me and God there is nobody at all, so I don't have to honour you, on the contrary you ought to honour me.« And with that he turned his back on the prince.

This instance and others like it are told about the Chechens with a good deal of relish. They are always in a chronic state of feeling themselves insulted by their fellow-creatures, and maintain that nobody can be considerate or respectful enough to them as a completely free people. There is some justification for this feeling since all their neighbours are plunged in feudalism. But an insulted Lamaroi is the most dangerous thing you can run up against in the mountains, much more dangerous than the leopards that are still to be found in the forests of Chechenia and Ichkaria. He is like a man running amuck. With bloodshot eyes he will gallop through the hills on a fiery charger, roaring at the top of his voice and throwing himself about in the saddle like a man possessed. In his mad course he will attack and kill anyone who crosses his path. The grounds of this excitement in a Chechen are as often as not absolutely irrelevant. A glance or an insufficiently respectful movement is quite frequently enough to make the man boil over with fury, seize his dagger, and strike down anybody within reach.

This habit of being insulted by everybody is possessed to a high degree by all Caucasians, Georgians, and Azerbaijans. The results of being insulted also work themselves out along similar lines with them.

But still there is no people that achieves white heat so easily as the Lamaroi. Moreover, the word used by the Caucasians for the state of »being insulted« does not quite hit off the nature of this condition. A Lamaroi may put up with considerable insult and injury to his honour without so much as leaving his house. But on the other hand he may often wake up in the morning in an access of rage. He is then insulted »by his dream,« as the people have it. If an offended Lamaroi is unable to run across anybody else, he turns his weapons against himself just to be able to let loose and see blood.

You have to know your Caucasian psychology very well, to spend much time in safety with the Lamaroi, or indeed with any of the other hill people.

A European can hardly hope to succeed even with the best will in the world. With the most peaceable of intentions he is in danger of conjuring up an insult and all that is consequent upon it. In Russia this characteristic of the Lamaroi was well known. In the military schools, in which the Lamaroi were willingly accepted because of their military ability, this circumstance was taken into special account. Caucasian weapons were kept ready for the Lamaroi in a special room, together with some furniture and other wooden articles. As soon as one of the future officers fell into a state of »being about to be insulted,« he was set upon with lightning rapidity by the guard and shut up in the room before anything worse could occur. He could then chop up the furniture with a sword or a dagger as much as he liked and make firewood of them.

Generally he had worked it all off after an hour or two, upon which they sent two of his own countrymen into the room in all seriousness to sue formally and ceremoniously for peace and to fix up the practical question of the price for the insult, according to home custom.

The price, even at the military school, was always a banquet to be given in honour of the insulted person. When some such definite conclusion to the negotiations had been arrived at, the Lamaroi left the confinement room proudly and victoriously, and the servants brought round new furniture for the next frenzied man. These measures were supremely reasonable, because, if the Lamaroi cannot satisfy his urge to let himself go on something, he will keep looking for a chance to take it out on the offender. So the Russians invented the wooden phantom as an object of revenge for their cadets. The idea might be tried out sometime as a solution of great international squabbles.

It is difficult to explain clearly to a European what comes into the category of an insult to a Lamaroi—and in a more limited sense to all Caucasians. Abuse never is, because, if a Lamaroi says he has been insulted by a word of abuse, he means something quite different. Even slander does not count as an insult. But any kind of injustice does, be it never so slight; and also anything which implies the smallest degree of degradation: the merest implication that he—the Lamaroi—cannot do something or other which another man can do with ease. But above all every kind of indifference, every undervaluation or scorn, or even a movement which implies any of these things is an unbearable injury.

It would, for instance, be a dreadful insult to a Lamaroi who was relating something if you were to tell him that you were not interested in his story, or not competent to pass on it. So that if, for example, a Lamaroi is telling a police official about his cow, which is sick, and asks for some medicine, the official must not reply in a matter-of-fact way: »My dear fellow, I am honoured by the confidence but I don't know a thing about cows.« In such a case, he must get some substance or other, such as a piece of sugar, and offer it as a cure, explaining very politely at the same time: »If this piece of sugar doesn't help, then my knowledge is—to my extremely painful regret—exhausted. I fear you must seek help from another, one who knows more about it than I do.« Then he must name the other person—preferably a veterinary surgeon —and assure the Lamaroi expressly, politely, and repeatedly of his entire sympathy.

I shall never forget the circumstances of one affront which took place in my presence and which only ended without bloodshed by the merest chance.

This event occurred some years ago, and not in the Caucasus at all, but in Germany at a world-famous spa where invalids (and healthy people as well) came every year from all parts of the world to amuse themselves. I was also staying there and happened to make the acquaintance of a Circassian prince, who considered it necessary, for reasons which were not quite clear even to himself, to favour the spa with a visit that year. Everybody goes through a cure there, prescribed either by a doctor or from some other such quarter.

The prince's imagination was not sufficient to prescribe something for himself. So he decided, as others did, to ask the advice of some luminary of medical science. He kept putting off the visit and finally arrived in the waiting-room of the famous professor three days before his departure. As he could not speak a word of German, and the doctor was not very well up on his Circassian, I accompanied the prince. I knew that it was not compatible with princely dignity to be kept waiting in a waiting-room, so I had announced the visit beforehand in order that we might be received without fail. The doctor examined the prince, asked a few questions, which I translated in a considerably sweetened form, and finally prescribed the following: hot baths for the feet, sun-lamp for the head, walking, and a complete abstinence from nicotine. All this was supposed to last six weeks. By way of precaution I translated everything word for word in the hope that the prince would be too proud to compromise himself by asking questions (although he had obviously not understood more than half of it) and would go peacefully home in dignified silence. Unfortunately, I was very far from the mark. The prince seemed to be really worried about his health and inquired calmly whether he was to take the sun-lamp for the head in the form of pills or drops. He had been accustomed to swallowing powders or some kind of medicinal drops at home.

And now we both of us started—the doctor as a specialist with me as a translator—trying to explain the use of foot baths and sun-lamp to the prince. The nurse, who remained in the room during the examination, went so far as to get the necessary articles and to attempt to explain their use to him. As he began slowly to understand, his face coloured gradually until it became a threatening dark red colour. »I am to put that thing on my head? And wash my feet in that? And all this from a woman and an unbeliever?«

I did not translate these words, because the tone in which they were spoken was enough. I was just about to reply to the prince with something soothing when he began to show the first signs of »being insulted.« With a fierce yell the »poor invalid« sprang to his feet, tore the glasses off the nurse's nose, trampled them to splinters with his feet, swept everything off the doctor's consultation desk, and began to get rabid. To start with, he made for the old nurse, overcame her, and threw her on to the sofa, where he treated the poor thing, whose face was buried in the cushions, in the manner that one chastises a naughty child. No amount of struggling was any good. The grotesque picture of the raging prince uncouthly and persistently slapping the unhappy nurse on her posterior is unforgettable to me. She was frightened to death and ended by uttering low wailing cries into the cushion. Finally the Caucasian let her go and turned his attention to the doctor, who had been standing there as dumb and stiff as a post, looking on at this scene. With a swift movement he smashed the box for the sun-lamp treatment over the doctor's head, picked him up like a child, and literally threw him out into the waiting-room. The weeping nurse and I precipitated ourselves after him. Luckily for us, I was still just able to lock the door behind us so that the prince was now left to himself shut into the consulting-room.

The first thought of the doctor was for the police, and the second for the insane asylum, because the yelling that issued from the room really led one to think there was a lunatic there. It is scarcely possible to describe the trouble I had to explain to the doctor, the nurse, and the attendants who had hurried to the spot, what the grounds of the prince's behaviour were and to persuade them to be indulgent. From his point of view he was entirely right.

A foreign woman and an unbeliever had decided that, instead of giving him medicine, he was first to be recommended to wash his feet. This was especially insulting, because the prince, precisely because he was a Mohammedan, was required to perform a ritualistic washing of the feet five times a day. It was true he did not do it, because he was not a particularly rigid observer, but that only made it all the worse that Christians (yes,

Christians!) should attempt to force him to the observance of his religious duties by apparently implying that his illnesses were merely a punishment for his weaknesses and for the neglect of his religious practice.

The other prescriptions of the doctor were of course equally insulting. For the inference to be drawn from the recommendation that he should take walks was the invidious one that he was too poor to buy himself a car. And finally the insinuation that a free prince should stick his head into a thing that looked like a yoke for oxen was the absolute limit, the very acme of deadly effrontery.

After I had explained all this to the doctor and he had set himself to reckoning up the damages with much shaking of the head, I knocked timidly on the door behind which the shouting had diminished slightly. The knock was answered by a curse, but a curse which no longer sounded so threatening; I opened the door softly and dared to enter the room. The prince was sitting on the floor busily tearing up notes which he had found on the doctor's table.

I was obliged to talk with him in vain for some time to persuade him to come home with me. It was not until I admitted openly that I entirely agreed with his point of view, and was just as enraged about the doctor's behaviour as he was, that he began to be more tractable. We remained a little while sitting on the floor, discussed fully the rotten state of Europe, and thought with longing of the fair Circassian land where affronts of this kind were absolutely impossible. Finally the prince stood up and left the room with proudly uplifted head. The doctor handed him the bill rather uneasily in the waiting-room. He did not deign to look at it, but pulled a bundle of bank-notes out of his pockets and threw it contemptuously to the doctor, remarking majestically as he did so: »Nothing but the streaming tears of your repentance can wash the filth of your insult from my countenance.«

I did not trouble to translate his words, but took him home and advised him to desert this rotten country of Europe as quickly as possible. The doctor, for his part, dismissed the idea of a prosecution in view of the Caucasian's title of prince, although the bearer of this title had shown himself very little worthy of respectful treatment.

As for myself, I was quite pleased that the prince had not been a real Lamaroi, or Chechen, otherwise the story would have certainly been much worse and would probably not have ended without bloodshed. This is only an example of the Caucasian state of »being insulted.« Whoever knows the Lamaroi can certainly tell dozens of similar stories from his own experience.

Unfortunately, it is not always possible to arbitrate a case of insult peaceably; it usually ends with bloodshed and wounds, during which, as has already been said, innocent bystanders are often made to suffer. But if the insult is very grave and the paroxysm cannot at once be relieved by some powerful discharge of emotion, more especially if the insult originates with several people, as in the case of a decision at court, or of a repeated theft committed by several people, then the Lamaroi becomes an »eternally offended man,« a monster, a terror of the mountains.

The man who is insulted permanently calls himself an Abrek, which means »one who has taken the oath.« But there is an important difference between him and the other Abreks, the cheerful, simple, ordinary brigands. Chiefly, the difference is the famous oath of the man who is permanently offended, according to which he must order his whole life. This oath, which is spoken at midnight, after prayer and sacrifice, in the courtyard of the temple, runs as follows:

»I, the son of an honourable and free father, swear by the holy place which I honour, to remain for so many years an Abrek, a man eternally offended. All these years I will spill human blood and have mercy upon no man. I shall pursue human beings like wild animals. I swear to steal everything from my fellow-men which is dear to their hearts, to their consciences, and to their courage. I shall stab the baby at its mother's breast, set the last shelter of the beggar in flames, and everywhere, where joy has reigned till now, there will I bring sorrow. If I do not fulfil this oath, if love or pity shall creep into my heart, then may I never see the grave of my fathers, may water never come to slake my thirst, nor bread to still my hunger, may my corpse lie upon the roadway, and a filthy animal befoul it.«

In most cases the Lamaroi keeps his oath. He rides through the mountains, lurks behind rocks, attacks and kills everybody, including his own relatives. He carries out his revenge upon mankind pitilessly. He can, of course, also take a limited oath, becoming an Abrek only against certain special persons or special classes, for example against judges, or against Russians.

After the Abrek years are past, if he is still alive and well, he goes to any district in which he is unknown, marries, and lives his allotted span as a peasant. But he is very seldom successful in remaining unknown. He is generally discovered. There are too many blood avengers on his track, and they get him in the end.

The Lamaroi are proud. They are a community of people numbering about two or three thousand and living in the most primitive state, but honestly considering themselves the best and most famous people on earth and always grimly attempting to prove it. This is not easy, for many Lamaroi clans have no history to boast of and just as little to be ashamed of. They know nothing at all about their past, and several scholars go so far as to maintain that some of the Lamaroi races have only emerged within recent years.

The emergence of a Lamaroi tribe is simple. Some clan or other loses its way from the steppes of Asia into the Caucasus, is driven out of the valleys, and finds refuge in the high mountains which are already inhabited by old free Lamaroi. As the latter have no organization whatever, it is not difficult for the new-comers to conquer the natives. The clan remains in the mountains from then on and runs wild in an astonishingly short space of time. Their former tongue mingles with the speech of the conquered people, who for their part often speak two or three languages already.

After less than a hundred years, a new homogeneous people has formed itself which uses a new language and refuses to admit to anything in common with anybody else. A hundred years is quite sufficient time for the Lamaroi to forget his origin and to bring forth legends which baffle the most penetrating investigators.

Naturally, all of these tribes try to establish their greatness in some especial way. Since they are not in any remarkable way superior to their neighbours, they have picked on the matter of language as the honourable and distinctive mark. The Lamaroi cannot boast about anything else so he snatches at this excuse. He will maintain with a superior smile: »Our language is the most difficult in the world.«

The Lamaroi are universally agreed in this opinion. Each of them wants to claim this honour for himself and declares calmly: »If I can talk the most difficult language in the world, it is a sign of the great intelligence which is in me, and the great deeds of which I am capable.« The Ingushes, the Avars, the Chechens, and the Abkhasians are the most arrogant in this respect, and they are not altogether wrong, for their languages are as a matter of fact among the most difficult in the world. The language of the Avars, for example, has no letters which can be represented in a normal alphabet. The Avar words are rendered by different kinds of tongue clicks or by peculiar noises which remind one of the gurgling of water coming out of a bottle.

Worse still is the Tabasar language, which is so difficult that the Tabasars themselves only learn it with great difficulty. The present-day natives maintain that at the moment their language is only being mastered to a very limited degree. The last Tabasar who could speak really well died fifty years ago. They use a neighbouring language by preference but, when they have to use their own, they are obliged to take great thought and to speak with measured pauses, otherwise they are unable to utter phrases which are grammatically correct.

There is nothing more complicated than the grammars of these languages which have been assembled for scholars with terrific difficulty by enterprising philologists. It is as good as impossible to find alphabets for these languages. Foreign philologists have as a matter of fact constructed a philological alphabet for the majority of them, but it is useless in practice. For years the Ingushes themselves have been trying to find an alphabet for their language. All the signs have been tried but so far without success.

A short while ago the first Ingush newspaper appeared with a Latin alphabet. Even the most educated Ingush was unable to read it. Since there are no rules or precedents for spelling, every article is written in the way the author thinks best, and according to grammatical rules which are known to him alone. Even the Circassians cannot find an alphabet for their language. And for this very reason they give themselves terrific airs and say: »Our language is too noble to be chained by signs.« And yet, all these tongues, the Ingush, the Tabasar, and the Avar, are not nearly so hard as the Abkhasian, which is spoken by a fairly numerous and intelligent race of people on the shores of the Black Sea. A famous German philologist of the last century, Baron Uslar, who devoted his life to the successful study of Caucasian languages, once wanted to explore this language too. He journeyed to Abkhasia, spent two years there, and said later that he—the philologist—not only had not learnt Abkhasian, but had no idea how the Abkhasians could understand one another.

It is impossible to pronounce Abkhasian words, although the individual sounds are perfectly normal ones. The relatively simple word for »to pray« runs in an exact transcription »stshisdydsvfeit«; »to lie down« is »amtzsgfyeit« in Abkhasian, and »to hide« is »itchilsimtsakhty.« Undoubtedly the palm goes to the Abkhasians in the competition for difficult languages.

But this opinion should not be openly admitted in conversation with the Lamaroi, because it might be taken as an insult, as a terrible injury to a well-authorized national glory.

The insulting or offending of national or personal pride, together with its consequences, cause the Lamaroi to deal with each other with every imaginable precaution.

Everyone takes the greatest care in his association with others to avoid the slightest suggestiveness and exerts the most unheard-of tact in the smallest matters. Even the Europeans who travel through the mountains are amazed at the perfect politeness of the savage Lamaroi. This politeness and the fear of insulting somebody lead in many districts to a strange custom. If a poor Lamaroi goes without adequate means to a foreign village, and has neither cattle nor lodging, he need not immediately set to begging from the inhabitants of the village. Begging leads only too quickly to an insult and dishonours a free Lamaroi for that reason. He has, therefore, by virtue of a sacred tradition, the right to steal from the other inhabitants of the village for seven years without incurring punishment. Everything he steals belongs to him and forms the substance of his future business. At the end of seven years he is as a rule just as well off as the other dwellers in the village and can now in his turn be robbed with impunity by the new-comers. It is only if, after seven years, the man cannot hold back from his beloved habit of stealing that he becomes punishable.

This authorized thievery is only one of the many examples of how the fellow-feeling and tact of the Lamaroi may often touch on the grotesque. If, for example, a Lamaroi has made a large bag of game when out hunting and he meets another Lamaroi who has been less successful or even had no intention whatever of shooting anything, then the lucky hunter must immediately hand over half of his booty to the other, regardless of whether he knows him or not, for otherwise the second man might be offended, because he felt inferior to the fortunate hunter. The marvellous sense of tact may carry the communal feeling even further. If a beast belonging to a Lamaroi dies, it is customary for the neighbours to replace the loss. Even in the case of damage by fire or some other agricultural misfortune, the inhabitants must repair their neighbours' loss as quickly as possible by their own labour.

It can be seen, therefore, that the most backward Lamaroi, take him all in all, in spite of the Abrek oath and the attacks of frenzy, by no means belongs to the completely barbarian races. There are no absolutely savage tribes in the mountains, with the possible exception of one semi-mythical race known as the Okochoki and supposed to inhabit the jungles of the south-west Caucasus between the main range and Svanetia. Their very existence is a matter of dispute and conjecture. Okochoki is simply the Mingrelian word for »wild men.« The wild forest-dwellers are credited with knowing absolutely nothing of clothing, weapons, or domestic utensils, nor of articulate language. Whether they exist or not, these naked savages are held in unholy horror by the neighbouring Abkhasians and Svanetians, who consider them the offspring of men and devils.

Even outside the land of the Okochoki there are districts in the mountains which have never yet been visited either by natives or by Europeans. What they contain for the explorer can at present only be guessed at. Perhaps there are other entirely unknown tribes, or the ruins of dead cultures or unexpected riches which will belong to the discoverer. The Caucasians themselves are not curious; they take no steps to find out about the secrets of the mountains. And Europeans dare not trust themselves in the unknown land. Meanwhile, scientists and scholars are at the moment sufficiently occupied with the already discovered and by no means completely solved problems of the Khevsurs, Pshavs, Abkhasians, Tabasars, and other mountain peoples, so their thirst for knowledge and for adventure demands at the moment no new discoveries. Conclusive information about these unknown regions must be left to the future.

18.

THE VILLAGE OF POETS

MAKING ENDS MEET in the mountain aul is exceptionally difficult and demands unspeakable efforts on the part of the peasantry. They cart mould up the mountain sides in sacks and lay out paltry little patches of arable earth on the naked rock for planting maize. These crumbs of earth are fostered and cared for like a treasure. The fields are small and narrow, as the structure of the mountains obliges them to be. There is a saying that a peasant from a mountain aul can, as a rule, cover his miserable little field with a wide Caucasian cloak, and the following story is usually offered as a concrete illustration:

A peasant went into his field to work and took off his coat to offer up the usual prayer before beginning his daily task. There was a slight wind blowing and his coat lay spread out on the ground. At the end of the prayer the peasant no longer saw his field. Had it vanished? Had the wind or an evil spirit carried it off? He sought for a long time, without finding his clod of earth. There was no doubt about it now; magic must be at work. Terror seized upon him. He decided to fly to the village and get help. He grasped his coat to go, but lo and behold! beneath his coat the field came to light again and was returned to him.

Where do these people get their means of subsistence? The cattle only partially nourish the villages. Hence everything which the cattle does not produce must be obtained by brigandage. The Caucasian despises every kind of work other than agriculture. At the outside, public opinion permits him to become a smith, preferably an armourer. The smithy and blacksmiths in general are sacred to the Caucasians, and many famous men of the past are spoken of as being smiths by profession. When a Caucasian wishes to honour anybody, he says to him: »You are a smith.«

The most sacred of oaths are made in the smithy upon an anvil, and the mystic conjuring up of spirits also takes place there. But all Caucasians cannot be smiths. Consequently the inhabitants of a particular village who possess neither land nor cattle are of necessity forced to pursue a specific craft—saddlery or hat-making. And this craft is the monopoly of their village. They wander throughout the country for nine months in the year, selling their manufactures, and then return back to their work for the remaining three months. For generations each craft has been confined to a single village, where it reaches a very high degree of artistic perfection.

The most interesting village of this kind is found in Sanghesur, in the southern part of Transcaucasia. It is the famous Armenian village of Khudsorek, of which all the inhabitants know but one single, joyous, and immortal craft; they are all trained professional poets. From their earliest years they are educated up to this profession; they learn Persian, the language of Eastern poetry, and also the complicated rules of prosody. All winter through they sit in their village and write. But as soon as spring comes, they take their lutes and travel into distant lands—to Daghestan, Azerbaijan, Georgia—wherever sounding strophes are beloved. And where are they not loved in the Caucasus?

These poets—like the native poets of Daghestan—are called Ashuks, which signifies not merely »poets« but »lovers.« To the Oriental way of thinking every lover must be a poet, and to be recognized as a true poet one must write, dream, and yearn for some inaccessible love. In the East, too, love is compared to a flame, and a Caucasian legend tells of a poet whose consuming love was so genuine that he, his beloved, and his house were all burnt up in the conflagration of it.

The poets from the village of Khudsorek, however, do not burn up with love. They travel from village to village, recite the products of their craft, and receive a princely fee. But even they have their worries. The designation of »craftsman« is not an especially honourable one for the Ashuks; and, therefore, every one of them strives to rise from the rank of craftsman to that of a god-inspired artist, that is to say, a genuine Ashuk.

For the Ashuks are divided into two classes, the false and the genuine. The art of a false Ashuk can be learnt, that of the real one, never. The genuine Ashuk is inviolable throughout the Orient; he may with impunity say any kind of impertinence he likes to any ruler; he may even sing cynical songs in the presence of women and claim any kind of fee he wishes. The pseudo-Ashuk is first of all trained and educated in his art in the village of Khudsorek; the real one needs no teacher, and therefore need not even come from Khudsorek. Among the genuine Ashuks all branches of the population are to be met with. Even princes of high degree are not ashamed to go through the country as Ashuks.

But—how does a man become a genuine Ashuk? If he is not born to it, there is only one way; he must call upon the protector of poets, the Prophet Elias, to perform a miracle and raise him—the supplicant—to the state of a genuine Ashuk. But the Prophet Elias can only perform the miracle once, within one hour, upon a certain night in the year. That night is the night of Kadir in the month of Ramadan. The month of Ramadan has thirty nights, and nobody knows which is the night Kadir.

In this night nature goes to sleep for an hour. The streams cease to flow; evil spirits no longer keep their watch over buried treasures; and the men born in that hour are destined to be rulers and wise-men. If the poet calls upon his patron and protector at the right moment, Elias will appear and give him to drink out of a cup, and say: »From now on thou art a real Ashuk and thou shalt see all things that are in the world through my fingers.« But it is, as I have said, impossible to know which is the night Kadir or at what time on that night Elias will fulfil the petitions of the poets. Consequently, one does not often hear of such metamorphoses.

But even the spurious Ashuk has nothing to complain of in his lot. His hearers regard him also as a higher being and put much more faith in his words than they do in those of a prince, a priest, or an official.

Whoever desires to accomplish something in the villages of the Caucasus must have the goodwill of the Ashuks, preferably of the genuine Ashuks. This is not always easy as a matter of fact. For Ashuks, too, suffer from megalomania and treat the ordinary mortal, including their own colleagues, in a decidedly capricious and condescending manner, just as the mood takes them.

When two Ashuks come together in one place, the matter never ends without competition and strife. All the inhabitants assemble on the village square, form a circle, and in their midst the two Ashuks swagger about, abusing each other in the roundest terms. First one will mock at the other's clothes, then at his appearance, and finally at his talent. The final stab, the stab to the heart, is when he maintains that his opponent is without »convictions« and that he only poetizes for the sake of money.

At last, when the stock of witticisms has been exhausted, the actual struggle, like that of Homeric heroes, begins. Somebody from the crowd suggests a theme, and one of the Ashuks begins his song. Suddenly, in the midst of a verse, he breaks off, and his opponent has to supply the missing rhyme and continue the song. When the song has been brought to an end after several interruptions, the popular game of question-and-answer begins. One Ashuk puts a question in verse, and the other must solve it in the same rhyme and metre. Finally the Ashuks must perform a Commedia dell' Arte, that is, they have to put on a play with a given subject-matter and improvise the dialogue. The winner receives his opponent's lute as his reward.

But when two Ashuks are not merely artistically at enmity but hate each other on purely personal grounds also, then this harmless duel may have more serious consequences. It is then not a matter of depriving the less gifted man of his lute and his reputation, but his head is also at stake. The peaceful poetical competition thus becomes a mortal duel in verse. The Ashuk possesses no other medium but words wherewith to destroy his opponent. He may not kill him—if the other is an Ashuk like himself—for that would be an admission that he was afraid of his talent. The two opponents come forward publicly and sing their songs. The wise-men are now required, in the capacity of unbiased critics, to determine which of the two is the more gifted and has the greater right to live or the greater claim upon a woman's favours. For one of the two the criticism is in this case equivalent to a death sentence. The victor is given the executioner's axe and must cut off the head of the loser in the presence of the critics. Such duels do not happen any more now. Poets, they say, are grown soft. They no longer know how to hate, and they have not sufficient faith in their talent, nor do they dare to let their lives depend upon the success of their poems.

In former days poetic duels were very widespread, and even today songs are sung in the poets' village of Khudsorek and verses are recited of the old courageous bards who lost their lives upon the field of poetic honour. I have no doubt whatever that these duels of versification which, as far as I know, occur nowhere else in the world would make some of the finest chapters which could ever be recorded in any literary history. A poetic tournament, in which life is at stake, claims the whole being, the entire creative power, all the fantasy and personal magic of a poet.

There are in the Caucasus two other poet villages apart from the famous Khudsorek: Dash-Kenda and Ali-kuli-Kenda. The inhabitants of these three villages used formerly to possess special privileges. They were not called up on military service and only paid half of the customary taxes. The guild of poets possessed great prestige in the Caucasus. Even now these poets continue their carefree wanderings; they work in the winter-time, and travel through the villages in summer, gathering in their fee in their large gourds and waiting for the night of Kadir to come when Elias will raise them to the state of genuine Ashuks.

The man I want to tell about now was without doubt a real god-inspired Ashuk. This strange and little-known story has admittedly nothing to do with the three poets' villages, but it cannot be omitted at this juncture while I am on the subject of poets.

The affair happened about eighty years ago in the heart of the Caucasus, in the region of the present Republic of Daghestan. In those days the Russians were still carrying on a bitter struggle with the mountain tribes, who had, under the leadership of Imam Shamil, declared a holy war against the Tsar. On the border of the mountains towards the Caspian Sea, the Russians erected the fortress of Grosny (now a famous

139

oil field), from which from time to time punitive expeditions were undertaken into the mountains. Life in the fortress was of an even and monotonous tenor; the young Russian officers were bored; and some of the more romantic spirits were bold enough to make trips into the hills, although this was strictly forbidden. The Murids—Caucasian warriors—sat behind every rock, waiting for someone to ride by, and then carried the officers off and killed them with great cruelty in their mountain villages. The colonial war was in full swing at that period.

One day a young officer, but lately arrived in Grosny, rode out of the fortress, determined to see something of the romantic hills in a short ride. Since it was forbidden voluntarily to leave the fortress, he had to undertake the journey on his own responsibility, in other words, he had to ride out alone into enemy territory without escort. It was an adventure which had previously been successfully accomplished, and subsequently also, and so it by no means constituted an attempted suicide. But the young officer was unlucky. Just beyond Grosny, indeed beyond the first hill, a shot rang out, a bullet whistled past the officer's head, and in the same instant a noose was thrown over his shoulders. He crashed from his horse and the Murids trussed him up. The adventure had taken a nasty turn.

The treatment of Russian officers in the mountains was not of the best. Usually, when they did not come of wealthy families, and could not therefore pay a high ransom, their eyes were put out as a preliminary, then the nose and ears were cut off, and finally they were rendered shorter by the length of their own heads. This procedure was entirely according to the hallowed traditions of all colonial wars. The young officer unfortunately came of a family of impoverished nobility, and was in addition a Christian, so that he had no especial mercy to expect.

As usual, the prisoner was brought to Shamil's governor, Naib Sado, who ruled over the neighbourhood of Grosny with sword and Koran. Naib Sado was the descendant of the great liberator Mansur. He was pious, warlike, a scholar, and known throughout the mountains as a man of especial wisdom. In the course of his entire life he had never spared a Russian. This had also earned him the favour of the great Shamil. The Murids who had taken the officer prisoner knelt before the Naib and demanded their reward: twenty pieces of gold or the right arm of the unbeliever.

This too was a sacred tradition, for a right arm nailed to the door was the pride of the whole family. The Naib had never disregarded such pious and important customs, and it was not to be expected that he would begin now. He arose, looked first with wonder and then in perplexity at the prisoner, turned his countenance towards Mecca, uttered a prayer, and then said with dignity, as became a learned governor of the holy Imam: »Believers who take prisoners in the holy war shall be rewarded of Allah. But today I proclaim that this right hand shall not be cut off nor these eyes put out. The man who stands before me is very pious and pleasing to Allah. I, Naib Sado, grandson of the Sultan Mansur, feel this to be so, and I declare my words to be in accordance with the Koran. Take the unbeliever back to the gates of Grosny, loose his bonds, and ye shall be rewarded of Allah.«

According to mountain law, the Naib ought now to have been punished himself. But for this once the authority of the grandson of Mansur triumphed over the normal procedure.

According to orders, the prisoner was set free before the gates of Grosny. He went back to his regiment and had himself immediately transferred to a more peaceful district. He never told anybody of this adventure. This was the only request which the Naib—who valued his reputation—required him to fulfil. The officer explained his absence as due to bad roads, on which he had lost his way. And yet this man who had been freed from the certain death of a martyr corresponded to his last days with the pious rebel Naib Sado.

The young officer's name was Count Leo Tolstoi, and Nard is the name of that presentient Naib's grandson, who told the story recently in Constantinople. It has, however, so far escaped the vigilance of biographers of the writer, though a bundle of Tolstoi letters are preserved in the family of Sado, the discovery and publication of which will some day be the task of Russian scholars. Whoever knows the short stories of

Tolstoi will remember how he there describes the imprisonment of Russian officers and the hospitality of the mountain people. Nobody realized until lately that the Russian author knew both from personal experience.

Tolstoi is not the only writer whom the mountains have attracted. Russian and European writers visited and still constantly do visit the Caucasus, undergo everything which the Caucasian authorities will allow a European traveller to experience, and then praise the hills in their books. Many of them must be satisfied with lesser adventures, such as those experienced by Alexandre Dumas during his Caucasian travels.

Alexandre Dumas came from Paris direct to the Paris of the East—to Tiflis—and took a house in the main street of this entirely European town. His Georgian colleagues received him with all the honour due to a prominent Western author. Dumas (who had put on Caucasian dress with a gigantic dagger, sword, and revolver on the very day of his arrival) astounded the Georgian writers by his—even to the natives—amazing capacity for filling himself up with unheard-of quantities of wine.

Shortly after his arrival, Dumas, yearning for the heart of the Orient, began to demand robbers and harems. Since both were at that time unobtainable in Tiflis, his hosts were in a great state of embarrassment. It was very painful to have to refuse anything to a guest of world-renown. Attempts were made to divert Dumas: he was taken to the opera, to the municipal theatre, and to balls, where native princes in dress coats started back in terror from the wild »Asiatic« (as Dumas with his weapons looked to them), while the ladies at first inquired whether a new principality had been taken under the protectorate of the Tsar, and had sent its prince to Tiflis in the person of that barbarian over there.

Dumas for his part was also unsatisfied. Frightened faces, men in frock coats, and inquisitive glances from beautiful women; of them he had seen enough in the Paris of the West. In the Paris of the Orient he desired something new. It was out of the question, however, to take Dumas into the real mountains, or to the real mountain people. For, as they could scarcely be expected to know anything of the fame of the Western Ashuk, it was to be assumed that they would rob him and take him captive at the first opportunity. The Government would then have been in the unpleasant position of having to expend a hundred thousand roubles for the release of the French writer. The mountain people would have taken this armed and piratical-looking poet for a European king at the very least and screwed their demands of ransom up to the craziest levels.

But the laws of hospitality urged the Georgians one day to invite the author to the citadel of Mtskhet. Mtskhet lies near Tiflis, in what is probably the most peaceful district of the Caucasus. For at least a century it had never heard any shooting at all. But still the fortress looks very grim. It is surrounded by mountains and mountain streams and makes a very fair setting for an attack by brigands. In the town of Mtskhet, near the fortress, there is also a grubby house of pleasure. Just before the author's arrival, the house was thoroughly cleaned, fumigated, fitted out with carpets, and its inhabitants clad in silk and imitation jewellery, so that the place might have a regular flavour of the harem of a Caucasian prince. During the night, Dumas slipped out with his good friends to the »harem,« was delighted with the amiabilities of the well-rewarded houris, again drank enormous quantities of wine, and had the »danse du ventre« (which does not exist in Georgia) performed, while he followed it delightedly with the air of a connoisseur.

During the return journey, on the bank of the river, he suddenly saw twelve savage figures rushing out of a hut. They surrounded the writer (who decided that he was being attacked by the eunuchs) and took away his weapons and those of his friends. Death was imminent. Dumas became sober and faced the worst with manly courage. This was after all what he had been looking for. He would not flinch, but die courageously if he had to. However, for once the affair ended happily. Fortune did not desert the great novelist. After a silent pause, the brigands approached their captives with even sterner looks than before, and said: »This time we will grant you your lives. But never dare under penalty of death to show yourselves again in our neighbourhood.«

143

It was fortunate that the disarmed author—who was congratulating himself that the brigands had not discovered his purse—followed this advice and never again returned to the place where he had been attacked. If he had, he would have seen by the light of day the peaceful sign upon the frowning robbers' den which announced »Police Department of Mtskhet.« The robbers were Russian policemen who had been ordered to treat the Frenchman as he seemed to wish.

Dumas returned to Paris entirely happy. He is by no means the only tourist who has been delighted by the Caucasus in a similar manner.

19.

THE EMPIRE OF THE JEWS

SCARCELY ANY RESEARCH can be conducted as yet into the manner in which the curious Empire of the Jews arose in the sixth century after Christ. But one thing is established –a Jewish emperor once ruled from the steppes beyond the Volga to the shores of the Caspian Sea, and bore the title of Kagan. For two hundred years the Kagan was the most powerful man of the East; everything was subject to him, and even the Christian kings were forced to pay him tribute. He built synagogues and rabbinical schools, and he fought and converted the heathen tribes, tolerating no Gentile in his vicinity. And yet he, his court, and his people were not by any means of Jewish origin. They called themselves Khazars and came of the great race which for ages had inhabited the steppes of Mongolia, Siberia, and East Turkestan.

To this race, which is generally called the Ural-Altaian, belong practically all those tribes which have left their native steppes from time to time in the course of several centuries to pour in an irresistible stream over the tribes of the West. Attila and his Huns, the horde of Jenghiz-Khan, the Turkish and Tatar conquerors, all came from the steppes of Central Asia. And the Khazars, those strange Jews of the steppes, belonged to that group of people. They had not a drop of Semitic blood in their veins and are consequently the only major race in the world's history to be converted by the Jews to their own faith.

The history of this Jewish empire and of its rise and fall is very little known. It was a typically nomad empire, created by an aristocracy powerfully swayed by the robber-instinct, and radiant with the glory of a meteoric fame which lasted for a few centuries only and then faded swiftly, vanishing without leaving a trace, as the star of a new conqueror ascended over the steppes.

The Orient has known a myriad such empires; the short span of a single century is usually enough to destroy the last trace of a world-power of this kind. Nomads seldom build stone palaces; they live in tents and differ but little from their successors with whom they blend without any difficulty.

But the case was different with the Khazars: they retained their speech from the steppes and preserved the purity of their nomad stock. They also learned from their missionaries, the rabbis and merchants, how to build cities, open bazaars, and carry on trade and how to unite continents with slim caravan routes. According to old legends and traditions, a rare and flourishing culture developed on the shores of the Volga and the Caspian Sea in the capitals of these converts to Judaism.

The Kagan, or Emperor, surrounded himself with all the glory and magnificence of which the Orient is capable. These magnificent court-holding emperors were compared by the enraptured rabbis to the kings of the Old Testament. At the approach of spring they always fell to planning campaigns for the release of the Holy Land. But this never got beyond a pious resolution, since the good Jewish warriors and generals, in common with all their successors and predecessors, preferred to plunder the neighbouring lands, collect their tribute there, and then to return after a successful expedition to the well-bred contemplative life of pious Turks amid their desert tents and the palaces of their commercial cities.

It is a mystery how these Khazars came by their Judaism since they were originally Shamanists like all Turks. Most probably they met with Jewish colonists on their campaigns in the Caucasus, or in Transcaucasia, and adopted this foreign religion just as light-heartedly as their relatives, the Seljuk Turks, adopted Islam.

With all the zeal for activity characteristic of fresh converts they felt themselves bound to spread the new faith, and it was not long before many races in the highlands of the Caucasus had adopted the Jewish belief of the Khazars.

Later on the Khazars came into contact with the Russians, who were not yet Christian at that period, and it is conceivable that the Russian

Grand Duke and all his subjects might thus have been converted to Judaism for all time. Certainly, negotiations were being carried on about it. If the Kagan had given more attention to these wild north-western heathens of Russia, it would have been very easy for him to effect their conversion, and Russia would never have known the pogrom. But the Kagan had more important things to attend to just then: he was suing for the hand of the fair daughter of the Georgian King. And when the latter refused her to the Jewish-Mohammedan emperor, the Kagan attacked Georgia, laid it waste, converted several clans, and then returned to his fabulous city of Itil.

But the Jewish-Khazar power was not to last long. The Arabs came from the south and conquered the Caucasus; they were followed closely by the army of Jenghiz-Khan from the east, and in his world dominion the last Khazar clans were dissolved. They remembered the race to which they belonged, but they swiftly forgot their Judaism and soon relapsed into paganism. In the company of Jenghiz-Khan they conquered Turkestan, Persia, China, Afghanistan, Russia, and Hungary, and finally returned again as Mohammedans to the steppes of the north-west Caucasus, where they now form two races, the Kumyks and the Nogai Tatars.

Not all the Jews, however, were converted to Islam; it was only in the case of the Turkish Khazars and the Caucasian races which had been recently made Jews that the new religion triumphed comparatively quickly. The Semitic Jews, who lived in small numbers among the Khazars, remained true to their old belief. They withdrew into the Caucasian mountains, that haven for the defeated, and gradually became wild in the unusual and rough surroundings. But they have remained real Jews down to this very day, and are known to every traveller in the Caucasus as Dagh-Jughutlari (Mountain Jews).

The Kumyks, Nogai Tatars, and Dagh-Jughutlari are, however, by no means the only relics of the Jewish empire.

All Caucasian peoples without exception have taken over some legacy from the Jews: here an Old Testament word used by them in their prayers, there some custom, such as levirate marriage. In any case, the

Jewish facial type is remarkably widespread among the population of the Caucasus, and in a purer and nobler form than is often to be met with among purely Jewish peoples. Savage, brutal warriors, knights and brigands, would be indistinguishable from Galician rabbis or workers if they were dressed in the correct clothes. Many Caucasian races confess their Jewish origin with pride and are considered honourably distinguished by it. It is true that one must generally accept facial characteristics alone as sufficient proof of this blood affinity since any other historical evidences for their statement are not forthcoming.

The Georgian clan of Guria, which constituted an independent, strictly feudal state until quite lately, is especially tenacious about this claim. It is true that the Gurians are less like the Jews than any of them, but the word Uria in Georgian means a Jew, and Uria is reminiscent of Guria. This serves all who need it with an ample basis for their theory that the Gurians are Jews by origin.

These races, of course, bear hardly any relation to the real Jews, the Uria or Dagh-Jughutlari. The Mountain Jews are a self-contained Caucasian race, leading the life of all the Caucasian races, but not mingling with the others, and possessing a few, if not many, customs which are peculiar to themselves. They have long ago forgotten the former glory of Khazar dominion and live now as a primitive people, principally consisting of illiterates who refuse to believe that they ever lived down below in the plain and ruled an empire together with the Turkish nomads.

At first, when one visits the villages of these Jews, one notices no departure from the manners of other communities. The houses and the dress of the inhabitants do not differ at all from those of the Caucasian villages, and even the house of God completely resembles the mountain mosque.

But once inside a house, as one is being received by the father of the family with the usual bowing, the difference becomes noticeable. The wife of the host appears with a basin of water, inclines herself before the guest, and draws off his shoes. She then washes his feet, according to the Old Testament rite, and, if he is an especially honourable person, she dries them with her own hair. That was the custom of their fathers in the Holy Land, and it is practised by the sons still in the mountains of the Caucasus.

Everything in the house is governed by the Old Testament. The Mountain Jew knows no other laws. During the week they carry swords and daggers, which they lay aside only on the Sabbath. Like the rest of the Caucasians, they till slightly more soil than they require so as to give alms to thieves and the poor who do not beg.

The Mountain Jews have a small school in every village. The rabbi is both a teacher and a sacrificial priest. But they have no very high opinion of knowledge, for even the village rabbi is not especially expert in the law, and answers all questions about laws, customs, and history with the words: »Ma amgaares« (I am an ignorant man), and adds humbly: »Ask the Khakham-Bashi,« that is to say, the Chief Rabbi in Derbent.

This Khakham-Bashi, whose abode is in Derbent, is the Mountain Jews' only authority, their highest resort in all questions of life, and the only person in the Caucasus who knows and interprets the law of the fathers in its full extent. When the Khakham-Bashi (the word means the »supremely clever«) dies, all the Jews go into mourning, collect money, and send delegates to Jerusalem or Constantinople to find a new Khakham.

The language spoken by these Jews is a Persian dialect, which is also spoken by Azerbaijan, Bokharan, and Persian Jews, but the names which they bear are so very Old-Testament that they are very difficult for a European Jew to pronounce. The commonest men's names are: Nakhshon, Ufch, Banoiou, Zufanya; the women's names are: Avigail, Serakh, Panina, Kerengapukh, Jemina, and so forth. Most of these Jews are peasants, handworkers, and small merchants, who do not like leaving the mountains and think it inconceivable that there are other Jews in the West who never have more than one wife, for among them polygamy is permissible.

In spite of the obligation to be hospitable which exists among the Mountain Jews, I do not advise anybody to make a visit to their villages.

The reception which they give to a stranger is trying to the patience of others besides Europeans. The washing and drying of the feet with the hair is but the first of the wearisome ceremonies which precede the most important one of all, the meal. This is carried out as follows:

The guest sits on the floor in the middle of the room. By his side are all the most notable people in the village. The host and the younger people must neither sit down nor partake of the meal with them. The host and his sons serve the guest, and the rest of the young people stand at the door and gape at the stranger in amazement. After endless washing and praying the food is handed round. Fruit comes first: melons, peaches, pears, pomegranates are all considered appetizers; immediately after the fruit comes the second course, garlic, which is handed round and consumed in enormous quantities on bread. Garlic and fruit are the favourite dishes of the Mountain Jews, but garlic is regarded much more as a medicine: it is supposed to strengthen and maintain the virility of the men.

After these two courses, the Jew hands his guest mutton fat, which is considered a special delicacy. It is impossible to describe the taste of this dish; only a fellow-sufferer can conceive of the self-control that must be exercised by the unprepared guest at this juncture. And it by no means concludes the menu of the banquet. The chief dish is yet to come, a freshly slaughtered sheep. Mutton roasted on a spit in the Caucasian manner tastes delicious, and the visitor harbours the most deceptive and beautiful hopes at this point. But all in vain. The dish is not passed to the guest of honour, or not until the chief course is at an end. To him is due the dish of honour, to wit, the boiled head of the freshly slaughtered sheep. He may divide it with the older diners, though the custom of the Jews dictates that he must consume the best part of the head himself, and this consists of the sheep's eyes. He is required to pick them out with his knife and relish them with every evidence of delight.

It is impossible to decline this honour. The host would take the refusal as an insult. It is permissible, however, for the guest to rise from table immediately after the fruit, but in that case all of those present must do the same, and are not allowed to eat anything more all day. After the course of sheep's eyes, a sequence of dainties of the same nature are handed round. And after that the company turns to the sweets, and the banquet closes with pure honey. Then everybody sits and waits until the guest belches, upon which they all follow his example. At this the meal is at an end.

The sons of the host bring water for rinsing the hands and mouth, and the young men, who have been standing against the wall all this time, are now permitted to fall to on the remains. Women do not appear during the meal.

A reception of this kind need not give one anti-Semitic tendencies, however, for similar customs pertain in all Caucasian villages, with local differences that are entirely insignificant. In any case, it is only the trained eye which can possibly distingush Jew from Gentile in the hills.

The Jewish woman, however, is more easily recognizable on account of an especial sign. She wears her hair hanging in a bag which is attached to her head. It is more improper to show one's head without a covering than to go about naked in the streets. Only a woman's husband may take the bag off his wife's hair; if anyone tears his wife's bag off by force he is prosecuted as a violator of women. This custom, as a matter of fact, also exists amongst other Caucasian people, only that their women wear a tightly bound head-scarf. This, of course, only holds good for those tribes whose women wear long hair. There are clans in the Caucasus among whom not only bobbed and cropped hair is the feminine fashion, but some to whom women are only tolerable with closely shaven heads.

The Jewess also differs in character from the other women in the mountains. She appears to be very quarrelsome, often has brawls with her husband, and disputes frequently with her friends. She also has a habit of weeping in most of her spare time, and it is very rarely clear what these crying orgies are about. If, for example, several young Jewesses, girls of sixteen to eighteen years of age, are seen sitting side by side crying loudly and they are asked the cause of their grief, they will cry all the louder for a while, and then one of them will sobbingly embark on the sad story of how her brother suddenly fell ill and died within three days. When pressed, she will give you to understand that her poor brother was scarcely six months old, and, if you sympathetically inquire still further into the matter, you will learn to your amazement that the whole thing took place twenty-five years ago, or at a time when all these unhappy girls were still unborn. It is hardly possible to believe in a genuine sorrow under circumstances of this kind. »It is a custom with us,« a Mountain Jewess told me, »to weep frequently, especially when several of us are together.« The men are so accustomed to these tears that they almost regard it as a breach of good custom if a woman has not wept for a long time.

Though these Jews have forgotten even the legends of the old Khazar empire, the neighbouring tribes still tell stories to show how dangerous it is to undertake anything against the Jews. I shall repeat one of their tales here:

In the vicinity of the town of Kuba, there is a village called Kola-Chulakh. As I was once passing by, I saw a building not far from the road which looked like a palace and was uninhabited despite the fact that it was in good repair. »What kind of a house is that?« I asked my companions, but they ignored my question with dark looks.

»I should like to look over the house,« I said, and reined my horse in. At this a terrific excitement took possession of my companions, who all began talking at once and yelling all kinds of unintelligible stuff. I could only understand the words of my servant, who swore that he would rather die than allow me so much as to set foot upon the threshold of the building. I was now not to be pacified until they told me the story of this remarkable house.

»Many hundreds of years ago,« they said, »a large Jewish colony lived in Kola-Chulakh and its neighbouring villages. When Nadir-Shah of Persia was trying to conquer the Caucasus, the Jews left the turbulent plains and withdrew into the mountains, having first sold their homes and their fields to their neighbours in Kola-Chulakh. Some little while after the Jews had departed, the Khan of Kola-Chulakh decided to build himself a new palace. So as not to be obliged to get stones specially from the mountains, he ordered the workmen to use the grave-stones from the Jewish cemeteries for his new construction. And so his palace was built of Jewish gravestones. But three days after the palace had been occupied, the Khan of Kola-Chulakh died, and soon after-wards his family and all the inhabitants of the palace followed his example. Even the horses in the stable died an unnatural death. And a successor to the Khan, who defied fate and moved into the house, also died very soon afterwards.

»Since then the palace has been uninhabited. Nobody now dares to set foot in it. The Mohammedan population, who were afraid of further punishment, sent for the Chief Rabbi from Derbent, who by his prayers turned God's wrath away from the Mohammedans of the village.«

But this respect is not extended to the former Jews, the lineal descendants of the Khazars. Their clans, the Kumyks and the Nogai Tatars, lead the most primitive of nomadic existences but are distinct in many other respects from the other nomad tribes. These ultimate sur-vivors of the world-conquerors are a psychological enigma, a remark-able and incomprehensible survival from olden, times which has so far been almost entirely neglected by research.

The most interesting are the Nogai Tatars, who at this date do not amount to more than ten thousand souls. The Nogai race has experi-enced and achieved everything which it is possible for a race to experi-ence or to achieve. Many thousands of years ago, it left its home in Cen-tral Asia together with the other Turkic tribes and wandered into mazes of glory, power, and decadence. In the thousands of years of their histo-ry, the Nogai people learnt to know and to revere every religion in the world. They were in turn idolaters, Buddhists, Jews, Christians, and set-tled finally upon the youngest world religion, Islam. And yet none of these religions was able to obtain any marked influence over the Nogai Tatars. Neither rabbis nor monks nor mullahs could make them pious. They remained what they actually were, proud nomads, with very little instinct for the abstract or for religious fervour or deep meditation. There was never a great sectarian or a religious leader among the Nogai people. They changed their religion every century or so, according to the example of the senior member of the clan, and in every other respect they asked for nothing more than to enjoy their liberty undisturbed.

Whatever god the Nogai Tatars served, they never ceased to be warriors. Led by the Kagans of the Khazars, and the great Mongolian Khans, they wandered through the steppes of Asia and of Europe fighting for their overlords, conquering strange lands, founding and destroying empires. They ruled in Russia for two hundred years, plundering towns and churches, and intermarrying with the daughters of the Grand Dukes.

Then came Jenghiz-Khan, the greatest of the great, and they fought ceaselessly on all the frontiers of his world dominion: in China, in Persia, in Hungary, in the steppes of South Russia, and in the mountains of the Caucasus. The race changed its home continually, now pasturing its horses on the banks of the river Don, now by the walls of Tatar cities on the Volga, now setting out again from there to the Crimea, then back again to the steppes and ending in the plains of the north-western Caucasus, by the reedy banks of Caucasian streams.

Judaism, Islam, Christianity, the great Mongols, power over two continents, battles in all parts of the world, and wanderings through interminable steppes; all this the Nogai Tatars witnessed and lived through. And with it all they have grown tired. They have exhausted their strength with thousands of years of war and of wandering, of religious and cultural change.

Today they are dying out. Nothing in the world can prevent their extinction. Their numbers have been steadily dwindling for fifty years, and it is only seldom that children are to be seen in their tents. The men and women of this ancient people are unfertile. And even if now and again in some tent a weak yellowish-brown child is born into the world, it generally has sad, quiet eyes, slow, impotent gestures, and a thin, weak little voice of which it rarely makes use.

The old race of the steppes knows full well that its hour has struck. And it has come to terms with itself. The wise-men of the race say sadly: »In a hundred years there will be no more Nogai Tatars. God is angry with us and will tolerate us no more upon the earth.«

The years have completely altered the character of the people. There is nothing left today of the mighty warriors who shook the world under the leadership of Jenghiz-Khan. The Nogai of today is no warrior, and no hero, he is hardly even a man any longer. His pale expressionless face is framed in sparse withered hair, or more often it is completely hairless. The small slits of eyes look out dully and sadly upon the world. They are no longer the eyes of human beings; they are the eyes of a quiet patient sheep to whom everything is indifferent, boring, and superfluous. The Nogai Tatars breed sheep. Wherever they go there are sheep with them. It is easy to compare their eyes with those of their flock. Their faces are always slightly swollen in appearance and the forehead low; they stoop as they walk and pay no heed to anything that may cross their path. When a Nogai speaks with strangers his entire appearance takes on a look of naive astonishment, which does not leave it for days afterwards. But he very rarely does speak, being sparing of words, not on principle, but because speech really is difficult for him if it is not about the familiar things of his own immediate surroundings. He reflects for several minutes before answering the simplest question, and then he answers slowly and carefully. His tongue moves with difficulty, and he stutters at every moderately complicated phrase. His thoughts keep deserting him, and he is quite incapable of concentrating on anything for any length of time. He very rarely laughs, takes joy in nothing, and treats everything in the outside world with the indescribable indifference of one who is finally and completely sated.

Even the primitive sensation of jealousy is unknown to the Nogai. The honour of his wife is, like everything else, a matter of complete indifference to him. If his wife's honour does usually remain unprofaned, it is purely and simply because the other Nogai Tatars are too apathetic to exert themselves in the slightest over another's wife. Yet the Nogai women are often very pretty, have a serene, amiable disposition, and would certainly appeal greatly even to a European if they did not so frequently obey the widespread custom of wearing rings in their noses.

The Nogai Tatars, descendants of the greatest warriors of all Asia, are now the greatest cowards that are to be met with anywhere in the world. Anyone can insult a Nogai, or steal his cattle, and he will look impotently on and wail without offering the slightest resistance. His weapons are always useless and rusted. It takes a quite extraordinary amount of ill-treatment to arouse his anger, and in battle he will run away at the smallest danger even when his forces outnumber the enemy a hundred to one. He is equally incapable of work and spends his whole day loafing about. He drinks huge quantities of tea, chats with his neighbours about the trivial details of everyday life, and is incidentally decried as the greatest cynic in the Orient.

Dirty, cynical stories—of which he knows an endless number, relating them with much joy—can alone still stir and entertain him, though as regards their subject matter he himself is known as a person of very limited possibilities. The pleasures or distractions known to the Nogai Tatars are few. They are even ignorant of dancing and games. The young people saunter around the tents in the evening and stare mutely at the sky in complete boredom; they can think of nothing to pass the time away.

In spite of this unheard-of degeneration and this dull vegetable existence, the Nogai Tatar considers himself an ornament of the universe. He proudly rejects every innovation which might to some extent uplift him in his miserable existence—for he is very poor. If you suggest anything of this kind to him, he looks at you with a tired, melancholy expression, and says in so many words: »We need nothing new; we have already had everything that a people can have; and anything we may not have had is superfluous.«

Nogai families of distinction carry coats-of-arms to this very day which resemble to a large extent their oldest European counterparts and lend a remarkably feudal character to these disappearing clans. Coats-of-arms are otherwise practically unheard of in the Orient. These proud *déracinés* have long forgotten that they were once Jews. And yet one of the most numerous and comparatively vital families in the land bears the name »Chi-Jughutlari,« which means »pure Jews,« and is certainly a reminiscence of the days of the Khazar dominion. The heraldic device of these »pure Jews« is the mathematical symbol of infinity. It is a very curious thing to see one of these »pure Jews« with a typically Mongolian face and Mohammedan praying beads. And yet the »Chi-Jughut« is very proud of his racial purity and looks with arrogance on his other compatriots as »not sufficiently pure Jews.« Furthermore, all Nogai Tatars are so fantastically unclean, or more exactly, so stinkingly dirty, that even their neighbours the Kumyks, who are not especially fastidious, avoid all contact with them.

Everything that I have said ought to mark down the Nogai race as the dullest and least intelligent of Asiatic tribes. But on coming to close grips with this poverty-stricken people—which up to now very few persons have had the curiosity to do—some very remarkable facts emerge. These idiotic, stupid, hopelessly moribund sheep possess, incredible though it may sound, a literature which I can unhesitatingly designate as one of the most important folk-literatures of Asia. It is not a literature composed by separate poets; it is not the artistic production of an individual; it is a true folk-epic, depicting the centuries of Nogai history in a remarkably interesting evolutionary series. The ancient greatness of the race has been preserved in the traditional epics and is recited by folk-singers on clear moonlight nights to the devoutly attentive people.

It is impossible to reproduce the primitive beauty of these songs. In the hoary language of the Turkic nomads, which is still used by the Nogai Tatars to this day, they describe the might of Jenghiz-Khan, they tell of the glory of his successors, of the great Khans; they picture the bloody battles and the magnificent feasts of the victorious Golden Horde.

The Nogai people have lost everything: wealth, office, and honour. Only their songs are left them, and their songs have a curiously enlivening effect upon them. It sometimes happens—not, it is true, very often—that the Nogai people, after listening for some time to their bards, awake suddenly for a few hours to their historic greatness. The amiable, melancholy cowards are converted in an ecstatic fit, by a sort of mass psychology, into courageous heroes. They spring on to their starved horses and ride into the steppes which suddenly resound with their old, wild war-cries. There they attack any stranger they meet with and, drunk with victory, they tear him literally in pieces, howling as they do so.

The ancient power of the steppes is resurrected, though in a ghostly, faded caricature. Then the frenzy subsides again as quickly as it came; the narrow eyes resume their dull, sad look; the carriage becomes stooping and the complexion pale; the Horde halts and retreats timorously. And that night the old men may be heard groaning with anxiety: »Alas! what have we done!«

Any literature or song that can accomplish this much is certainly magnificent, even if untranslatable into Western speech. The inner music of every strophe is magical, and so are the heavy dignity of the rhyme and the robust brutal beauty of every phrase. The people who made this literature were not only great warriors but also really great poets, with an indescribably fine feeling for words and a subtle lyric sensitivity which, though they can be appreciated today only by philologists, are indeed surprising as characteristics of the »Terror of Asia.«

Today both are disappearing—the Nogai Tatars and their songs. The wonderful literature of a world-empire will be forgotten. In two more generations the last of the Nogai Tatars, that most un-Caucasian of races, will have disappeared from the earth. Yet still they say: »We need nothing more; we have achieved everything that a people can achieve. And now God will tolerate us no longer.«

20.

HOW THE CAUCASUS
WAS CONQUERED

IF YOU OPEN THE MAP, you see a frontier line which starts east of Germany and runs north and south, disappearing amid the ice of the North Pole and the waters of the Black Sea, reappearing again in Armenia and Siberia, and enclosing altogether one-sixth of the entire surface of the earth. Within this line is written »Russia,« or, if the map is a new one and Poland is registered on it, »U.S.S.R.« People who have retained from their youth and schooldays the sense of the ultimate indisputability of the lines of a map will have learned at one time that the Caucasus belongs to Russia, and will be of the opinion that the Tsar's viceroys were stationed at Tiflis even in the dim and remote past, signing proclamations and hanging captured brigands.

This schoolroom knowledge and these lines of the map are deceptive. It is barely one hundred years since the Tsars began the conquest of the Caucasus. In the history books it is written: »In the year 1874 the conquest of the Caucasus was completed.« Many decades have passed since then, and when the greatest of all revolutions broke out in the fourth year of the World War, the conquest was far from being complete. It is scarcely to be supposed that it ever will be.

The Russians occupied only the large towns and the strategic points; only in the peaceful valleys of Georgia and Armenia did the Tsar's word hold good. Farther into the mountains, among the tribes of Daghestan and of the so-called Greater Caucasus, the power of the Russians was purely nominal. Patriarchal law and the power of the princes and elders stood for more there than the countless orders issuing from the great palace in Tiflis, whether they were reinforced by punitive expeditions and vain threats or not. But even this limited power was acquired by Russia only after lengthy fighting, countless campaigns, and brutal devastation. The gulf that separates Russia from the colourful world of the Caucasus is too wide, and it will not be until the last Caucasian is dead that the mountains will really be subjugated.

The history of the Russian campaign of conquest, varying often enough as it does from the grotesque to the cruel, and from the cruel to the frivolous, cannot be omitted from any book on the Caucasus, especially as there is so much that is remarkable and essentially Oriental in this history.

The first harbinger of a conquest of the Caucasus was Peter the Great's famous Caspian campaign. The Tsar was tempted at that time by the waters of the Green Sea, which were apparently without a ruler and whose shores ran far into the Caucasus and stood nominally under Persian dominion. At that time civil war was raging in Persia, and the Russian troops marching along the ancient Caspian military road met with no serious opposition. The independent rulers of the district, the Shamkhal of Tarki, the Khans, and the Princes, bowed remarkably quickly before the power of the Tsar. The whole of the eastern plain of the Caucasus up to Baku was very soon in the hands of the Russians. The Tsar then rejected the uninviting prospect of penetrating into the mountains, declared Daghestan and the East Caucasus conquered, and concluded a treaty to this effect with the Persians. Soon afterwards the Russian troops withdrew, and the newly acquired territory was placed under the governorship of a general.

The whole thing was accomplished in a few months, and in the joy of victory the Russians failed to notice how tremendously pleased the Persians were that they could hand over to the Russians this restless, unprofitable, and, in the last analysis, entirely independent land of brigands. The conquest did not bring the Russians much good luck. After the death of Peter the Great, his far-reaching Oriental projects were forgotten, and nothing remained but anxiety about this gigantic district which defied all authority and for whose piratical onslaughts the Persian Government could no longer be held responsible.

The successors of Peter the Great, determined to be rid of the burdensome fruits of their brilliant conquests, entrusted resourceful diplomats with the difficult task of palming the Caucasus back on the Persians. The diplomats rigged up an imposing conference and boasted all their lives afterwards of how they had finally been successful, by means of their diplomatic skill at bribery and corruption, in again saddling the Persians with a country the size of Germany as a component part of their empire.

The modest Russian occupation was then withdrawn with all speed, and the Government at St. Petersburg breathed again at the prospect of at last coming out of that grim Caucasian affair with a whole skin. Daghestan and Azerbaijan (which were by no means as uncultured at that time as the Russians thought) scarcely noticed the change of government. Instead of a Russian occupation, an equally unassuming Persian occupation took its place; the native princes felt themselves no more disturbed in their sovereignty than before. The Shah remained what he always had been: a ruler who lived a very long way off, and of course occasionally laid waste tracts of land and set up new princes instead of the old ones, but had otherwise very little to say. The Russian adventure was forgotten after a few years.

Some decades had elapsed when Sophia of Anhalt-Zerbst, the famous Semiramis of the North, the brilliant Catherine, ascended the throne. She bothered her head less, if anything, than her predecessors about the Caucasus and the strange lands beyond the great mountain wall. It was not until she was beginning to get old that fate obliged her to interfere in the history of the mountains. Fate in this case took the shape of the young Count Plato Subov, the last lover of the old Empress. Subov, the handsome favourite, was the most powerful man in Russia and yet he had his troubles, too. It was true that the Tsarina's love was his, and that she permitted him unlimited power over her land in return for his affectionate attentions. But still there is nothing more variable than the favour of a Tsarina, even if she is close on seventy years of age, as Catherine was. The twenty-five-year-old Subov and the seventy-year-old Empress were the most jealous lovers in all Russia. The Empress would not allow a single pretty face to come near Subov, and Subov would not tolerate any good-looking, uncastrated young male to approach his warmly beloved Empress. Years went by in unruffled bliss while Subov continued to supply the old lady with caresses. True, he was often disgusted with himself as he returned home from these services, but in return he ruled over a sixth of the world.

But suddenly a rival cropped up whom he could neither banish to Siberia nor annihilate in any other way. It was his own brother, now grown up, the angelic Count Valerian Subov. The Empress's eyes rested ever more lingeringly upon the youth, and Count Plato's expression became ever more worried as his stock went down. Everything possible was now done to keep the young man out of the Tsarina's bed. He was married off; when there was war, he was sent to the front; and, when there was peace, he was sent abroad for a cure. But nothing could afford sufficient security. In this dire necessity Subov major finally decided to do something drastic to keep Subov minor permanently away from the court. The twenty-two-year-old Valerian was made a general and immediately promoted to be the Tsarina's viceroy on the Caucasian frontier, and lastly he was favoured with the childishly simple task of conquering the Caucasus, Persia, India, and, if possible, Turkey as well, for the Russian crown. Count Plato convinced the Empress that the task presented no difficulty whatever, and Count Valerian went to the frontier with the fixed hope of adorning his brother's statesmanship with these desired and fabulous lands.

Thus began the grotesque second Russian assault on the Caucasus.

Count Valerian was a temperamental young man who believed that, if one became a general at twenty-one, it was essential that one should be proclaimed conqueror of Persia at twenty-four. His opponents, the warlike Caucasians, called him the »Baby General.« The campaign began according to tradition at the same spot from which Peter the Great began his conquest, and the memory of it has remained to this day perpetuated in all kinds of Caucasian jokes and droll stories. Was the Caucasus, the land which had defied all the heroes of world history, to bow the head before a baby?

The mountain people had good cause to laugh. They never even thought of a serious war. Subov was received with festivities in every town. The princes did him homage and compared him with the great Macedonian, and in return they cashed in on the extravagant gifts with which the Count showered them. Gigantic silver keys were quickly prepared by resourceful craftsmen and ceremoniously handed over to the radiant conqueror by the princes, always with the same remark, to the effect that Peter the Great had received the same keys in his day. The princes had learned that the handing over of city keys was a custom in the West and they wanted this generous conqueror to be well pleased. The fact that the Russian soldiers were incidentally attacked and plundered many times over remained a mere detail by comparison with the dazzling successes of the promising youngster. The reports which he sent the Tsarina from the seat of war were most enthusiastic: »The conquered people weep tears when they hear Your Majesty's name, and they fall to the ground and give thanks to the Almighty for allowing them to be contemporaries of Your Majesty. Even to think upon the possibility of being permitted to kiss Your Majesty's hand makes them the happiest people on earth,« and so forth.

Count Valerian apparently was really intoxicated by his victories. He hardly ever put his nose out of the door of his magnificent tent, or at least he failed to notice how the district which he was conquering became continually more trackless, and how he heard less and less from the outside world every day. True, the numbers of his soldiers diminished day by day, but then the protestations of the native princes became every day more and more flattering.

The Apollo of St. Petersburg was lucky. Just as the catastrophe began to reach a climax in Daghestan, just as the homage began to cease and the attacks to increase in the most threatening manner, a second and much more significant catastrophe happened to Subov. The great Empress died and her son Paul, who had sworn to drive out all his mother's lovers and banish them to Siberia, ascended the throne. The two Subovs were at once deprived of their positions.

The pretty boy Valerian left the scene of his glory in headlong flight for his estate over the Volga. His army was annihilated by the Caucasians who surrounded it. Only a few fragments of it were able to reach the Russian frontier after terrible hardships. Thus ended the second Russian campaign in the mountains.

The actual conquest of the Caucasus, the deliberate and brutal colonization, begins with Alexander I. He it was who started the never-ending Caucasian war, which even his last descendant did not bring to an end.

At that time two lines of the Georgian royal family, sons of King Erekle by different mothers, were at war. Georgia was an independent kingdom under the mild sovereignty of Persia. The ruling King George XII found himself hard pressed. As he could discover no interest in Persia for the internal affairs of his country, he turned to Russia with the request that she should place troops at his disposal for suppressing his brothers. In payment he promised to recognize Russia instead of Persia as the sovereign power of Georgia. This chance to get a firm foothold in Transcaucasia was very welcome to the Tsar. Russian troops invested Georgia and assured the invalid King of his throne. Their leaders swore, in the name of the Tsar, never to violate the independence of the Georgian crown. »It is not that we may extend our empire, which is in any case the greatest in the world, that we undertake to protect the kingdom of Georgia,« so ran the initial words of the manifesto which the Tsar had carved in bronze and set up in Tiflis.

These bronze tablets still adorn the principal streets of Tiflis and have proved themselves more lasting, not merely than the throne of Georgia, but than the throne of the Tsar as well. Soon after the guarantee of Russian protection, King George XII died, and in spite of the manifesto, in spite of the promise of the Tsar, the independence of the Georgian kingdom was revoked and the land was declared a province of Russia.

The rebellions which then began were brutally suppressed, and the royal family was driven out and annihilated. The last queen (who, in spite of a harem education, carried on the war against Russia, and, aided by one of her daughters, stabbed a Russian general with her own hand) was banished to Siberia. Peaceful Georgia lay devastated. The thousand-year-old independence of the country, which even the Shah and the Sultan had not dared to attack, was now gone. But the Georgians' battle for freedom lasted on into the sixties of the last century, when it stopped for forty years, to flare up once again in 1905.

Georgia, however, is not the whole of the Caucasus. All around it lay independent countries: Guria, Imeretia, Mingrelia, the principalities of Daghestan, and the Khanates of Azerbaijan. The Russians considered it absolutely necessary to conquer these places in order really to »protect« Georgia, according to the promise of the Tsar. And thus the sixty-year war for the mountains began, the struggle between the Russian giant and the hundreds of little, split-up, peaceful, and in part even Christian peoples of the Caucasus.

Frequently enough in olden times, the Caucasus had been visited by foreign oppressors. Assyrian cuneiform script which has been found in the earth testifies to ancient campaigns. Greek coins recall rich and warlike colonies. In the heart of the mountains there are Latin inscriptions, the rocks of Daghestan commemorating the presence of Pompey, the Imperator, and the Caucasian campaign of the iron legions. The Genoese towers, the Moorish palaces of the Arabians, the Byzantine churches and the ruins which were made of them by the hordes of the cripple Tamerlane; all these proclaim a history which has known the greatest among all the world conquerors. Nebuchadnezzar, Darius, Alexander, Pompey, Attila, Jenghiz-Khan, and Tamerlane, all of them were adversaries of the mountain people in days gone by.

And now came the Russians, the Europeans, and quite outdid the deeds of their famous predecessors. The Christian generals raged over the mountains with blood and iron; villages were razed to the ground; whole peoples were destroyed; the medieval »scourge of God« was resurrected with an increase in terror. The conquest certainly did not come easily to the Russians. One general after another was called back from the hills as incompetent. Cannons had to be transported over vertiginous heights. Deep precipices, rugged cliffs, and snow-capped peaks threatened the Russians from all sides, and behind every rock, on the edge of every precipice, lurked the enemy, the armed Caucasian fighting for freedom. Those sixty years which the Russians required to conquer the Caucasus saw the most terrible, the most bloody colonial war of all time. It is unfortunately known to Europeans from Russian sources only.

The first Russian expeditions into the mountains, which began immediately after the conquest of Georgia, were unsuccessful. It was not until the Tsar appointed General Ermolov, the hero of the Napoleonic war, as his viceroy in Tiflis that the organized campaign began. Ermolov, who was one of the most remarkable people in Russia, deserves to be discussed more fully here.

He felt himself to be a Roman proconsul in the Caucasus. That was his only weakness. He procured himself a harem of native beauties, whom he acquired legally, and he persuaded the Tsar to grant legitimacy to the children deriving from this harem. He had an almost perfect mastery of the figurative politenesses of Eastern intercourse, addressed his opponents as »Pillars of Righteousness,« and never hesitated, if necessary, to overcome his enemy by cunning or treachery, or to slaughter thousands of prisoners. All this impressed the Caucasians immensely. Ermolov was the only viceroy who was looked up to and respected in the mountains, in spite of the fact that he was the most brutal and bloodthirsty of adversaries. The Caucasians recognized the fact that the wily soldier was their peer. In addition to all this, Ermolov was a clever man and one of the best acquainted with the Orient, possessing as masterly a knowledge of Eastern politics as he had of Eastern warfare.

The following story is significant of those days, and of the clever politics of the General and the people with whom he had to deal. Shortly after his appointment as viceroy, Ermolov betook himself to the court of the Shah of Persia, in order to settle the question of frontiers and the influence of Persia upon Daghestan. He was coldly received at the court of the Shah, but finally gained the confidence of the tyrant and his ministers by incessant gifts and continual quotations from the Persian poet-princes. But from the business standpoint, this great lion of a general was unable to move the Persians, who refused to meet him half-way on anything.

Then Ermolov invited the Persian Minister for Foreign Affairs to a conference in his magnificent palace. In the course of the discussion he asked with a forbidding countenance: »Is Your Excellency then unwilling to yield on any point?« »Yes,« answered the Persian. Ermolov rose, seized his head in his hands, and began roaring like a tiger; then he leaped with both feet on the divan, put his tongue out at the Minister, and laughed in a menacing way. After that he broke a few chairs and finally announced that he was not General Ermolov at all, but a direct descendant of Jenghiz-Khan, the conqueror of Persia. With that he tore open his coat and disclosed on his breast a recently painted spot of some kind, declaring it to be »the mark of the great Khan.« The Minister crept out of the room on all fours, astonished and frightened to death, but overjoyed at having got out of the affair alive.

In the next room he was awaited by the General's secretary.

»I must confess something to you,« the secretary said gravely. »Our General is a brave soldier and a descendant of the great Khan, but he is also unfortunately a little bit mad and inclined to outbursts of rage. He is exceedingly dangerous when he is in this condition. The Tsar himself is afraid of him, and that is why he sent him to Persia because he seemed to him too dangerous as a madman and a descendant of Jenghiz-Khan.«

The Minister listened timidly to the secretary's words, and at the same moment he caught a terrific tiger-like roar from the next room, which caused him to leave the house and rush back to the imperial palace, whence he returned shortly and explained as gently as you please that His Majesty was in full agreement with all the General's proposals. The latter grinned with satisfaction, though he took care to let out a savage roar or two before the treaty was actually signed.

He knew that the people of the East respect nothing so much and fear nobody more desperately than they do a maniac. »Never contradict a madman,« says the Koran. And how much more difficult to contradict one who is a descendant of Jenghiz-Khan and a trusted servant of the Tsar. Who knows what a madman may not do if he is capable of making life difficult for his own lord and master? It were better to give in and accompany the raving General back to Russia with honours. »God protect us from a lunatic,« says the old proverb.

Later, when other ambassadors came, the Persians always exacted their word of honour that they were of sound mind. Ermolov, however, had gained his objective. His lunacy served him well on another occasion. Russia has to thank the General's brain-wave for her dominion over the three principalities of Shirvan, Shekeh, and Karabakh. The three princes were hereditary allies of the Russian crown, and, since the population was very loyal to the princes, Russia was unable to turn the autonomous principalities into Russian provinces. So Ermolov determined upon a peaceful Russification of these principalities. The princes were invited to visit the General and, when they arrived with valuable gifts, they were royally received at the Russian camp within the General's magnificent tent. The tall stature, broad shoulders, and leonine hair of the General made a deep impression on them. But, instead of taking their presents into his possession, he hailed a passing shepherd and exchanged them for a couple of sheep which he caused to be slaughtered on the spot; then he wrapped himself in one of their skins. At this the princes bowed low, kissed the General's hand, and hurried back in all haste to their own countries. There they assembled their friends, packed up all their belongings, and, accompanied by their entire families, left their districts as fast as they could go. »We are afraid to live under the authority of a madman,« they explained in terror.

The General wished for nothing better; he declared the principalities which had been deserted by their legitimate potentates to be Russian territory and occupied them with his troops. All this occurred in the year 1822.

These grotesquely idyllic circumstances did not last long. The never-ending war became gradually more brutal and more bloody. The Russian soldiers lived in the mountains for whole decades, and when they died they left their children behind to continue the struggle for another generation. Finally the two opponents became indistinguishable from each other in habits, mental character, and outlook, and those who were known as »old Caucasians« among the Russian troops finally earned the designation by becoming typical Caucasian hill-bandits.

At length, after a thirty-year war, just as Russia was on the verge of completing the work of subjugation, a remarkable movement started in the heart of the Caucasus, in Daghestan, which annihilated the Russian labours of thirty years, and turned the whole of Daghestan into an invincible stronghold for several decades. For the first and last time in its history, Daghestan changed from a collection of enemy peoples into a unified, independent state with an autocratic ruler at its head. The movement which made this possible was called »Muridism«; its followers were the Murids, or people of the Tarikat. And the man who ruled over Daghestan for thirty years, defying the Tsar and preaching the Tarikat, was Imam Ali Shamil, the King of the Mountains, the celebrated hero of the Orient, the first man to preach and fight for the »Awakening of the Orient.« His text was Islam militant and the Tarikat, which is the strictest form of the religious life.

His soldiers, the Murids, were essentially fighting monks, members of an order which embraced the entire male population of Daghestan.

The life of Shamil is like a fairy tale. That which the medieval monks failed to do, of which Ignatius Loyola dreamt, and to which Catholicism was unequal, was accomplished by this warrior and scholar of epic proportions—to wit, the subjection of an entire country to an abstract religious idea. For thirty years Daghestan became one enormous monastery full of armed monks, who knew no other law than the bidding of their prior, the Imam. For the first time in the history of humanity the principle of theocracy was here brought to perfection. At the head of the people stood the »Master of the Faithful,« the Imam, the chief worshipper, and behind him were the Murids of the Tarikat. After them came the ordinary Murids, the associates and helpers in the righteous struggle for God and Freedom. Universal military service, brutal penalties for the slightest offence against religion, the stoning of anyone who omitted a single prayer, and death to anyone who smoked, together with a stringent military-religious organization such as had never before been known in the Orient; these were the means of government adopted by the Holy One of Daghestan, the man who caused the Arabic inscription, »Whoso thinks of the consequences will never be brave,« to be inscribed upon the badge of the Order which he issued to his warriors. Shamil lived for fifteen years as a pupil of the wise-men in the seclusion of a cell in the mosques. He studied the Koran, the holy writ of Islam. For fifteen years he was a pious monk and scholar, and then became a warrior and a fighter, declared a holy war upon the »Gasavat,« drove the Russians out of the mountains, and suddenly created a living theocratic state out of the graceful Arabic script and the age-old wisdom of the saints of antiquity.

The conquerors of the land had no idea of how Shamil's work began. The last uprising of the mountain people had been put down, and the bastions and garrisons of the Russians stood in the very heart of the mountains. The Russians thought they could rule the mountains from their fortresses and were really under the delusion that they governed the country. All was quiet. The native princes held court and paid tribute. Respect for the Russians increased every day. Banditry was on the decrease, and nothing gave any cause for anxiety; there was not even the customary ferment in the hills.

But suddenly, without rhyme or reason as far as the Russians could see, the Holy War started. The Russian garrisons were destroyed, and the native princes who would not renounce their office were driven out or murdered.

From now on there were to be no more princes or nobility, and no ruler except the Imam, the founder of the new state. At first the Russians thought it was merely another of the usual bandit raids, and as usual they sent out punitive expeditions. But when the latter were annihilated one after the other, the danger was manifest, and the birth of a new state was recognized with astonishment. Punitive expeditions were of no avail now.

An army which seemed to have come into well-organized being overnight and to be quite invincible now faced the Russians. The battle between the theocracy of Daghestan and the absolute monarchy of Russia lasted for thirty years. Russian armies were continually being beaten, and the Russians frequently gave up the struggle only to take it up again later. Meanwhile, in spite of the theocracy, Daghestan was practically growing to be a modern state. The principalities were abolished;

the land was divided into provinces; and every inhabitant was provided with a passport. A uniform system of justice based upon the Koran was introduced; blood feud was forbidden; taxes were regulated; munition factories, printing presses, and mints were built; and brigandage was done away with. For the first and last time in the history of Daghestan, it was possible to ride through the mountain gorges in safety and to register at the police station in the most remote settlements. Even the confusion of languages disappeared because Arabic, the language of the Koran, was proclaimed (partially at least) the official business and governmental tongue.

This remarkable religious and political renaissance in Daghestan did not last for long. A free land in the midst of the conquered Caucasus did not suit the Tsar's book at all. Since nothing could be accomplished against the organized people of Daghestan by means of skirmishes and expeditions, and since Shamil was stronger than the Russians in open warfare and had advanced almost to Tiflis, Russia discovered a solution which was indeed not recognized in European strategy but was supposed to be effective here in the mountains. It was decided to divide the land into zones and to proceed systematically against them destroying all villages, fields, and springs, killing all the cattle, and murdering all the people in each one. Thus the kingdom of Shamil might gradually be shattered step by step. Every zone that was conquered must be laid waste so that its re-conquest would be of no help to the enemy. Every Daghestan native was to be killed, so as to weaken the Murids progressively by a process of attrition over a number of decades.

This humane method of warfare was consistently pursued. All Daghestan, even if it took years to accomplish, was to be turned into a desert waste. That was the password of the most cruel of all colonial wars. And this password was really obeyed. The poisoning of springs, the murder of women and children, the destruction of painstakingly tilled fields, and the deforestation of the land, all at the Tsar's behest; these are things which cannot be described here in a few lines. Russian and Caucasian sources give quite enough information on the point, as they do also about the romantic and knightly prowess in the battles on the mountain heights, and about the foolhardy exploits of the Caucasians and the blood and misery of the »penetration by zones.«

To cut a long story short, the war came to an end after thirty cruel years: the kingdom and the life work of Shamil lay in ruins on the ground. He himself, having put up a defence to the very last on the snowy summit of Mount Gunib, was forced finally to drag his battered limbs, wounded in eighteen places, into the enemy's camp. His one condition was that no Mohammedan should witness his surrender.

The Russian soldiers who took him prisoner afterwards stood row upon row before his house and reverently kissed the hand of this saint of a foreign faith whenever he came out. They had never known a ruler who led the life of a saint as he did, who remained poor, fought bravely and heroically himself, and after thirty years of power had nothing but a terribly wounded body that he could call his own.

The King of the Mountains would have died of hunger if the Tsar had not paid him a pension. He died eventually in Mecca. He was and he remains the greatest hero in the awakening Orient and the pioneer of all those who are fighting for the liberation of the East.

The freedom of Daghestan and of the whole Caucasus was now done with for many years. The battle was never given up, it is true; new insurrections kept blazing out here and there. The freedom-loving bands of Abreks, who carried on the fight, rose up again and again in the mountains, but the result of the battles became ever more hopeless.

Then, in the year 1917, the great revolution broke out, and all the fruits of the Russian conquest were lost for years. It was not until this event occurred that the Russians realized what weak roots their forty years of tyranny in the land had sent out. The most fanatic of Russians could scarcely maintain nowadays that »the Caucasus is a part of Russia.« At the most he might declare that the Caucasus »should be a Russian colony.« But that implies a new war, more penetration by zones, more blood, more misery.

That is the story of the conquest of the hills, the bloody tale of a hundred free peoples combating the colossus of the North. It was followed by a period of comparative peace, which Russia used for raising the cultural level of the country. This process consisted in driving out the inhabitants of all the best properties and settling Cossacks in their place. A start was made in the construction of roads and cities and in the opening of factories and the erection of monuments, but most of these attempts ran a more or less grotesque course and always ended in disaster.

The Russians succeeded in doing something really important in one place only: in the North Caucasus in the neighbourhood of the mountain Besh-Tau, where the famous Caucasian health springs are. Four towns were built at Besh-Tau. The most beautiful of them, Kislovodsk, was far superior to the most worldly European spa in luxury and magnificence. Villas and palaces formed a town which contained some of the finest gardens in the Orient. Three full days are necessary to view the great park in Kislovodsk. The whole town is a unique wonder of nature, created by the princes and bankers of St. Petersburg for their leisure moments. Courtiers, monarchs without thrones, feudal nobility, statesmen, and generals used to stream into Kislovodsk every summer. Cossack settlements were laid out around the town so that a substantial standing army could look after the peace of this most heavenly of all cities. The cream of Russia, by which of course is meant feudal Russia, chose Kislovodsk as its favourite holiday resort and saw to it that it was well cared for and protected.

I visited Kislovodsk several times. In the very year that I was becoming acquainted with the great mountains and the auls and princes of Daghestan, my journey concluded at the baths of Besh-Tau. Since these baths and the feudal town have now lost their old glory for ever, I will resurrect them from their oblivion here.

21.

NARSAN – THE BLOOD
OF THE GIANT

THE FAMOUS CAUCASIAN HEALTH SPRINGS lie in the north of the mountains in the land of Kabardia. In the vicinity of the springs, however, there were no Kabardians left. They had been driven into the mountains, and supplanted by the Russian Cossacks who guarded the four health resorts from attack.

The Kabardians did not let themselves be driven out unresistingly. The struggle lasted for years until the Russians took firm hold in the valley of Kabardia and tricked the princes of Kabardia into submission by cunning treaties. In this case it was the princes—for Kabardia was the only Caucasian country where until recently neither priests nor the family had anything to say. Everything in Kabardia belonged to the seven famous princely lines, who regarded neither the Sultan nor the Shah as in any way their peers.

A Kabardian prince is the embodiment of all Caucasian ideals in the eyes of Caucasians, the exemplary type of all the virtues of this earth, an untouchable person who must be treated as if he were sacred. The princes of Kabardia are fully aware of their dignity, for no one disputes the fact that the Kabardians are the most chivalrous people in the world and their princes the noblest lords in the whole Orient, than whom all the potentates of the world are lesser beings. Their families ruled for two thousand years without one single prince being murdered by his subjects, or even an attempt to do so being made. Everything in the land of Kabardia belonged to the princes; they might take whatever they chose from their subjects, even their wives. When they journey through the land, everybody who meets them must stop, however much of a hurry he may be in, and accompany the prince until he is dismissed with a proud gesture. When the prince blows his nose, everybody present must do likewise, and, if he is obliged to answer the call of nature on a journey, all his companions, the whole court, indeed every person that is visible in the region, must follow his example on the highroad. But if, on the one hand, the prince owns all of his subjects' property, it is also true, on the other hand, that everything the prince possesses may belong to his subjects. Every Kabardian has the right to seek out his prince and more or less unceremoniously exchange daggers or hats with him, or take any other object out of his house. If the prince forbade this, he would be decried for his haughtiness and declared to have forfeited his dignity.

The Kabardians then—who are a branch of the great Adigheh people—lived for centuries in the valley of medicinal waters, until they all withdrew—princes, counts, nobles, peasants, and soldiers—into the mountains, where they continued their feudal existence. In the valley where the Russians came, there was nothing left but the baths of the Kabardian people, and the legends which are connected with them. I shall give one of the legends, about the origin of the springs, in a literal translation.

Many thousands of years ago—say the Kabardians— when the earth was still young and fair and no shadow of past suffering lay upon the surface of it, there were no human beings, no men and no women. No single being dwelt in the endless steppes, in the dark depths of the sea, and on the distant isles; the mountains alone, dark, enormous masses of sand and stone, had the breath of life within their breasts. The little hills, graceful and supple as spoilt women, and the mighty giants, tall and powerful like men armed with sword and helmet.

The mountains at that time were free and mobile. They wandered through deserts and forests, looked at themselves in the great green mirror of the sea, and told strange tales to one another, of which unhappy humanity today knows nothing.

They would often gather together, and then the great solemn heights would pay court to the little hills, who tried to coquette shyly and timidly with their mighty friends.

The mountains enjoyed their rendezvous most when they took place on the small strip of land between the Caspian Sea and the Black Sea. Many a beauty was to be met with there, slim lovely ladies, whose description is not within the compass of human speech. Only the eagles upon the high peaks of the Caucasus still remember the past and often sing in savage cadences their praise of the stony beauties of the mountains, but we men do not understand them.

There was once a woman who was known for her charm by all the mountains among the giants of the Caucasus, the Himalayas, and the Alps. Mashuk was her name.

She was slim and young and proud, like so many beautiful women. Only two of the giants dared to come near her. Their names were Elbruz and Tau. Their summits reached high into the heavens, and they were the first to greet the sun at morning and the last to bid him farewell at night. But the beautiful Mashuk was proud and teasing; she promised her love first to one, then to the other, and the thing happened which always does happen in such circumstances: the giants, burning with jealousy, started a quarrel. Elbruz fell upon Tau like a terror from on high, like an image of the wrath of the Almighty, but Tau defended himself bravely. The two mountains fought with fire and sword; the earth trembled beneath their steps; and the red reflection of their strife radiated to heaven and over the whole world.

The battle lasted for five hundred years, and the flames from the hearts of the giants grew bigger and bigger, and blood flowed down their bodies in streams. But at last Elbruz was victorious. With all his strength, he struck at Tau with one last sword stroke. Tau could not withstand the terrible blow; he broke into five parts and fell down at the feet of his proud opponent. Thus from the mighty Tau (mountain) was created Besh-Tau (five mountains).

But the joy of the victor did not last for long. When he presented himself to Mashuk, he found not a young maid but an old woman with deep furrows in her face over which rolled crystal tears.

The battle of the giants had lasted for five hundred years. No woman's beauty can wait for love so long. Mashuk's youth was past, and now she was mourning over her departed life, and the death of the handsome Tau, and the bloody wounds of Elbruz. Since that time thousands of years have passed. The mountains are now old and tired. They no longer walk about the earth. White hairs cover their heads, and deep folds lie upon their faces. Other creatures, smaller and thinner figures, live now upon the wide fields and in the green forests. They wander about the earth and fight with each other and wait until the day when, dead and petrified, they too shall resign their place to still younger beings.

But the tears of Mashuk and the blood of Elbruz still flow upon the earth. High up in the mountains in Kabardia, near the stricken giant Tau, Mashuk stands, and from her depths flow the famous tears, the healing springs of the mountains, where those who are sick with love and old age may find health and recovery. Even the blood of the grim Elbruz is famous, perhaps more famous than the tears of Mashuk; it is called »Narsan, the blood of the giant.« Whosoever has been cured of love and of old age goes to Elbruz, in the town of Kislovodsk, to the mountains of Besh-Tau, and bathes in the icy blood which restores to him his strength and beauty.

Princes, ministers, aristocrats, and lieutenants of the guard did so with especial pleasure, in the company of the most exquisite beauties from Russia. They built villas, set out gardens, and succeeded in creating a mode of life in the mountains which was possible only in the Russia of the old days and in the last years of the empire, when there were still Cossacks to watch the luxurious nook, and when the Caucasian vassals of the Tsar still did not dare to plunder the place from out their mountains.

In Vladikavkaz, the Russian city at the edge of the mountains on the end of the renowned Georgian military road, the luxurious railway begins which connects the watering-place with the rest of the world. The traveller, from the heart of the mountains or from the centre of the Tsar's empire, who wished to know the charms of this pearl of cities was here met by salon cars such as were unknown in Europe.

I too boarded this train, together with my servant, and took leave of my outriders and of the primitive life of the mountains. A whole day we travelled in our salon car through the mountains, with scarcely a stop. The conductor appeared every half hour at the door of the compartment and asked in English, French, and German whether we were in need of anything. This selection of languages was doubtless merely a matter of prestige because scarcely any of the passengers used a European language. At the frontier of the spa district, the train stopped at a junction, and the passengers got out and read on the walls of the waiting-room the official notices regarding visits to the baths.

§ 1, ran as follows: Jews are forbidden to enter Kislovodsk.

§ 2: Jews travelling for the purpose of staying at spas must obtain permission from the Minister of the Interior.

§ 3: Jews who belong to the Russian nobility may visit Kislovodsk. And finally:

§ 4: The ownership of land in Kislovodsk is not permitted to anyone who is not a Cossack or a member of the nobility, unless with the special approval of the Minister of the Interior.

These four paragraphs and a dozen similar, complementary ones showed clearly enough the significance of these precious medicinal baths. Feudal Russia wanted to be alone as far as possible and at the outside to meet only native-born Caucasian aristocrats.

In the great park at Kislovodsk at the height of the season it was then possible to meet all the vassals of the Tsar. The Emir of Bukhara promenaded in the uniform of a Russian general, surrounded by a circle of gaily dressed courtiers, and looked askance at the Khan of Khiva, who, swathed in silks, proudly sipped his orangeade in a cafe. Nine blonde Mingrelian princesses conversed with the son of the last ruler of Abkhasia about the blessings of the Russian administration, and the Shamkhal of Tarki made a wide detour when he met his neighbour, the Uzmi of Karakaitag, because the latter was considered »Red« and might have compromised the ever-cautious Shamkhal. Somewhere else, a brother of the disgraced Sultan of Elissu followed Prince Krym-Girei, the civil Governor around and assured him that he had always been at bitter enmity with his brother and had consequently been unnecessarily deprived of his estates.

Frequently the whole distinguished company would spring to its feet in a row to gaze with awe upon His Imperial Highness, the Viceroy, who was pleased to take a walk in the park from time to time. By the side of His Highness strolled the princes of the realm and the old nobility of Russia, staring with haughty contempt at the native princes, the so-called »People of the Bodyguard.« For the Caucasian princes constituted the famous bodyguard of the Tsar, who trusted them more than he did the whole Russian nobility.

The chief attractions, however, were not the princes, not the cautious Shamkhal, nor the much bedecorated Emir, but the ladies, the female representatives of all the peoples of Russia who streamed to the Caucasus. They came to gaze at the wild Circassians (for in Russia all Caucasians were called Circassians) and to fall in love with a Tatar prince, enjoy the peril of a possible abduction, and finally go back to St. Petersburg and tell thrilling stories about the wild land. In order not to leave these women unsatisfied, though everything »wild« had been extirpated in Kislovodsk, some guaranteed savage brigands were artificially produced and exhibited.

The ever-complaisant Georgian princes set themselves to the task and used suddenly to play at being wild in the midst of the peaceful summer-bathing life, by snatching their daggers from the sheath, uttering inarticulate noises, and rejoicing whenever the terrified Russians spoke anxiously about the »hot-bloodedness of the Caucasians.« Kislovodsk is in fact the first town in the world to invent the genuine guaranteed wild man, a species which also found recognition in Europe later on. Today, there is scarcely a single town of moderate size in Western Europe which does not possess an Oriental night club with a wild Circassian at the door.

Kislovodsk was a fairy-tale city even without the Cossack villages, the well-paid wild men, and the romantic ladies of St. Petersburg. Everything which to Europeans has a »Southern« connotation, and constitutes the secret dream of every Northerner, finds embodiment in this great valley of the Caucasus: tropical plants, tropical forests, foaming mountain torrents, picturesque people, the cliffs and gardens of the great Narsan, the chilly blood of the giant which no one leaves without being healed. In the broad park between trees and mountains stood marble villas, equipped with every European luxury. There was never such a mixture in the world between the romance of the East and the super-culture of the West as was shown in the luxurious spa of Besh-Tau. It may be said without exaggeration that anyone who did not see Kislovodsk before the year 1917 does not know the full beauty of the old world.

In addition to the beauty of the spot, and the colourful Russian-Caucasian race mixture, Kislovodsk was unique in another way: it was the meeting-place of primitive, half-savage Caucasians who were suddenly inspired to invest themselves within twenty-four hours with all the advantages of European culture. The almost incredible barbarians from the gorges of Pshavia, or Kistinia, or God knows where, utterly unlike the Russianized Georgians, would suddenly appear in Kislovodsk with their endless trains of relatives, look on timidly for a day or two at the way their more advanced compatriots used their knives and forks, and then would bravely grasp the implements themselves in the entire conviction that they had nothing more to learn even from a London dandy. These genuine savages, however, behaved with all the modesty one could possibly wish for; they let their wives go about without veils and were amazed at arousing the surprise of the people around them by some apparently quite harmless idiosyncracy.

A day or two after my arrival in Kislovodsk, I was sitting on a bench in the great park on a quiet summer afternoon and observing the odd Eurasian mixture before me as it strolled about, confident in the comfortable security afforded by the Cossacks. Next to me on the same bench sat a young lady with a pretty dreamy face and the typical Caucasian wasplike waist. She was unveiled, which indicated a certain European tendency, but she wore the dress of Daghestan and a chain of gold coins, which was entirely Oriental. It is not the thing in the Caucasus to speak to strange ladies, and still less is it customary for them to address unknown young men, so that I had no expectations of getting to know my fair neighbour. But fate decided otherwise.

A small error, which I did not think it necessary to explain, effected the introduction. An error, I may say, which was not especially flattering to me. The young lady mistook me for a girl. I was young in those days and beardless and wore Circassian dress and, as many women went about Kislovodsk dressed as Circassians for some unknown reason, I was often taken for an Amazon. Such was now the case. My young neighbour looked me over for a while, then leaned across to me, and said in the language of Azerbaijan, which is the international language in the hills: »Dear girl, of a surety thou hast not yet made acquaintance with a man?« At that she took on the expression of the woman of experience who is about to impart some wise advice to an innocent.

Somewhat taken aback, I agreed, in soft maidenly tones, that I had not in point of fact yet had experience of a man. So she sighed deeply and informed me that the time when I should sacrifice my maidenhood to the man of my choice was certainly not far off. »And then no more shalt thou wear Circassian dress. But it is to be hoped thou wilt not be forced to come to Kislovodsk to visit doctors everlastingly, as I am.« And she sighed again, more sadly even than before.

As her face was fresh and young and did not seem to indicate any inward suffering, I advised her sympathetically not to put too much trust in European physicians, but rather to enjoy this charming life in peace. »I am not ill at all,« she replied; »I only go to see doctors because my husband wishes me to. And he is undoubtedly in the right.«

»Your husband is very fond of you then?« I said, and blushed like a girl. »Perhaps,« said the lady, »but he only takes me to see the doctors as a punishment for my frivolity and not out of love.«

Somewhat surprised, I now asked how this solicitous care for her health could also be a punishment for frivolity, and received the prompt reply: »My husband does not take me to see the doctors on account of my health at all.« »Well, what for then?« said I. The young lady blushed, and hung her head, and then said shamefacedly: »So that they may cut off my nose,« and, when she saw the somewhat idiotic expression on my face, she added: »He doesn't want to do it himself.«

I now understood to some extent what she meant, but it was not until we had talked for some time that I fully comprehended her husband's odd demands. The lady was an unmasked, publicly exposed adulteress, and her husband was a respected Daghestan nobleman who was very particular about his honour, but also considered himself the very embodiment of European refinement. According to mountain law, a man may cut off his wife's nose as a punishment when he catches her in flagrante delicto (which, be it here observed, is at least better than murdering her and being subsequently acquitted, as in Europe).

My neighbour's husband had wanted to do this when he discovered his wife in this precarious situation. But he remembered himself in time. It seemed to him irreconcilable with the refinement of a European (as he wanted to think himself) that he should obey this barbarous custom. He felt bound to give his people a good example in his capacity as a man of advanced culture. »I shall not cut off thy nose,« he told his wife publicly, »because blood-poisoning might set in. Besides which, it hurts. Thank God, these are enlightened times in which we live. I shall go with thee in summer to Kislovodsk where there are famous European doctors, and they shall cut thy nose from thy face according to the rules of their craft.«

The people who heard it were amazed at the hundred-per-cent European attitude of the husband, and the young woman began slowly to prepare for her trip. When they got to Kislovodsk, the husband visited all the most famous European doctors, but was always forced to return with much shaking of the head. All the doctors indignantly refused— despite the high fees which they were offered— to perform this strange operation for the restoration of Daghestan honour, and one of them—a professor from St. Petersburg—even threatened to inform the police. The husband could not understand why the doctors, who were Europeans and men, every one of them, had no sympathy with him, and for some weeks now he had been dragging his wife about relentlessly to all the doctors in the city. His wife, in philosophic calm and stoic remorse, let him do as he liked, but she whispered in my ear that, if no doctor could finally be found, her husband would probably end by forgiving her lapse. He had already become much nicer to her, especially since a real Russian general, whom she had met in society, had kissed her hand in front of everybody and enthusiastically said: »Such a finely modelled nose! Only a lady of the mountains could have such a nose as that.« Her husband was apparently very favourably inclined towards Russia. I took leave of the lady, without discarding my incognito, wished her the successful retention of her finely modelled Daghestan nose, and expressed the hope that my future husband would also have European leanings.

A few days later, I met her in the company of her husband. He was a tall, elegant-looking man with enormously long moustaches, the melancholy eyes of a calf, and the self-possessed air of a man who can give a good reason for all his actions. As far as I know, he did finally forgive his wife's lapse and returned with her in the end peacefully back to the mountains.

At the time I was in Kislovodsk, an incident of importance stirred the entire Caucasus and more especially the luxurious spa itself, in which the heads of the land were assembled. Despite the fact that it was the height of summer, and despite the fine weather and the beautiful surroundings, the inhabitants of the spa were in a ferment. Old friends suddenly refused to greet one another, and races which had previously been friendly threatened to jump at each other's throats. The entire Caucasus seemed to fall into two factions. A dispute, which was already beginning to disturb those who were in power in Russia, was brewing between the Armenians and the Georgians, who had suddenly become bitter enemies.

The grounds of this enmity were curiously enough neither political nor economic. It was now purely and simply a matter of a questionable old stone of absolute irrelevance which had been lying about useless and unnoticed for thousands of years and had been suddenly brought out into the light of burning actuality. Some scientific expedition, consisting of globe-trotters rather than scholars, had found an old inscription on a stone which no member was able to decipher. The inscription was copied and laid before several important scholars, who estimated its age at three thousand years. As regarded the writing itself, some of the experts thought that it was old Georgian and others identified it as old Armenian.

This was quite enough to unloose a quarrel between the two races. Clever columnists deciphered the inscription in the twinkling of an eye and discovered that it spoke of an ancient world-empire, and they declared without any hesitation that the Armenian (or the Georgian) race was the oldest and most developed people not only of the Caucasus but of the whole world. (Their decision depended upon their nationality.) The newspaper discussion was very fruitful in consequences. Neither party would yield prehistoric priority to the other. The more simple among them positively came to blows over the matter.

It was a good time for the journalists. The otherwise severe censorship was uncertain how it could forbid a scientific discussion and dared not interfere. This was a windfall for the Armenian and Georgian press. »It is unheard-of presumption,« wrote an Armenian newspaper, »that such an idiotic, degenerate, dull-witted people as the Georgians, who can thank us for whatever culture they may possess, should suddenly dare to maintain that the inscription testifying to our glorious past and deriving from a period when no Georgians even existed belongs to them,« etc. To which the Georgians replied: »The Armenians, who have forgotten that we possessed a culture in the far distant past comparable to that of Egypt (as the newly discovered inscription proves abundantly), have attempted a clumsy deception by manipulating the facts to such an extent that« etc., etc.

The news of this learned discussion soon penetrated to the lowest classes of the people, and the peasants were soon maintaining in all seriousness that a diamond had been found which was as large as a mountain and belonged either to the Georgian or the Armenian people. The stone was to be sold abroad, and every Armenian (or Georgian) would then receive a thousand roubles. The prospect of receiving a thousand roubles a head put the peasants in a warlike mood, and each of them was prepared to destroy any race that wanted to arrogate the great stone to itself.

Even people who had otherwise nothing to do either with science or with culture took part in the polemic. For example, I once heard a pretty Armenian girl in Kislovodsk maintaining very earnestly that she, as a representative of the oldest human civilization, was not disposed to associate with such primitive people as the Georgians. As we could not be considered to share either of these civilizations, her confidence was repeated to us from both points of view. Every day we saw representatives of both nations at my father's house, each of them very anxious to pass on a new and nicely worded piece of mockery as soon as he could get it out. They all began with the words: »You know that we are the oldest civilized race on earth.«

Those who were not concerned in the affair became confused to such an extent that the usually cautious Khan of Khiva, for example, suddenly declared himself to be the oldest civilized person in the world and was offended because everybody did not agree enthusiastically. He, therefore, departed overnight from Kislovodsk back to his native land. Even the Shamkhal of Tarki, the most timid man I have ever seen in the world, went red in the face and made enigmatic allusions from which it was gathered that he, the Shamkhal, was also some three thousand years old and was making a painstaking search for the stone on which it was all recorded.

This dispute about culture threatened to develop into a widespread and extremely uncultured squabble fraught with serious consequences. The Government found itself impelled to interfere in deadly earnest in the quarrel between these two »oldest civilizations.« A scholar of world-renown was delegated from St. Petersburg and commissioned to decipher the inscription once and for all. Afterwards, it was asserted that the Government had exerted special pressure on him, because his interpretation was unfavourable to both parties, and stated that the inscription was neither old Georgian nor old Armenian, but an Assyrian cuneiform to the effect that the Assyrian army had once penetrated to the innermost part of the mountains under the guidance of Armenian and Georgian slaves. Thus the great quarrel came to an end.

Later on, of course, there were sceptics who wanted to verify the affair, but the stone with the inscription had disappeared in the meantime and nobody knew where it was. It was said, heaven alone knows why, that it had been taken away at the bidding of the German Kaiser.

Both sides declared themselves satisfied with this peaceful version and soon began to threaten each other in a much milder way with: »You wait and see! They'll be able to read it correctly in Germany.« But civic peace was very zealously preserved as a rule in Kislovodsk, and it was not again disturbed until the revolution. The Khan of Khiva returned, and the Shamkhal thought it necessary to make a statement in the papers to the effect that he was by no means three thousand years old or even getting on that way.

22.

THE CASTLE OF
LOVE AND BETRAYAL

THIS IS THE ROMANTIC NAME of a rock which rises like a castle up over a steep precipice not far from Kislovodsk and is the favourite excursion centre for those who wish to bathe their weakened limbs in the cold stream of Narsan. Proud aristocrats have had their names painted on all the most inaccessible parts of the rock, and on a neighbouring boulder a Persian prince who was on his way to St. Petersburg wrote the following verse in Persian:

> The world, dear brother, is a vale of tears;
> Lay thy heart at the feet of the Creator,
> Put no faith in the pleasures of life;
> He hath made and unmade many such as thou art.
>
> *Prince Khosrou-Mirza*

This unworldly sentiment, however, did not keep the prince–a great rogue–from swindling the Tsar in masterly fashion when he got to St. Petersburg.

An old legend of Kabardia is connected with the rock and is told today all over the Orient, in Persia, Turkestan, and in India. Translated, the legend runs as follows:

It is said that the Sultan Mahmud of Gasni, Master of the World, made unto himself a crown of fairy tales. How many jewels graced this crown is not known, but every stone of it betokened a fairy tale.

It is further related that the poet Firdusi–king among poets–once asked the Sultan for the meaning of these stones and was told by him the following tale:

In the Caucasus, where the blood of the giant Elbruz flows over the earth, a great cliff stands upon the shore of a deep black sea. A youth and a maiden once sat upon a high summit of it. Their faces were pale in the rays of the moon, and sorrow was reflected from their eyes. »O, my love,« said the maiden, »we see each other today for the last time. Tomorrow, I must wed a wealthy prince and the rest of my life will be like living in a dungeon.« And from her eyes the tears flowed big and clear.

»My maiden,« spoke the youth, »when the white lilies unfold their petals, they whisper thy name. The wind taketh it and carrieth it upon the wide hills, and the shepherds, when they hear it, play a song of praise to thee upon their flutes. Beloved, life is worse without thee than the life of a leper in the deep dungeons of the Shah of Shirvan. Where thou goest, dark roses blossom forth upon the earth and the scent of them maketh warriors to be brave and noble.«

For a while the youth was silent, and his eyes filled with tears. Then he went on: »Beloved, the deep, black sea is here before us. Freedom sleepeth upon the bed of it. Let its dark waves cover us, and its depth join us forever.« Then the maiden replied: »Without thee, I shall not live. A shield of dark water is the best protection for us against evil men.« And they decided to leap into the water together. They arose, and by the light of the stars the young man sprang into the depths. From the watery surface came a groan, the groan of the sea as it greets its prey.

The girl also drew near to the precipice, but she only looked down into the depths with curiosity, and thought: »How fortunate that I am rid of him; now I can marry the rich prince without hindrance.« She dried her last tears and ran, singing for joy, down the narrow mountain path.

So the tears of the youth and the maiden were left alone in the rays of the moon upon the summit of the cliff. Then the Lord of the World created a pearl from the tears of the maid, but from the tears of the youth he created a diamond. Then spake the Lord of the World and said: »Thou, Pearl, art made of the deceitful tears of deceitful eyes; in truth thou hast deserved a curse.« And the pearl hid itself for very shame upon the bed of the dark ocean. But the Lord blessed the diamond and hid it in the depths of the mountains of granite that are warmed through and through by the light of the sun in summer. From that time forth, the pearl dwelt in cold and darkness, and grew pale and dim from the curse of the Lord; but the diamond which God blessed was warmed through in the depths of the granite mountains by the light of the sun and glowed like a piece that had been broken from the celestial rays. People say that clear pearls bring tears to the wearers of them, but that those that wear diamonds smile because they perceive in them the rays of eternal light which God had blessed.

Thus spake the Mahmud, the son of a slave, Sultan of Gasni, Master of the World. He took his crown and pointed to the tip of it. »In that I am King, I wear both, the pearl and the diamond, for I must know all things, the cold tears of darkness and the shining laughter of the sun.«

And the poet Firdusi bowed before his wisdom. But since he was a great master, he would not repeat the tale of another; and therefore this is not to be found in his Book of Kings. But the people of the Caucasus, the wandering poets and the travelling princes, are not so distinguished, and they tell the tale of the Sultan to anyone who will listen to it.

This story, and the cliffs in general, with the inscriptions on them, have a dangerous effect on the most sober temperaments. It caused a fat, drink-sodden Russian general, for example, to paint up the inscription: »Suicide is as offensive to religion as an illegitimate love affair. It is far better to give one's blood fighting for God, Tsar, and Country.« It took quite a long time to scratch the inscription out afterwards.

But even more trouble was taken in draining off the mountain stream where it flows past the »castle,« searching it thoroughly, and then turning it back again into its old course. The search was for nothing more nor less than the gold pen with which Goethe wrote the *West-Eastern Divan*.

The reason why the river at the Castle of Love and Betrayal was considered the right place to look for Goethe's pen needs explanation. It is said that Goethe sent his gold pen to the poet Pushkin, who was reputed to have travelled through the Caucasus with it. While he was there, he visited Kislovodsk; he was writing a poem on the top of the Castle when Goethe's pen slipped out of his hand and sank in the river so that he was not able to finish his poem.

Although literary historians had not in the least established for certain the question of whether Goethe had ever really sent his pen to Pushkin, a few romantic souls with plenty of time on their hands decided to search the riverbed. Unfortunately, nothing of importance was found except a few empty fruit tins, but the gold prospectors none the less considered themselves important research workers in the field of literary history.

When I visited Kislovodsk and the Castle of Love and Betrayal, a remarkable story was unfolding itself which has nothing to do with Love or Betrayal but which kept the summer population in a state of excitement for weeks on end. Between the Castle and the town there stands a pretty villa with white colonnades, a trim garden, and great shiny windows through which the luxurious appointments inside the villa may be glimpsed. In it dwelt a notorious Caucasian profiteer and stock speculator together with his family, servants, and other retainers. The profiteer was as rich as he was distrustful. But his distrust was not confined to private individuals; it extended to all the banks as well. He swore he would never trust them with one penny of his, his whole life long. The safest hiding-place for money in his opinion was one's own pocket.

His house was therefore an absolute treasure chamber. The safes were heavy with gold; the portfolios were stuffed with bills and bonds; and he himself never left his house without a gigantic bundle of banknotes, so that whatever happened—if, which God forbid, the house should burn down—there would always be something left to him. It will be seen that he was very careful and ready for anything. In addition he was a prince and possessed a few former subjects somewhere in Daghestan to whom he gave a few pence every now and again and who therefore owed him obedience. The old gentleman's distrust of banks was talked of all over the Caucasus and led directly enough to an event which, of course, everybody foresaw as perfectly natural except himself.

One day the house was visited by burglars. The safes offered due resistance, but one of them was nevertheless broken into, and it was quite enough to satisfy the thieves, since it contained valuables to the extent of a hundred thousand roubles. The old profiteer was thunderstruck. Not because the loss had ruined him—there was enough wealth hidden away in the other safes—but he simply could not grasp the fact that somebody had taken possession of his money. At first he raged, and then after a while he convoked his faithful subjects and bade them get his money back if they valued their lives. Otherwise, they would be punished, firstly, by his all-powerful damnation and, secondly, by the instant suspension of his miserly payments.

His subjects made objections and pointed out that they were after all not trained detectives, but they were particularly afraid of their master's whip, so they finally bowed low and promised that they would recover the stolen money. Two weeks passed, and then the servants came back, all radiant with joy, into the presence of their master and handed back the money which they had recovered. Overjoyed though he was, the old man had first to overcome one small disappointment, for his gold and his valuables had changed to bank-notes in the meantime. On the other hand, his hundred thousand roubles had grown into two hundred thousand. He had therefore received a bonus of one hundred per cent, which was certainly a sufficient remuneration for his vexation.

The old gentleman was now satisfied and gave every servant a silver coin, promised him God's blessing, and locked up the money. As he now became doubly cautious and neither left his house nor received anybody, he did not discover the excitement that had broken out at the spa in the meantime. After the theft had been perpetrated at his house, there began a series of daredevil incidents of the same nature, such as had never been known before in that brilliantly protected and distinguished resort. Various timid but financially powerful persons received threatening letters or unannounced visits from masked gentlemen. The result of the letters and the visits was always a certain reduction of the power of their capital. Reasonably enough, only such gentlemen were visited as were not likely to make an outcry except post-factum, thus enabling the visitors to get their winnings away into safety between times.

But the outcry was all the greater—post-factum. These distinguished Russian gentlemen, who were suddenly robbed in the fresh summertide, appealed to the Russian authorities, with bitter complaints about the impertinent Caucasian bandits who were not content to stop with their first impudent burglary at the house of the rich profiteer. The investigations of the police continued to be fruitless. The wrong-doers were sought among the banditry, among the notorious thieves in the gambling dens of Tiflis, and even among the criminals of St. Petersburg. Nobody, of course, thought of the humble servants of the arch-profiteer, not even their master himself. It was not until months after the thefts had ceased that it was learnt that the bereaved gentleman bore no further grudge against the thieves, that on the contrary he was rather grateful to them for returning the stolen property at a hundred-per-cent interest. But the sum involved— two hundred thousand—was precisely that which the various Russians were complaining that they had lost.

The profiteer never thought for an instant of returning the money; on the contrary, when they pressed him for it, he pushed off together with his servants.

The whole affair was hushed up, even when a few clever people stubbornly maintained that even the theft at the profiteer's house was just part of an imposture and that the idea of robbing his neighbours to cover a fictitious loss originated with the man himself. This sounds a little odd, but it is not entirely improbable. Anyway, the indignant gentlemen in Kislovodsk soon forgot their loss; no poor men were affected by it.

That summer in Kislovodsk was the last aristocratic season that the little nest of luxury saw. The next summer, instead of Grand Dukes and aristocrats, there were only intimidated people who had been driven out by the revolution, and who still used their old titles but had otherwise very little semblance of the old glory. But even here in this heavenly spot they found no peace.

The noblest health springs in the world—for that the springs of the Caucasus undoubtedly are—became the setting for many a bloody scene. Very soon, the twenty-five-year-old commander of the White Guard, General Shkuro, arrived, accompanied by his notorious »wolf pack,« as his soldiers were called. Shkuro happened to discover two Jews in Kislovodsk who had not been baptized. This discovery resulted not only in both of the Jews being hanged, but further resulted in every tenth inhabitant of the town being marked down as a Bolshevik and forced to mount the scaffold which stood in the centre of the park. Shkuro raged for several months and then went north to attack the Bolsheviks. Somewhere or other, he was defeated, and his opponents, the Communists, took possession of the feudal town. And now every fifth Cossack and every second visitor to the springs was promoted to the rank of monarchist and treated in the Cheka with the usual revolutionary punishments.

The spa became a morgue.

Later, the Kabardians or the Ingushes somehow turned up, gathered in hordes, fell upon the town, and plundered whatever there was left to plunder. Their hatred was chiefly directed against the Cossack villages, which were razed to the ground, and the ruins hacked into small pieces and burnt. The Caucasian peasant plough was then drawn across the Cossack village so that no one might find the place where it had once stood. One day was enough for the practised Kabardians to turn a Cossack settlement into a ploughed field. The Cossacks themselves were destroyed, though they defended themselves bravely. From every village some of the best soldiers were forcibly removed from the fray and sent to the interior as soon as the battle seemed quite hopeless, in order, as they said, that the Cossack stock might be continued.

Kislovodsk suffered cruel visitations from the Whites, the Reds, and the mountain banditry. The trees of the wonderful park were extensively cut down, the houses were burnt, and the priceless treasures of Narsan ran from broken conduits out upon the street. There was nothing in Kislovodsk to remind one of the old times when the Grand Dukes and the vassals of the Tsar bathed in the blood of the giant Elbruz and strolled importantly in the park in the full consciousness of their rank.

Today Kislovodsk is half-way to being restored in a primitive manner. But the old brilliance is gone. There is no Tsar, there are no proud aristocrats. Communists come to the town to pass their fourteen days of leave and scratch their names in awkward writing on the bark of the remaining trees with the sign of the hammer and sickle below. Then they go back and tell colourful stories at home about the strange town that used to belong to the princes of an empire that has passed away.

23.

THE ART OF HEALING
IN THE MOUNTAINS

HUNDREDS OF EUROPEAN DOCTORS waited upon distinguished clients in the watering-places of the Caucasus. Sanatoria were splendidly equipped, and tired visitors could have their inherited or specially acquired illnesses treated according to the latest dictates of European medicine. What medicine was unable to accomplish was accomplished by the health springs, of which there were thirty others besides Narsan in the region of Kislovodsk alone— a profusion that is scarcely met with anywhere in the world.

But beyond the Cossack villages which protected the springs, beyond the villas and the luxurious hotels, the realm of western science came to an end. In the citadels, the auls, the snow-capped mountains, amid the clans that inhabit these mountains, the healers of the unbelievers were accorded very little faith. At the outside, a degenerate prince or a half-Europeanized merchant would call in the assistance of the doctor. The others, warriors, women, children, and old men, avoided all intercourse with the Hakim. They were afraid of the unbeliever and hid themselves when he travelled through the hills; they were silent when he asked after their diseases. It was firmly fixed in the mind of the hill dweller that the medicaments of the West were all prepared with pig's fat, and such forbidden poison as that might only be taken when certain death was imminent. But the sick Caucasian did not immediately think that death was at hand. Why should he? He had his own doctors, who performed wonders as great as those of Kislovodsk, and were not only pious Mohammedans but powerful exorcists as well, masters of the realms of darkness, of the demons and djinns which possess the sick.

For in spite of all the assurances which my eunuch made to the contrary, there are still djinns in the Caucasus. It is true that they do not sit upon the mountain tops, but they lurk in the valleys and the gorges, in the steaming jungles and by the marshy river banks, whence they attack the passer-by. They leap into his inward parts through the mouth, causing nauseous fevers, malaria, smallpox, bellyache, and the red spots of scarlet fever. They irk the women in childbirth and torment and destroy people, if the wise-man does not intervene in time to drive away the evil one and cure the sick person. The art of these wise-men the Caucasian trusts unreservedly; no failure, not even the death of the patient, can rob him of his faith in them.

A few kilometres from Kislovodsk, or Tiflis, where there are doctors and modern hospitals, the magician of antiquity still holds sway, practising his traditional craft according to its primitive rules, and loftily contemptuous of anyone who dares to doubt the power of his remedies.

In one respect the magicians really do deserve unqualified admiration: there are scarcely any better healers of wounds in the world. A man may be covered with dozens of wounds, shot through, stabbed and hacked about by the weapons of the enemy, but the mountain magician never gives him up; he smears him with ointment of his own making, bandages him up in masterly fashion, and regularly, in nine out of ten cases, he restores the seemingly dead to life. The fact that he murmurs exhortations to the spirits while he is at it and spreads out his hands mysteriously above the patient need not upset one. Even the European doctor has traditions from which he will not depart. But it remains a fact that more than one Russian general and dozens of Russian officers who were wounded in battle and despaired of by their own doctors were saved by native magicians to whom they were taken. And when a great man, a prince, an Abrek, or a fighter in the cause of liberty, returned from the field of honour all covered with blood, the mountain magicians used to carry him up to a lonely peak by means of an excellent stretcher and there they cured him, all diagnoses of European doctors to the contrary.

But the Caucasian is only an expert as a wound doctor, though, of course, wounds are far more common in the mountains than anything else. You must take care not to trust the Caucasian upon any matter of internal ailments. The medicine which he gives his patient is often quite peculiar, and its nature is determined by the fortune of the client. Hill medicine is often terribly expensive. The patient is expected to swallow down real little diamonds, or diamond dust, for example, as a cure for diseases of the brain. Powdered turquoises are administered in large quantities for severe pains at childbirth, and pearls in vinegar are supposed to be of assistance in all cases of heart trouble.

Gems in general play a considerable part in mountain, medicine. Moonstones, alexandrite, sapphires, emeralds, as well as brilliants are among the steady stock-in-trade of hill doctors. There are two kinds of gems, the male and the female. For the cure of one illness, male opals must be used, and for another female ones. Only a specialist can establish the sex of stones. A complicated science sets forth in innumerable theses the relationships of stones to one another, including their efficacy, and above all their origin, all of which is addressed to the reader in serious, unadorned phrases. According to them gems are living beings who inhabit deep gorges and are inaccessible to man; they multiply in a natural way just like all the rest of Allah's creatures. The hereditary enemies of the stones are the eagles. Soaring above the clouds, they look down into the depths of the gorges to search for the stones which live there and, when they find them, they pounce on them, grip them in their talons, and disappear into the sky. With the gem in their claws, they fly over the mountains, delighting in its flashing colours; they torment it till it dies and then they throw it to the ground where poor humans greedily gather the remains of the eagle's plaything. At least, so the story goes in the treatises of the mountain people which are written in Arabic and are current all through the Orient.

It is not to every patient that diamonds can be administered. But the Caucasian doctor is also a mullah and, as a priest, he has remedies at his disposal which are easily as good as the best diamonds of the male sex. For instance, the smoke of a Koran burnt at the bedside of the patient is a wonderful cure for all illnesses that are caused by evil spirits, and it is of especial value if the Koran be written by an expert hand in beautiful writing with no errors. A Koran of this kind is expensive, but less expensive than a gem.

The Caucasian, however, like everyone else, knows that the chief task of the doctor is prophylaxis, the prevention of disease. For that there is a simple and effective expedient. A strip of parchment is scribbled over with prayers and magic formulas and worn tied over the heart with a string. This parchment must be, when it is unrolled, precisely the length of its owner's foot to within a millimetre. If the wearer of the parchment does fall ill in spite of it, then it is merely because it was not made exactly the same length as his foot. But when the illness is already present, and the evil spirits have effected an entry to the body of the patient, and the correct gems are not to be found, then the old simple medicine and magic of the Caucasus is brought to bear with its specifics which have remained unaltered for centuries.

Every age and each sex has its own peculiar remedies. The knowledge which a Caucasian doctor must possess in these matters is wide enough in itself to earn him the respect and honour due to a real wiseman. I will give some instances of Caucasian remedies which have been of assistance to the people since olden times.

First of all, croup, which occurs frequently among women and children. The cure for this is simple. Two threads are drawn across the bed of the sick person and burnt; the ashes are thrown into water with which the soles of the patient's feet are then painted. At the same time, a cup of boiling water must be stood at the head of the invalid and red-hot iron thrown into it three times in succession. Then the patient is cured.

Diseases of the mind are more difficult to deal with. If water with prayers dipped in it has no effect, musicians must be hired to play Caucasian dances for a whole week without stopping, and to these the patient must dance. If that is no use, the illness is incurable.

Diseases of the eyes are more complicated still. To cure them, the doctor must have seven irreproachable virgins. The latter form a circle in the midst of which the invalid sits. In front of him is placed a basin of water, into which the virgins dip their fingers and moisten their own eyes while they sing under the doctor's leadership: »Heaven is clear, why should the eyes not be clear.«

Against heart- and lung-trouble, milk and honey are administered mixed with salt, and, in cases of high fever, the doctor prescribes a bath in sour milk. These are all prescriptions for adults.

Children's cures are many, but there is one initial remedy which is always used:

A cow is slaughtered; the belly cut open and the entrails removed; and then the child is stuffed in in place of them. If the child gets red after it has spent a few hours inside the cow, then its recovery is assured. It also helps to change the name of a very sick child, because the evil spirits are confused by the pseudonym and leave his body. It is essential, of course, to know whether the disease emanates from evil spirits or from God. In the second case, human assistance is vain, and there is nothing for it but prayer and waiting upon God's aid. It is only when the case is particularly serious that universal exorcism is resorted to, but it is very dangerous and is recited at one's own risk.

The exorcism runs, in the Georgian language, as follows : »Anisani Banisani, Mamaverli–Kaniani ... Sachletiha, Khvthisitha, Mammisatha da zisatha da Culisa Tzmindisa. Amin.« The exorcism must be pronounced three, five, or eight times, a series of figures, oddly enough, which are the components of the Golden Section, of which assuredly none of the exorcists can possibly have heard.

As for the far more important prophylaxis, its principles are common knowledge like those of the laws of the fathers and the code of knighthood. If, for example, a child dies before it has been given a name, it has boiling water poured over it and is beheaded, in case it should come to life again, because that would be a sure sign that all its relatives, beginning with the mother, would die within a very short time.

The umbilical cord plays a considerable part in the prevention of disease; it must on no account be merely thrown away. The place in which the umbilical cord is deposited determines the child's future. It is best to retain it until the child is grown up. Then he may wear it, sewn up in a cloth, on a string round his neck. This is a powerful protection against all evil. The umbilical cord is always in great demand anyway, especially among women. By wearing it under their clothes next the stomach, they are protected against pregnancy. And on the other hand, a woman upon whose body an umbilical cord has been severed becomes pregnant. Small wonder, therefore, that at a childbirth, the next room is full of women waiting for the umbilical cord so as to have it cut on their bodies, or on the other hand to wear it afterwards beneath their underclothes.

Lastly, in the case of an epidemic, it is a good preventative to strew one's bed with flowers before going to sleep and to divert the disease by placing sweets and toys in every corner of the room. And the sex of the disease must be considered as one does so, because there is a male and a female sex amongst illnesses just as there is amongst jewels. Measles, for example, is a female disease and requires sweets. Smallpox, however, is a male disease and can be turned aside with a jug of wine. During an epidemic, the parents of a sick child must avoid sexual intercourse, because this might have the effect of offending the disease. It is very effective in the case of scarlet fever to dye a cock and let it run about in the sick person's room.

But in the cause of truth, it must be stated that medicine in the hills does not consist exclusively of such peculiar remedies as these. There are, for instance, excellent native remedies against fever and equally efficacious ones against diseases of the stomach, and, in establishing important legal decisions, the doctors often have interesting information to offer.

I once witnessed the following gem of legal medicine in Daghestan.

Before the Kadi of the village in which I was staying, there appeared an inhabitant who accused his next-door neighbour of assault. Some years previously, his neighbour had apparently hit him on the head, and as a result of the blow headaches had latterly developed. »My skull is cracked,« said the plaintiff, »and I demand three cows and eight sheep as damages.« The accused repeatedly denied his guilt, so that the judge, who explained later that such cases occurred every day, was obliged to appeal to medical knowledge. The doctor was called in, and the expert evidence began. First of all, the plaintiff's head was shaved smooth, and then the doctor took out his dagger (even doctors always carry weapons) and cautiously removed some skin from his skull so that a broad piece of skull bone was exposed. The doctor touched it with his fingers; then he drew the skin together, took needle, thread, and scissors from his pocket, and sewed the wound up again. During the whole of the evidence, the patient sat on the ground and quietly smoked his pipe. »Yes,« said the doctor finally, »it is quite true; the skull is cracked; it could only have happened as the result of a blow.« At that the accused was at once sentenced to pay the damages.

Similar examinations are daily events in the hills, and there are persons so litigious that they will permit such investigations to be performed frequently on themselves without apparently being any the worse for it.

The Caucasian on an average attains the age of eighty to ninety years. Centenarians and even older persons are by no means uncommon. Of course, this high average is not decisive proof of the benefits of the Caucasian craft of healing, but in view of such longevity no very serious reproaches can be made against it.

The fact that this craft flourishes in the near vicinity of civilized towns like Tiflis and Kislovodsk is not especially surprising. It is only one of the many contradictions in Caucasian life and is on a par with the Socialists who are horse-thieves and the princes who play at being Socialists.

Europe has left a few grains of its culture in the Caucasus, seeds which form little European islands impotent against the ocean of Asia. European towns live unnoticed and without influence among the hills, sufficient unto themselves with their civilized or half-civilized populations. The Caucasian does not recognize their inhabitants as of equal rank with himself; rather he looks down on them as degenerates who can never comprehend the mountains or their traditions, and are therefore themselves not worth understanding.

Stories, even of very recent years, about the hill dweller are always filled with a dark romanticism, with a remarkable monkish, piratical point of view which no neighbouring culture can supplant or destroy. They illustrate the conscious culture and poise of the mountaineer. If they strike one as excessively coloured and even perhaps as a little gaudy, then let us say that it is the fault of the hills, that is, if the reader should happen to be—as the Caucasians have it—a degenerate city dweller incapable of comprehending mountain life.

24.

TRUE STORIES FROM DAGHESTAN

MOUNTAINS, DEEP RAVINES surrounded by snowy peaks, and in the midst of these, upon the edge of the void, like buds upon the cliffs, the castles and the auls! One on top of the other the houses stand, linked to each other by narrow trails, each house a fortress poised upon the precipice. When the foe draws near, every home has to be separately stormed, and not the men alone, but the women and the children too, defend them. They hurl down heavy stones and furniture and leap after them, attacking the enemy even with their teeth. When the house has been won, the fighters fly to the next and carry on the battle from there. It is not until the enemy has penetrated to the last house that the defenders withdraw to its small balcony, fire off their last cartridges, and leap, with their wives and children, into the gorge. There are no braver warriors in the world than the men of Daghestan, and it is not for nothing that the Persian proverb says: »When the Shah is mad, he attacks Daghestan.«

The Persians know what they are talking about. Their Nadir-Shah conquered the whole of India and a hundred kingdoms and then marched upon Daghestan, where he was defeated, not by men, but by women who opposed him alone. The men did not consider the Persians of sufficient rank to give battle, so Persia's bravest warriors had to flee from the womenfolk, even the very Shah himself, the subduer of India.

Since then, no Shah has dared to go to Daghestan. High up in this land, impregnable and girt about with steep mountains, lies the aul of Dargo, the chief town of the Darghi, the centre of the endless war which Imam Shamil, the Master of Daghestan, carried on against the Russians. At seventy-five years of age, Imam Shamil stood at the height of his power. The whole of Daghestan, the lands of the Chechens, the Kabardians, and many others obeyed this one man and became one state under him. No king in the Orient could compare with him. He was surrounded by hundreds of courtiers. The Sultan and the Shah sent him worshipful letters, and the Tsar himself treated with him as an equal. In every mosque his name was held in respect, and every man who entered his palace had to kiss humbly the hem of his garment.

The Chechen people were hard pressed by the Russians. Their land is some distance from Dargo, the seat of the Imam, and, when they asked him for assistance, he was at that time unable to afford it to them. »Defend yourselves and die in the battle,« he wrote, and so the Chechens defended themselves. At last, however, they grew weary, for the battle was hopeless and never-ending. The Tsar was for ever sending new bodies of soldiers into the hills. But an awful oath bound them to Shamil, and they were forced to fight on. Terrible was the vengeance visited by the Imam upon every traitor. At last, the Chechens decided in their extremity that they would send a delegation to Dargo which would tell the Imam of the people's need and beg for a remission of the oath so that they might conclude a peace with the Russians. Later on they would fight for the Imam again when times were better. For the moment, provided his permission were forthcoming, they believed that peace was an urgent necessity. The Imam gave the delegation a friendly reception in Dargo; he issued instructions to them and spoke of the holy war and the duties of a Moslem, with the result that the Chechens dared not place the request of their people before him. The envoys sought out the most powerful courtiers and dignitaries of the Imam and offered treasures of gold and silver in abundance to whoso would dare to present their request to the Imam. But there was none found among the courtiers who would do it. Every one of them feared the wrath of the Imam.

At last the Chechens decided to visit the Khanum, the mother of the Imam, the only person before whom he bowed the head. He always fulfilled her every wish, always lent an ear to her requests, even when she pled for enemies and criminals. Shamil was a good son, a model for all the mountain country. It was with him that the proverb originated : »Accursed be he that maketh his mother to grieve, for surely Hell awaiteth him.«

The Khanum had a merciful heart. »My son rules over many peoples,« thought she to herself. »What are the Chechens to him? Let him release them from their bond.« So she promised the envoys to put in a good word for the Chechens.

When the mother of the Imam told him the request of the Chechens, his face darkened. He stroked his beard, meditated for a while, and said: »The Koran forbids that treachery be allowed; it also forbids that a man contradict his mother. My wisdom is insufficient for this case. I will pray and fast that Allah may look with favour upon me, and throw light upon my thoughts.«

For three days and three nights the Imam remained shut up in the mosque. The courtiers and generals, the populace, and the delegation of the Chechens stood in front of the mosque and waited day and night. At last the door opened, and the Imam appeared. Allah had manifested his thoughts to him. The face of the ruler was pale; his lips were tight, and his expression was taciturn. Again he stroked his beard, stretched forth his hand, and said: »This I proclaim to be the command of Allah: the first person who speaks with the Imam of this treachery shall be condemned to one hundred strokes of the rod.« He fell silent again and stroked his beard—and then continued: »The first person who spoke to me of this treachery was the Khanum, my mother. I condemn her to one hundred strokes.«

He signed to his faithful followers, and presently the mother of the ruler appeared in the courtyard of the mosque. The veil was torn from her face; she was thrown to the ground; and two warriors approached her with rods. But they only administered one blow to the Khanum. Horror-stricken, the Imam fell at her feet and wept bitterly. Then, when he had prayed, he said: »The laws of the Almighty are of iron, and none may gainsay them, not even I. But the Koran permits one thing: the children may take the punishment upon themselves, therefore I will take the remaining ninety-nine strokes upon myself.« The Imam of all Daghestan, the Lord of the Chechens and the Kabardians, the Master of the Faithful, bared himself in sight of the people, laid himself upon the steps of the mosque, and bade the soldiers: »Beat me. As true as it is that I am the Imam, so will I behead you if I perceive that the strokes are not laid on with all your strength.«

So Shamil received the ninety-nine strokes. A hundred strokes is the highest number that the Koran permits. Covered with blood, he lay upon the steps of the mosque; his skin was torn in strips but no sound rose from his lips. Horror-stricken, the crowd looked on: the generals, the warriors, and the populace. The faces of the Chechens became ashen. They turned back to their homes, and there was none that dared to betray the Imam again.

Thus were the mountains governed, and only thus could they be governed. Sixty years have passed since that time, and to this very day the visitor to Dargo is shown the steps of the mosque and told of how the Imam of Daghestan, the first man in the East, condemned himself in front of everybody to be beaten with a hundred strokes, and reddened the steps with his own blood.

This true story of filial love and duty, which might be a Roman legend, will never be forgotten in the hills, nor will its opposite, the story of the mighty prince of the aul of Andalal, a tale of betrayal and destruction. It is known to every mountain man, and always repeated whenever the talk turns to fathers and children, or to patriotism and war.

This prince was reputed to be a good man. He helped the poor, protected the weak, and sought to dispense peace and order everywhere. He was loved by his people and taught them many arts, opened schools, and spread prosperity. But the people set no especial store by this. The populace of Andalal was proud and self-satisfied, desired no instruction, and was vexed at having such a clever and outstanding man in its midst. For this reason, the elders came one day to the prince and declared: »Thou art a good man and a clever man, but we are grown weary of thee. The people will have none of thee. Leave us therefore immediately. If in three days thou hast not obeyed, the people will stone thee. But thy sons are good brave warriors, useful to the people. They shall stay.«

The prince was obliged to comply. He mounted his horse and rode through the aul, took his leave of everybody, sons included, and departed from his home followed by unfriendly glances. But hatred for his people was born in his heart. He was received with honour at the court of the Shah, whom he accompanied on his campaigns into Turkey, India, and Turkestan. He won fame for himself and earned the friendship of the sovereign. »In the valleys of Andalal,« he counselled him one day, »there are gems and gold in great quantities. The people of Andalal is small and weak. Let us conquer the land.«

The Shah agreed. An enormous army set out for Dagh-estan, warriors from Khorosan, from Shirvan, from Mesendaran and Azerbaijan. The best soldiers of Iran were gathered together. At the head of them rode the Shah himself and next to him the prince, the traitor and avenger. They reached the mountains, penetrated the land, and began the fight. The traitor was the leader. Every road in the land was familiar to him, every cliff was known to him, and yet the Persians were unable to carry off the victory. The men, women, and children of Andalal joined in the struggle. Every cliff became a fortress. The people defended themselves with heroic spirit, and in the midst of them the sons of the traitor, the exiled wise-man, fought for their home. The Persians were defeated. The warriors of Khorosan, Mesendaran, Shirvan, and Azerbaijan fled before the people of Andalal. First amongst them was the Shah, and last the princely traitor. The women and children pursued the fleeing army, and it was from women that the traitor carried away the wounds upon his body. The land of Andalal was laid waste; its fields were destroyed, its houses burnt, and a tremendous hatred blazed up against the man whom it had once driven out.

Ten years passed. The friend of the Shah grew old; he became homesick and wished to see once more his country and the people that hated him. So he left his palace at Teheran, drew on his old armour, and rode into his own land. Slowly he approached the aul and slowly he moved through the streets of his native town. When the inhabitants saw him and recognized him, they spat and shut their doors in his face. He rode all day through the aul and found no friend. Even his sons avoided him. Finally he dismounted from his horse and went to the Kadi, but the Kadi also would not greet him. Then said the traitor: »I have come home that I might make atonement for my guilt. Deal with me as the laws command.« The Kadi stretched forth his hand. »Bind the traitor,« he said.

On the next day the whole populace gathered and demanded judgment. The Kadi appeared, had the prisoner brought in, and proclaimed: »According to the law of the fathers, the man must be buried alive.« And the people said: »Let it be so.«

The Kadi was just. »What canst thou say in thy defence?« he asked the prisoner, and the latter answered: »Nothing, I am guilty. I have led the enemy into the land and I will make atonement for my sin. It is good that the people revere the laws of the fathers and deal out justice to me. But I ask that still more justice be done. The laws of the fathers say: 'He that fighteth against his father shall be killed.' My sons remained here and fought against me, yet they enjoyed the esteem of the people. I demand my right. Let my sons be beheaded over my grave, otherwise the people of Andalal are unworthy of their fathers.«

The sons of the betrayer were very much respected in the country. They had defended their home courageously, and were deemed the best warriors in the land. But the Kadi and the people took counsel and said: »So be it!« And so it was. The traitor's living body was buried, and his sons, the best warriors in the land, were beheaded over his grave.

The people in Andalal are proud of the decision to this day. Above all virtue, even above the virtues of courage and love of home, ranks (in the eyes of the Caucasian) the duty of the son to follow his father even in crime and treachery. All the children of Daghestan are told this story as an example so that they may know how to conduct their lives.

Such stories, and thousands like them, form the character of the mountaineer and make him brave and dutiful, revengeful and piratical. A successful robbery invests the hill dweller with great honour, and, when as a child his father gives him his first weapon, he hears the traditional phrase: »Let thy weapon help thee by day and by night,« that is to say, in legal and illegal ways. He has no greater joy than to raid and plunder the villages of his neighbours. The only pleasure greater than theft is that of vengeance successfully carried out, as the account of the robber-poet Kholchvar will show.

The robber Kholchvar was lured into a trap by the Khan of the Avars. He was overcome and exhibited in bonds on the great square of the Khan's capital of Khunsakh. The Avars stood all round him, mocking the robber, and then determined to burn him at the stake. While the pyre was being made ready, he was to sing a song for the amusement of the people. Kholchvar promised to sing and requested only that his bonds be loosened so that he might play his instrument. The famous song in which the sinister mountain knight expressed his soul ran as follows: »I, the robber Kholchvar, sing as I am about to die. Hear my song, ye people of the Avars, ye princes of the people, thou Khan of the land! Many people stand around me here; I see among them many women. These women are widows, for I have killed their husbands. Many children stand all around me and all of them are fatherless, for I have killed their fathers. In Khunsakh there are many virgins. They look at me through the lattices of their windows. I have kissed the breasts of each of these virgins, each of them I have dishonoured, I, the robber Kholchvar. And even have I stolen the trousers of the wife of the Khan. And now I stand before the pyre, and now hear the last stanza of my song. Sweet is my voice. It lureth away children thus—!« At that, the robber bent down and seized with both hands the two sons of the Khan who were listening to the song and jumped with them into the flaming pyre. The last stanza resounded from the flames: »Be silent, ye children of a whore, I, too, am burning with you. Hearken, ye Avars, thou Khan, hearken! Go tell it to my mother, how I died and how in death I took revenge, I, the robber Kholchvar.«

This man who was able to take his revenge even at the stake has become the ideal of every man of Daghestan who believes that revenge, robbery, and filial love are the greatest human virtues. Similar stories exist by the hundred, but these three may suffice to make the reader understand somewhat these mountain people who have been ringed round by Arabian, Georgian, Persian, and European culture for thousands of years.

To be sure, it is only in Daghestan and among the Chechens and the Kabardians, and one or two Georgian clans, that the old knighthood and romance persists today. In other parts of the Caucasus other conditions exist, and there are many tracts of country so completely Europeanized that they are beginning to cultivate the romance of the hills artificially. But very near by, spirits are still being conjured with sacred seriousness; enemies are being laid low, and girls abducted, with the calm matter-of-factness of a Caucasian doing his duty according to the laws of his fathers.

25.

PLEASE COME AND VISIT ME

WHEN THE GRÆCO-ROMAN TOWNS and colonies still flourished on the shore of the Black Sea, the Roman governors used to maintain a hundred and thirty interpreters permanently in order to keep up some sort of understanding with the population. But often these hundred and thirty did not suffice, and then two or three times as many interpreters had to be got in. One would translate to the second, and the second to the third, who would finally retail it to the Governor. It is not for nothing that the Caucasus was called by old geographers, not merely the »Land of Mountains,« but also the »Land of Tongues.«

It really is impossible to know which language to learn first in order to be understood in the Caucasus. In Daghestan, Azerbaijani is enough, but the western ranges of the Caucasus have no international language, and whoever travels there must, if he has not sufficient interpreters, depend entirely upon the expressive possibilities of his own hands and face.

Svanetian, for example, is undoubtedly a beautiful language, but I am not at all convinced that the mastery of it even in the Caucasus necessarily forms a part of a liberal education. The fact that I did not know the language did once cause me an unpleasantness, which was shared by a crowd of friends who went with me from Kislovodsk on a trip of some weeks' duration in the southwest territory, that is to say, to Svanetia, Imeretia, and Mingrelia.

We were riding on horseback over luxuriant meadow land, shut in on the left and right by mountains, which was to lead us into the valleys of the Rion. The friends with whom I was travelling were in the country for the first time, and even my constant companion, the eunuch, did not know his way about here. Our guide, an old Karachai knew the way all right, but not the conditions. The only ethnographical information he could give us was that the Svanetians were a savage race and that two weeks before they had plundered some Russian tourists who were travelling here like ourselves. But he also admitted that the Svanetians were the arch-enemies of the Karachais and that for this reason alone he could have nothing good to say of them.

We were contented with his arrangements and travelled on peacefully through Svanetia. But suddenly a tall man appeared from behind a hill and approached us with gigantic strides, and behind him at a seemly distance strode about a dozen other equally lanky figures. The man drew closer to us, and we got really frightened. He looked like the Devil himself, enormously big, with a pockmarked face and swollen lips, long teeth, and small watery eyes; in addition, he was fantastically ragged. His naked body peered through the rents of his fur coat. The whole impression was that of a ghost in a dream rather than of a man. This dreadful person took hold of one of our horses by the bridle and began to yell something in a threatening tone of voice, which was quite incomprehensible but seemed to be hardly pleasant. His followers came behind him, surrounded us, and nodded their heads at each of their leader's phrases, which became more and more insistent. We couldn't understand a word, and our guide understood nothing either, and observed in a melancholy way that the people certainly wanted to rob and kill us. This sounded credible enough, but was far from explaining what all the outpouring was about. In the end, we tried to interrupt the wild man's talk with a few words of our own. But neither did he understand us, and he simply got more and more excited and pointed to the meadow and to the mountains, beat his breast, and yelled all the louder. At the same time, his men seized hold of our horses and became more threatening every minute. In spite of all our efforts, we could not understand a word of the Svanetian's lengthy speech. But at last our Karachai guide had an idea, which was probably a rare occurrence with him. Even if he could speak no Svanetian, and the Svanetians knew no Karachai, it was still possible perhaps that they might be able to understand each other in a third language. He tried the Ossete language first, but without success, then the Adijheh tongue, upon which the gulf between us and the wild men was suddenly bridged, for they understood Adijheh. But nothing whatever was gained for us personally. The conversation had merely altered from a monologue on the part of the Svanetian to a dialogue between him and our guide. We still understood nothing. The two of them talked, gesticulating violently, bawled at each other continuously, pointed at us with their fingers, and got more and more agitated. We expected glittering daggers to be drawn from their sheaths at any moment, and blood feuds with all their consequences to break out on all sides of us. But just then one of our number seized our guide's hand, held him fast, and urged him not to speak further with the Svanetians until he had translated to us what had already been said. »Wait a while, master,« said the guide. »I want to say something more——« and the dispute started all over again. It was not until we had made repeated interventions, politely at first, and then rudely, that we managed to persuade the guide to translate his conversation. To our amazement, the words of the wild man were as follows: »I am a Svanetian aristocrat. Anyone here will bear me out. All the land you see belongs to me. I am very wealthy and a nobleman, and I beg you to honour me with a visit. Nobody has ever journeyed through this country without visiting me, and I swear that you will be well looked after at my house.«

So the sinister brigand turned out finally to be a hospitably inclined gentleman who wanted to take us back home with him in accordance with the customs of the land. »I can see that you are respectable people,« he added. »I am a respectable person myself, so come to my house. Nobody in the land will receive you better. These are not rags but my working clothes.«

And then, apparently, to make his meaning more clear, he continued: »I stand here almost all the time and wait for travellers, whom I then invite, but very few people pass this way, although anybody who does come always visits me.«

There was, therefore, nothing for it but to accept the invitation of the Svanetian aristocrat and to betake ourselves to his house under his guidance. We remained on our horses and the Svanetians showed us the way. They went on foot, but with such huge strides that they kept up with the horses without any difficulty. This swift pace is a racial characteristic of the Svanetians; they are the best runners in the world and, if they only wanted to, they could make their land famous on the international sports fields of the world. But on our way to the nobleman's house we did meet one horseman—an unusual sight among the Svanetians—the eight-year-old son of our host, who rode out to meet us just before we arrived at the village. He was a sturdy boy, armed to the teeth and a perfect rider for his eight years. But that is nothing astounding. I have seen five- and even four-year-old boys in the Caucasus who could use horses and weapons with complete mastery. At seven years, the children are usually taken into battle or on plundering raids. Our Svanetian's son did not look especially peaceful even when he greeted us according to all the regular rules of Svanetian courtesy.

After a short ride, we came to the Svanetian aristocrat's aerie. It was a fairly well cared-for stronghold, rising up from the top of a hill and surrounded, as is customary, with one or two mud huts. The castle was certainly not out of date yet, and served the same purpose for its owner as the strongholds of European princes in the Middle Ages. Once inside, we were obliged to convince ourselves of our host's wealth and high quality. From the top of the citadel he showed us his herds of sheep, his lands, and finally some stone on which his grandfather fell in battle with the Dadashkelians, the princes of Svanetia. His grandfather was apparently a rebel, as most of the Svanetians were. After we had done sufficient honour to our host's wealth and nobility by nodding of heads and clasping of hands, he took us into the reception-room of the castle, a large chamber whose walls were hung with the horns of wild animals. »I have killed many other animals,« the Svanetian observed, »but I sacrificed the best heads to God.«

Whom he meant by God remained obscure. The Svanetians are officially Christians, but customarily they sacrifice the horns of all the animals they shoot to the hunting god, whose temple is somewhere in the mountains. But the Christian church is not neglected for all that. On every hill, and at every crossroads, stand the strange Svanetian crucifixes. The vertical stem forms the head and body of the crucified figure, and the hands wave about in the air. The face has an expression of gruesome hatred and is painted in glaring colours. The crucifix is not, properly speaking, a crucifix at all, for it has no cross. It is more the statue of a person with outspread hands who looks at the passer-by with eyes which would cause the most courageous to shudder. The Svanetians, however, love these crucifixes and value them more highly than the holiest relics of the Georgian church. Our host himself was a pious Christian, and made the sign of the cross solemnly as he invited us to partake of some treasures of Svanetian cookery. We did so the more readily that Svanetian meals in no way accord with the wildness of the land, but could even grace a European table with honour. But it was not without effort that we were able to overlook the table manners of our host. The Svanetians are horrible eaters.

The thing which tastes best of all is the Svanetian hunting cheese which can be recommended for imitation in Europe. It is prepared in the following way: An ordinary Caucasian cheese is stirred to a doughy consistency in a pot with simmering butter. After this a little flour is poured in and the whole stirred up well with a stick until the thick tough mass is done. It is then twisted on to a piece of string in the form of a ring, and the string is in its turn wound round a stick which has been dipped in water; it is then put to cool. When the cheese string has set, it is taken off the stick and carried over the shoulder as nourishment on a hunting-trip. The cheese is elastic, never gets old, and tastes excellent. It is a perfect substitute for the European bread-and-butter, containing as it does both butter and flour.

We allowed ourselves to be served by our Svanetian host for several hours, and the other Svanetians also took part in our meal with the exception of the eight-year-old warrior, who had suddenly disappeared. We thought that he had ridden back into the fields, or that he was going to eat later on, but we were mistaken. As we were leaving the castle, after this handsome feast, we saw a remarkable picture on the threshold. The eight-year-old urchin had laid aside his weapons and was sitting on the ground, sucking the breast of a nurse who sat respectfully by him. The warrior and horseman was still an infant at the breast. The affectionate father watched the nourishment of his offspring happily and then said in a somewhat melancholy manner: »Unfortunately, we must soon wean him of the breast.«

We were polite enough to conceal our astonishment and learnt later that it is the universal custom among aristocratic Svanetians to nourish their children with woman's milk for as long as possible, as the latter is supposed to be especially strengthening. The nurses have to be changed constantly, at least once every six months. In addition to which the milk of one nurse is not sufficient for a well-developed suckling. After the third year, two and, later still, three nurses at a time are required to satisfy the appetite of the giant baby. The milk diet appears however to suit the Svanetians admirably. They flourish extraordinarily and grow up to be huge fellows of terrific muscular strength and longevity. It is a custom all over the Orient to nourish children with mother's milk for a fairly long time, but, as far as I know, it is not usual elsewhere to prolong it to such an extent as do the Svanetians.

We stayed three days in the house of the Svanetian nobleman, and then we bade him farewell, after he accompanied us to the frontier of his land. We travelled on through Svanetia as far as the valleys of Mingrelia.

The Svanetians, for my first knowledge of whom I have to thank this nobleman, are undoubtedly a curious people, but in no way mysterious as many Caucasian travellers maintain. They are simply a branch of the Georgians who have run wild. Driven back into the mountains, they have become split up and have completely lost their former significance. They are now nothing but a rich storehouse of conclusive information for the future investigations of old Georgia. Until recently, the Svanetians were divided into three parts, the Dadianic Svanetians, the princely Svanetians, and the famous free Svanetians. The Dadianic people were subject to Dadian, the King of Mingrelia. The princely Svanetians formed the principality of Svanetia proper, which was ruled by the family of Dadashkeliani until the second half of the preceding century. Lastly, the free Svanetians are those who live in inaccessible wild gorges, have no conception of government, are indescribably primitive, and occupy themselves chiefly with plundering their neighbours. They have never known any other profession but that of robber, and they justify this by the fact that they, the free Svanetians, are very poor, while their neighbours are rolling in wealth and can easily spare them something. The manner in which the free Svanetians became Russian citizens is worth telling here.

One day it was announced in Tiflis, the Viceroy's capital, that an unknown people–the free Svanetians–wished to send a delegation to the Viceroy to request him to recognize them as subjects of the great Tsar. The news was received in a very friendly manner. His Serene Highness the Viceroy condescended to smile pleasantly and wrote personally to the Tsar saying that »the Russian influence in the mountains was increasing every day.« It was true that nothing very precise was known about the free Svanetians, and even the ruling prince of Svanetia, who was at that moment staying at the court of the Viceroy, knew nothing very definite about them. This, however, did inot prevent the official newspapers from writing that »a people who have hitherto never recognized any ruler, whom Caesar, Mithridates, and Alexander failed to subdue, has now voluntarily laid its freedom at the feet of the white Tsar.«

These articles pleased the Viceroy very much, and the good humour of the court increased noticeably. Finally, the delegation itself appeared. When the Viceroy received the delegates, and looked upon the rough, unconquered mountain people, who were moreover Christians, and when they fell at his feet and swore that they would be true to the Tsar, the animated humour of the court increased to exultation.

The delegates were richly rewarded and even decorated with orders and finally sent back to their country with all good wishes. Behind them travelled Prince Eristov, the newly appointed Governor of the free Svanetians. The experiences of the Governor in free Svanetia, depicted by him in his rather dry report to the Viceroy, include certain interesting details.

The new subjects of the Tsar received the Governor as respectfully as they knew how. They knelt down before him, bowed, and asked him timidly but pointedly whether he had brought any vodka with him. The Governor was a little taken aback, but the Svanetians bade him again not to joke with them because they knew for certain that the Tsar put any desired quantity of free vodka at the disposal of every new subject for ten years. The gratuitous distribution of vodka, they said, had been an important factor in leading them to decide to become Russian citizens. The Governor was alone with his staff in the power of the Svanetians. In order not to upset the cordial welcome he had received, he divided up his entire supply of vodka and asked cautiously whether there was anything else they wanted. It then transpired that the Svanetians had a second request to make.

Their principal occupation was stealing, they said. It had thus far been a custom in the wilderness of Svanetia that, when the member of a neighbouring tribe discovered his stolen property in the possession of a free Svanetian, the latter was obliged to pay him back half of the stolen property if he was to prevent bloodshed. This seemed now to the Svanetians to be wrong and intolerable. They, therefore, requested that a law be issued to them with the signature of the Tsar according to which a free Svanetian should return only ten per cent of the stolen property in the event of his being discovered. This seemed to them to be fair enough.

The Governor was disturbed; what was he to do? A Governor's salary was high. And after so much solemn speechmaking, to return to Tiflis and renounce the government of the Svanetians would have been too shameful. He decided to gain time. »I shall write to the Tsar,« he said, »and inform him of your request. But, first of all, I should like to get to know your country and my new government, to visit your towns and villages and see the people.«

It was now the Svanetians' turn to be taken aback. »What people?« they said. »What villages? The whole people stands now before you. There are no more of us free Svanetians.«

Now the Governor was furious. This miserable handful of people, these two or three houses, were all that he had to govern. It was more than he could comprehend. And yet he had to swallow the bitter truth. The entire race of free Svanetians consisted of barely two thousand people, who lived in one single valley and subsisted by plundering their neighbours. It was simply a somewhat glorified gang of brigands who thought that they were going to profit by Russian rule in some way or other, and had appeared to the Government in Tiflis in the light of a great unconquered people.

The Governor returned with all speed to the capital and wrote his report to His Serene Highness. At the end of the report he proposed that a sergeant-major and ten policemen should be sent to manage the country. To this the Governor added »and a priest for the betterment of morals among the Svanetians.«

And that was what really happened. A decayed sergeant-major, ten questionable policemen, and a village priest were sent to the Svanetians with high salaries, and they sent back accounts for the erection of churches, the building of roads, etc. Everything was granted them. It has been estimated that the free Svanetians cost the Russians more money than it would have taken to settle the two thousand of them in Tiflis and provide them with a pension for life. The circumstances I have described apply of course to the free Svanetians only, and not in any way to the Dadianic or princely races.

Even today the territory of the free Svanetians is as inaccessible and wild as ever. But the free Svanetians do not regret having become Russian subjects. The money which the sergeant-major and the priest received was always divided with them in a spirit of Christian charity. The only loser by the whole business was the ruling prince of Svanetia, Konstantin Dadashkelian. For, after the free Svanetians had become Russians, it was suggested that he should also follow their example and lay his country at the Tsar's feet. But Dadashkelian was a ruler of spirit; he did not wish to renounce his crown. The negotiations lasted for a long time and concluded by the last regent of Svanetia stabbing the Tsar's representative and a personal friend, the prince Gagarin, with his own hand at the council table. He paid for it with his life. He was solemnly shot at Kutais, and his land was declared a Russian province. The other princely Svanetians, and later the Dadianic, became Russians too, but that, as I was able to establish during my visit to my »Svanetian aristocrat,« had scarcely any influence worth speaking of towards raising their cultural level. They have remained one of the roughest, wildest, and least known, as well as the most friendly, of the Caucasian people right down to the present day.

26.

RUINS, DEAD CITIES,
AND CHURCHES

IN THE SOUTH OF SVANETIA lie two former Georgian states, the kingdoms of Imeretia and Mingrelia. Both of them have an ancient history and a glorious past which go back to the days when the Greek Argonauts sought the Golden Fleece in Imeretia on the banks of the Phasis, which is now known as the Rion. The inhabitants of Imeretia are Georgians and maintain, like their neighbours of Guria, that they are descended from the Jews who emigrated to the Caucasus in the days of the Babylonian captivity. The philologists of Imeretia also quote a number of place names which are reputedly Jewish, and even the word Imeretia, the ancient Iberia, they consider to be nothing more nor less than a corruption of »Hebreher« or »Huber« meaning »in-comers.«

In point of fact, the Imeretians of today are outwardly indistinguishable from Jews and are universally considered the most resourceful and cunning barristers and orators of the Caucasus. Even the royal family of Imeretia is Jewish and claims to be the oldest, the noblest, and the most distinguished race of rulers in the world. It is the famous race of Bagration which can be proved to have been of royal rank for three thousand years. The Bagration family have been kings at some period or other in almost every country in the Caucasus. In the history of Armenia, Georgia, and many other states royalty of that name may be found; even in Paris in the burial-grounds of the French Kings there can be seen the grave of a Bagration who had been King of Armenia before he was driven out and came to live and die in Paris as a cousin of the French King. Indeed, the last Bagration lives in Paris today, not as cousin to the King, but as a chauffeur on one of M. Citroën's taxis. However, there is no more noble race than that of Bagration. All the princes of Europe and Asia, the Habsburgs, the Bourbons, the Romanovs, are mere petty nobility compared with a Prince Bagration. For the Bagratides are direct lineal descendants of King Solomon and King David; they are also descended from the prophet Moses. A collateral line is related to Jesus, so that they can therefore maintain with perfect justice that nobody in the world is their peer. The royal title of the family always ran: »I, blessed of God, Bagration, King by God's grace, Ruler of the land (here follows the name of the country), heir of our Saviour Jesus Christ, the son of Kings Solomon and David, the heir of Moses, the rightful Lord of Lords, etc.« The entire title would occupy three pages. The word Bagration means »he that cometh from the Mount of Zion,« and even if the official genealogy is not absolutely accurate, at any rate the three thousand years of overlordship and the Jewish origin of the Bagratides are historically proved. There is certainly no parallel to that in the whole of history.

During the nineteenth century, a Bagration emigrated to Russia, where he took part later on in the Napoleonic war. Alexander the First, Tsar of all the Russias, offered him the hand of his sister, which was refused by Bagration as an unseemly and unreasonable request on the Tsar's part. The daughter of one who ruled over one-sixth of the world was far from being the peer of a Bagration.

The Tsar's indignation was unbounded, and it was only the war which saved the haughty Caucasian from banishment. He was killed soon afterwards at the battle of Borodino.

The Bagration family ruled in Imeretia right down to the nineteenth century, and they ruled in a somewhat primitive way. To this day, the trees may be seen in their capital of Kutais beneath which the last King of Imeretia, Solomon the Second, held a court of law, and upon which the condemned were instantly strung up. This same Solomon was driven out by the Russians after a heroic battle.

Imeretia is very rich in legends. Some most remarkable ruins of old towns and temples testify to the fact that not all of the traditional stories are mere fairy tales. There are first of all the Christian myths. The number of churches which contain pieces of the true Cross, golden and silver nails with which Christ was crucified, the Chiton Christi, and other relics is endless.

The churches of this country are certainly among the oldest in the world, and the oldest of them all is the Martvili church, »the Church of the Great Oak.« It is supposed to have been built in A.D. 40 by the Apostle Andrew. A cloister adjoins it in which the Bishop of the Great Oak, the Chkondideli, has lived from antiquity. Chkondideli was the chief bishop of Mingrelia; he was always related to the kings and was, properly speaking, less a priest than a feudal baron. In the middle of the holy grove of oaks stood a fortress built of stones which had once been in the walls and pillars of heathen temples. The Chkondideli, like the other prelates of Georgia, possessed a standing army and had his own princes, nobles, and warriors to put into the field. Most of the Georgian priests are very warlike. It used to be difficult in former times to tell where the priest began and where the feudal baron left off. After a successful battle the leader who had just been smiting the foe would remove his armour, take up the cross, array himself in priest's vestments, and absolve the sins of those who had fallen. These priests gave a better account of themselves as warriors in history than the professional soldiers, the worldly princes who were too much inclined to apostasy. For the wars which Georgia conducted were principally religious wars against the Mohammedans, who surrounded this oldest of Oriental Christian lands on all sides, so that the warlike prowess of the priests was entirely in place even if it was not always directed against the Mohammedans.

In the neighbourhood of the seat of the bishops of the holy oak (the oak is honoured and worshipped as a holy tree throughout the whole of Mingrelia) are to be found the old ruins of the famous town of Niko-lakevi, which are now about to be investigated for the first time by an expedition of scholars. Nikolakevi is the oldest ruin in the western Caucasus and the most interesting storehouse of information as yet unopened by archaeology. The word »Nikolakevi,« which the place has carried as a name for thousands of years, means »the old town« in Mingrelian and is the literal translation of the Greek word »Archeopolis.« For the town to have been known as an old town thousands of years ago, it must have a considerable past. And it seems certain that the town of Nikolakevi will testify to such a past as this. In the opinion of scholars it is neither more nor less than the famous legendary town of Ea, the capital of Colchis, and the dream of all Greek adventurers. Here upon this spot the godlike Medea practised her magic spells; here the Argonauts landed; and here Jason searched for the Golden Fleece.

It is really a fabulous spot, which will sooner or later unquestionably become a place of pilgrimage for tourists and archaeologists. Things will perhaps presently reach the point where the old heathen and classical temples will have been dug up; a brass plate will commemorate the place where Medea bewitched Jason; guides, hungry for gratuities, will take strangers through the ruins; and heavy tomes will glorify the town of Nikolakevi. But that time is not yet come. The expedition which is to excavate the treasures of Georgia's past is still only on its way.

Classical antiquity lives still among the inhabitants of Mingrelia and Imeretia. Innumerable old sagas of the land are nothing but variants of Greek legends. The figures of the Mingrelians themselves are also of classical beauty, and Greek and Genoese blood may be assumed to flow in their veins. The centuries of Greek colonists, Italian merchants, and Byzantine conquerors will never wholly cease to influence the spirit of these people.

In the fifth century, Nikolakevi-Archeopolis was the capital of the Christian kingdom of Lasika, and in the sixth century Justinian, the mighty Emperor of Byzantium, built a great church there, the ruins of which lie today amongst the ruins of the classical age. Even the modest huts of the Mingrelian peasants and monks stand in the midst of ruins. The police commissioner who lives amongst them sees to the maintenance of peace among the inhabitants and will soon have a difficult task to fulfil: it will be his duty to find houses for the scholars who are coming to unlock the new world.

All around Nikolakevi, in Mingrelia and especially in the rocky ranges of Imeretia, and farther to the east in Georgia itself, there are ruins in comparison with which those of Nikolakevi are practically modern. These are the mysterious cave dwellings, cave towns and palaces, of a people of whom today the very name has been forgotten.

The most famous of these dead cave cities is »Upliszikhe,« the »City of God,« which is in the neighbourhood of the town of Gori; it is glorified by legends, and is considered the public property of the Georgians. Upliszikhe is a mountain of rock; its steep crags and walls rear up treeless and grey above the banks of the river Kur. At first you do not notice that you are in the presence of a dead city. It is only at the very top, at an inaccessible height, that a few caves are seen, small excavations in the rock wall to which all approach seems impossible. One single dark entrance on the edge of the river leads up to a shaft which can be followed only with an experienced guide, otherwise one becomes inextricably lost in the dark labyrinth of chambers, palaces, and streets within the rock city. The city itself is by no means the primitive dwelling-place of prehistoric cavemen. On the contrary, finely carved pillars support the ceilings of the halls, betraying the style and skill of an established culture. Ornaments and inscriptions cover the walls of the rooms; cupboards and recesses for lighting and heating purposes are in rows along the walls. But near by coarsely carved dwelling holes are to be seen with asymmetric windows and the undecorated walls of genuine troglodytes. Innumerable generations must have inhabited the town, for not only the style of building but also the inscriptions on the walls vary. Old Georgian writing is represented together with incomprehensible hieroglyphics which have not been deciphered to this day.

Some of the palaces of this rock town have two floors, with ceilings in the form of a cupola. Gigantic wine pitchers stand around as if they had been in use just yesterday. And yet it must certainly be millennia since the last inhabitants quitted this secret, invisible town carved in the rock. It is not known when Upliszikhe was founded. The very oldest Georgian documents speak of it, and scholars maintain that this labyrinth of a town was hewn out of the rock without steel instruments, and that it bears a striking resemblance to the old Pelasgian catacombs. At an estimate, they are three thousand years old, though the Georgians think otherwise. According to them, the great Queen Tamar was the builder of the town. But that is of no significance because it is well known that in Georgia every ruin, even if it be only fifty years old, is reputed to have been built by Tamar. Documents report that Alexander of Macedon visited the rock city of Upliszikhe, and many scholars see in its palaces a magnificent old temple of Astarte and Baal.

However that may be, the city remains a riddle, as does also another fabulous city which is supposed to be constructed in the bowels of the rock, deep in the earth under the river-bed. Nobody has been able to discover this second town, though the natives are convinced of its existence. The entrance-way, which is supposed to be as well concealed as that of Upliszikhe, has yet to be found.

The rock city, which can only be detected from above, must have been a completely impregnable fortress, with its bulwarks, its passages, and its caves. There are only two narrow, dark passages connecting the town with the outside world, and one of them is absolutely invisible to the most observant eye.

In the midst of the ruined city stands a church of relatively recent date. It is held in honour even now, though scarcely in a Christian fashion. After the wine harvest, the peasants of the surrounding villages come up to the church bringing heathenish gifts to the spirit of the dead city: great pots full of wine which are stood open by the side of the altar. The wine evaporates to the well-being of the god. The clergy of Georgia does not oppose this custom; it is tolerant and has to put up with much stranger blasphemies than that. The Georgian church adopted practically all the customs of heathen times, supplemented them by the ritual of the Greek church, and in this way created a religion which the people regarded as the root of all national tradition. For this reason the Georgian church is the centre of the spiritual life of the people to this very day, and the upholder of national honour and power.

The churches have remained unaltered throughout the centuries in the enduring architectural style of Georgia, though they are most of them extremely old and often dilapidated. The ground plan of the Georgian church is the cross. A slim octagonal cupola rises over the transept. All churches in the land are built on this principle. Frivolous changes of style are unknown to the Georgian; he despises the substitution of deceptive novelties for traditional, long-established custom.

In the evening, the Georgian girls creep up to the churches when they are empty. In their hands they hold a piece of string wound up into a ball. Their lips utter heathenish words as they kneel and pray before the entrance to the church, dropping the ball as they do so. In their hands they retain the end of the string; then, having kissed the ball, they crawl on their knees all round the church along the wall until they arrive back at the ball again from the other direction, upon which they knot the end they carried to what is left of the ball. If she is successful in this, the girl rises up joyous and confident, because she knows now that, before the year is out, she will marry one of her honoured heroes. The spirits of the church will see to it because the girl has imprisoned them with the string, and it is not until they have fulfilled her wish that they can leave the church again, fly to the villages, and take the pious gifts which the Georgians put out for them on the windows of their huts. The Georgian churches are often covered with a thick net of strings, so that one is obliged to lift one's foot high in order to get over the threshold. There are so many girls who want to get married.

Georgian saints certainly have a hard time of it. But the churches of Georgia do not merely house saints. Even the Italian churches do not contain more relics than the holy cloisters and churches of Georgia. In one church, for example, the clothes of the Saviour are exhibited; in another the oldest picture of Christ, painted by an apostle; and in one of the most famous of them the vine branch is shown which the Mother of God delivered in a dream to Saint Nino, who brought Christianity to Georgia. The most remarkable holy relic, however, is shown in an Armenian church in the neighbourhood of Mount Ararat. It is a piece of decayed wood which is supposed to come from Noah's ark as it settled upon the summit of Ararat when the flood subsided.

The holy legends of the Georgian people fill several volumes. They are unknown in Europe, although they are probably older and closer to the original form than many legends of the West. Oriental Christianity, which is so often penalized and sneered at, is reflected in these naive fables and is of a childlike piety, fantasy, and candour. It is the oldest form of Christianity in the world and was obliged to fight harder for the cross in the course of its existence than the churches of the west. Indeed the whole history of Georgia in the last two thousand years has been nothing but an unbroken battle for the faith, against enemies of other creeds who surrounded it on all sides. Georgia succeeded by its stubborn bravery in doing what the greatest Christian realm of the East–Byzantium–did not; it retained its Christianity. No wonder that the Georgian priest and monks became soldiers and learnt to be tolerant of their own countrymen and to accept the old pagan gods in exchange for the freedom of the land. The history of Georgia, therefore, knows no sects. The old water god, the goddess of the hunt, and the god of the harvest found their humble places by the side of the saints of Christ. No Georgian is shocked if in many districts the old gods are honoured with pious gifts and legends along with Saint George, the patron saint of the nation. In Pshavia and Tushetia, for example, these gods are not even cloaked in the disguise of a Christian saint, and their cult runs its course undisturbed by the side of the official cult of Christianity. In Tushetia they have actually kept their own priests, the Dadekones, who are not by any means always at loggerheads with the Christian priests. It is in any case difficult to establish where Christianity ends in Georgia and where overt paganism begins, for everything that is not Islam is at once termed Christian. Even the savage Khevsurs, who call themselves Christians only in order to emphasize the fact that they are not Mohammedans, but who admit no Christian priest into their country, actually figure in the official reports, as Greek-Orthodox Christians.

In the struggle for their beliefs, the Georgians have been able to preserve the pagan past of their country. The valleys of the western Caucasus have therefore become a veritable treasure house for cultural history, archaeology, and ethnography; Mingrelia, Imeretia, Svanetia, and Guria still harbour ruins whose discovery may be of as much importance as that of Babylon or Egypt. The Egyptians, the Assyrians, the Greeks, the Hittites, the Romans, the Byzantines, the Genoese, the Arabs, the Persians, the Turks, the Russians have ruled in all the valleys of Georgia. The traces which they left behind them, the towns which they built, and the customs which they introduced still lie undiscovered. Deep in the forests of Imeretia, on the banks of the ancient river Phasis, there linger still slender, crumbling columns, the remains of mighty fortresses and graceful palaces of marble, and inscriptions yet unseen by the eye of the scholar. The rustic scions of the mighty kings of yore pasture their flocks near by and shun with pious superstition the purlieus of a vanished glory. The famous land of the sorceress Medea still waits upon research.

27.

THE CRADLE OF HUMANITY

THE KINGDOM OF MEDEA, the future treasure chest of archaeologists and globe-trotters, abuts upon the chief range of the Caucasus, the land of eternal snow. Mountains higher than Mont Blanc rise there which are to this very day without a name, for they are low by comparison with the monarchs of the Caucasus, with Elbruz and Kasbek, and with Ararat, at whose feet, according to the ancient legend, the cradle of humanity lies.

The beauty of the broad stretches of snow is unmeasurable, and indescribable is the clearness of the mountain air. Who has once seen the panorama of the hills, or breathed the magic air of the Caucasus, will always long for it again, for there is no clearer air in the world and no more beautiful mountains. A man's eye may roam unbelievably far in that place. He can see across the whole of the Caucasus from the peak of one moderately high mountain, from the shores of the Black Sea to the gorges of Daghestan, the valleys of Georgia, and the land of the Cossacks. The mountain massifs stand forth nameless and innumerable. And even those that have a name and dwarf the highest peaks in Europe are only known to the specialist. Who has ever heard of the mountains Jimeras-Khokh (the mountain of Homer), Syrkhubar, Tepli, Zmiakomy-Khokh, and Palyvter? Unknown and unconquered, they rear from time immemorial their white peaks to heaven, surrounded by mystic legends. No man nor beast has trodden the eternal snow; no sound penetrates the awful silence of the giants. They are mysterious, and overpowering in their gigantic beauty. Small wonder indeed that the Caucasian gets piously upon his knees on days when the face of the mountains is veiled in cloud, and prays to the spirit of the giants with his forehead upon the ground. There is something holy and fearful and exalted about the mountains, which have been thought from time immemorial to be the boundary of the world. The ancients called these mountains *Kaf* and used to tell how they circled the world as a ring circles a finger.

In the Caucasus, close to the stars, Zeus fought with Typhœus. Here the Titans lived, and here it was that all the old gods were driven back, here that Prometheus stole the holy flame and the vultures rent his liver. Any traveller can see for himself the rock which is honoured by the natives on the borders of Abkhasia and Imeretia and upon which Prometheus lay bound. All the myths of the ancient Greeks have been preserved in the mountains. The variations under which they appear among the many tribes are innumerable.

»The Cradle of Humanity—here the nations began,« says the proud Caucasian; »here they arose for the second time after that flood to which not only the Bible but also all the races of the Caucasus testify.« The Ark of Noah glided over the Caucasus and grazed as it did so the summit of Elbruz. Elbruz was split into two halves, and the two peaks now rise up as a monument of God's mercy, Who split a mountain in two to save the Ark. At Ararat where the Ark landed the children of Noah lived, and the people of Ararat, the Armenian race, descends from Japhet's grandchild, Haik. Amiran was the name of the King of the Armenians, and he was a cruel tyrant, so that the Armenians drove him out. But the King kept constantly attacking his people, pillaging, murdering, and robbing. So the Lord of the World took pity and seized the cruel king and incarcerated him in the depths of the rocks of Ararat. He was bound with an iron chain. His favourite dog alone shared his prison. Day and night the faithful dog gnawed the chain, and the King would have been set free long ago if every Armenian smith did not strike three times with his hammer on the anvil and speak a magic formula every New Year's Eve. At that the chains of the wicked king are joined together again.

The neighbours of the Armenians also, the Georgians and the Azerbaijans, practise the same custom as the Armenians. Every smith in the Caucasus, regardless of the tribe to which he belongs, strikes his anvil three times on New Year's Eve, so that the evil king Amiran may not attack their neighbours, the Armenians.

The mountains which are the richest in legend, however, are—not Ararat—but the highest peaks, Elbruz and Kasbek. On the cliffs of Elbruz are chained all the giants who were driven out during the great twilight of the gods, and even today the Ossetes search the lonely mountain caves in the hope of releasing the chained giants and of receiving gold and gems as a reward. Elbruz even possesses an inverted version of the Barbarossa saga.

Protected by a guard, shut up within the mountains, sits an old king. Once every hundred years, the King asks: »Does grass still grow upon the earth, and do the lambs still find increase?« When the guard has told him that this is so, the King moans and strikes with his fist upon the walls of his cavern. Then the earth quakes and avalanches fall from Elbruz.

On the summit of the mountain lives the bird Simurg, the king of the birds. With one eye Simurg looks into the past and with the other eye into the future. He rules in the invisible kingdoms of Elbruz, in Djinnistan, the »kingdom of the djinns. The djinns of Elbruz are not evil spirits. They are fair maidens brought up by Simurg for the heroes of the future. Simurg knows the heroes of the future and chooses for each of them a Djinness or Peri. In the Elbruz also lives the unseen power of Gog and Magog, who shall come according to the New Testament and the Koran from out the underworld at the end of days and overthrow the kingdom of the righteous.

So much for Elbruz. No less interesting are the legends of Kasbek, the second highest mountain in the Caucasus. Kasbek is a chance name given to this giant by the Russians. The Caucasian races call it, each in his own language, »the Mountain of Christ.« On the peak of the mountain, invisible only to the eyes of the transgressor, there is a church. By the power of heaven, the tent of Abraham was set up within this church and in this tent stood the holiest of all relics, the cradle of the Saviour. Priceless treasures are assembled around the cradle, but only a really virtuous man may put forth his hand to them. Innumerable people have thought themselves truly pious and have paid for it with their lives. There were even priests and monks among these treasure hunters, and the last King of Georgia sent people to look for the cradle of Christ. But nobody has so far been sufficiently good. Even the Englishmen who made the first ascent in 1868 did not find the cradle. They saw nothing but old stone crosses standing upon the inaccessible massifs of the mountains in memory of a Christianity which had disappeared.

Over and over again, the conquest of the land of snow has been attempted; bold men are always to be found who will dare to enter the magic world of the Caucasus. The pious and sanguinary legends are slowly fading from the recollection of the mountain tribes, and yet the Caucasus is the land which will be the last to resign its characteristics. No man has yet been successful in becoming master of the mountains. The mountains know how to protect themselves. The gloomy songs, the mad pranks, the amazing people, and the immense mystical silence of the giants still constitutes a wall which separates two worlds—Europe and Asia.

Only in one case did the Caucasus give in. At the point where the mountains cease, a fruitful land begins which was still the home of innumerable races only fifty years ago. Rich villages sheltered a peaceful populace. Today this populace is gone. Innumerable clans and languages have lost their homes. The villages have vanished, and immigrants from the north have occupied the land, but it was not as the result of a conquest. An enormous bloodless migration of races took place here when a million persons left their country about fifty years ago to depart voluntarily into a distant land and merge with a foreign people. The native Caucasian tongues have disappeared, and many philologists are ready to shed bitter tears in vain over the irrecoverably lost opportunity for studying them. The story of the migrations is told in the Caucasus as follows: Five princes once decided to drive the Russians out of the Caucasus. These princes were the Ossete, Mussa Kundukh; the Tabasar, Mussa Uzmi; the Ingush, Zur; the Chechen, Saadulla Osman; and the Kabardian, Atashuk. The Kabardian prince Atashuk betrayed this conspiracy to the Tsar, upon which the latter decided to destroy the races from which the conspirators derived. But Kundukh and Osman sought to save the people. »There is no necessity to kill us,« they said to the Tsar. »We shall leave the land of unbelief, for the great Sultan at Stamboul will be more merciful to us.« Thus began the migration. One race after another wandered to Turkey under the leadership of Mussa Kundukh. They reached the land of the Ottomans on foot or by ship. But no happiness awaited them there. The land which the Sultan gave them was bad, the life was unsuitable to mountain people, brigandage was forbidden them; they starved and longed for their home; they died or intermingled with the Turks. Only a small fraction of these people was able to adapt itself, the Circassians, who formed the famous bodyguard of the Sultan and furnished Turkey with her best statesmen and Pashas until quite recent times. Mussa Kundukh also, the leader of this migration, died as a respected Pasha of the Ottomans. But his people, who had shot off their rifles three times in farewell upon the shores of the Caucasus, starved and suffered in Turkey, and succumbed without forgetting to praise the name of the General Mussa Kundukh Pasha, their saviour. Their land in the Caucasus was given over to the Cossacks.

Many years have passed since then; the Caucasian Government has made its archives public, and more is known about these events. All the leaders of the migration, with General Kundukh at the head of them, were well-paid agents of the Russian Government. For every Caucasian family that departed, they received a definite sum of the Tsar's good silver roubles. Every Caucasian who emigrated was mentioned in detailed letters, and the joy of the Russians was unbounded as the depopulated regions were put at the free disposal of the Russian Cossacks. Mussa Kundukh was a traitor to his people, as were also the other leaders of the migrations. But in spite of this, their memory is still kept sacred and honoured by the Caucasians who migrated to Turkey. These migrations or disappearances of entire peoples at the bidding of the Tsar, and owing to the treachery of the honoured generals and the Prince Mussa Kundukh, constitute a grim chapter in the more modern history of the Caucasus, a chapter which remains yet to be written.

This is the only case in which the hills gave in to the enemy and were obliged to take him into their midst. But it is far from being a victory over the Caucasus. It is unbelievable how quickly the air of the hills, the marvellous scenery of the Caucasus, changes the psychology of the conquerors. The Cossacks and the Russians who once drove out the people of the Caucasus and appropriated their lands have become genuine Caucasians in a few decades. »Caucasus-Russian« is now an accepted term, which has nothing whatever to do with Russia and signifies a race that differs very little from the other Caucasian people in its way of living.

One result of these migrations has been the remarkable fact that some of the Caucasian languages which are no longer to be found in the mountains are spoken far away in the plains of Syria and in the mountains of Lebanon by the successors of the emigrants. The Caucasus has been transplanted into Syria. The knights fight with their neighbours there, undertake thieving expeditions, remain true to the laws of their Caucasian fathers and the eternal custom of the blood feud. The homeland of the Caucasus still lures them, however, in spite of the fact that they are generations removed from it. In their songs they mourn for it, and in their fables, which they recount in their old language in the midst of Syrian Arab life, they still tell of the giant Elbruz, of the wicked king in his prison, and of the cradle of the Saviour upon the inaccessible peak of Kasbek.

28.

A MORE OR LESS EXTRAVAGANT CONCLUSION

I HEARD MANY WONDERFUL STORIES in the Caucasus about robbers, soldiers of liberty, buried treasures, and fair ladies. Perhaps a great many of them were fables. But nevertheless they are just as true as anything that can be proven by inscriptions, old manuscripts, or yellowing archives and registers. To learn to know the Caucasus one need not go a-burrowing among old parchments and doubtful museum pieces.

The things the Caucasian has to say about himself and his country are important, because no poet believes more implicitly in the products of his imagination than the Caucasian, who is quite capable of pointing calmly at a mountain and declaring that its interior is of solid gold. To him that is the truth, and he will reject any other kind of truth with righteous indignation. The difference between poetry and truth is not yet recognized in the mountains. Will the sad fact ever penetrate to them that not all mountains are of gold, nor every brigand a noble knight? For the Caucasian there is only one Caucasus, the one he sees and knows, and it is peopled with Crusaders, evil spirits, fabulous treasures, adventurers, and holy legends. It is a fairyland, and the people there are really not to be blamed if they assume that there are things in their valley just over the next range of hills which would cause a levelheaded investigator to smile.

The story which I should like to add now is, however, not »Caucasian« but historically true in the European sense, which requires that everything which happens shall be supported by documents. A fat, old, good-humoured Caucasian told it to me in the village of Passanaur upon the much-praised Georgian military road, which I used on the return trip from the kingdom of Medea to the luxurious town of Besh-Tau. But the story is not true merely because a Caucasian told it; there are police records which confirm it, and police records are not usually any more imaginative in the Caucasus than they are elsewhere. The story, too, is in no way fantastic but probably merely overdrawn. And I really do not know myself why it is the favourite story which I brought back from the hills. It merely enthralled me more than any other.

Here it is: A few years before the war, a robber named Kerim lived in the Caucasus, plundering travellers, attacking stations, and generally preparing himself in the usual way for the ultimate career of a Persian imperial adjutant-general. How he came to hit on his profession is not known. It is said that his father was shot by a Russian officer. This led first of all to a blood feud and later to protracted brigandage. Kerim, however, was what is called a noble character; he only plundered the wealthy, and even then only men. Towards women he was a gallant cavalier and, when he attacked a railroad train, he would rob the men down to their very shirts, but merely kiss the ladies' hands. He never touched them even if they had sacks full of gold with them. This naturally caused the men, whenever there was a hold-up, to turn over all their property to the women as fast as they could and to keep back nothing but a small sum for the sake of appearances.

Even in his battles with the police Kerim was always the gentleman. He did not kill an officer until he had warned him three times. The warnings consisted of first stealing the officer's clothes while he was asleep, then burning down his house, and finally shooting his horse. It was only after he had seen that these warnings were of no avail and that the officer continued to persecute him, that he killed him without mercy.

Whole regiments were sent out to capture him, but he was always able to escape the danger in time. It was not long before the enthusiastic Caucasians elevated him to the rank of a sort of national hero. At last, however, the Russian Government decided to adopt the time-honoured method of reward which had already delivered many criminals into the hands of the law. Fifty thousand roubles, a sum which is fantastic according to Caucasian standards, was to be received by anyone who would betray the brigand to the Russians. The news of the fifty thousand roubles spread very swiftly throughout the land, for the Caucasus affords the most amazing results in this kind of intelligence work. Any information spreads like lightning over cliffs and gorges, mountains and valleys. No newspapers are necessary; the news runs through the mountain paths and the glacier tracks as if by cable, and if you start to tell the latest news, brought direct from the town, in some godforsaken little mountain nest, the listeners laugh at you: »We know that, try telling us something new.«

And that was what happened in the case of the fifty thousand roubles. In a few days the whole of the Caucasus knew about it and laughed. Naturally there wasn't a soul in the hills who would have betrayed Kerim. Those who would have liked to couldn't, and those who could, wouldn't. This time the Russian proposition failed.

Years went by, and the money was still there for some traitor, and Kerim still went calmly about his business. But one day he fell ill, and the wise doctors of the hills said: »Thy time hath come; thou hast but four weeks to live.« Kerim thought for some time. A wise resolution was maturing within him. He went to a village which had always afforded him a secure hiding-place from the Russians and descended at the house of the poorest peasant there. It was his present intention to make this man happy, the poorest of the poor, the man who had so often protected him and saved him.

»Friend,« said he, »go thou into the town, to the Russian General, and say to him that in thy house sits the robber Kerim. Then the General will come to take me away, and thou shalt receive fifty thousand roubles.« The peasant started to his feet in horror. »I am not a traitor,« he cried. »I will not sell my friend.« But the robber persisted, and commanded that the Kadi be called and the elders of the village, and he explained to them how he intended to reward the peasant. »My life is worthless now,« said he. »I wish my friend to receive the fifty thousand roubles! Why should the money remain with the Russians?«

And that was what occurred. A whole detachment of Russian police appeared in the village, surrounded the house in which the robber was hiding, and arrested him after a long fight. Kerim died of his illness before he could be shot. But the peasant received the money shortly before his death. The robber's wish had been fulfilled and the treasury was fifty thousand roubles the poorer.

That is the moving tale of the robber Kerim, who rewarded his friend, the poorest of the poor, and who exchanged his ebbing life, a worthless thing, against fifty thousand roubles for the good of those who were in need.

There are, as I have said, thousands of stories about robbers in the Caucasus—brutal and romantic, bloodthirsty and tender—but none of them seems to me to equal this one. Perhaps it is because it seems almost untypical of the Caucasus, and yet it reveals the remarkable spiritual life of the Caucasian robber, the protector of the poor and soldier of liberty. The fat, kindly Caucasian who told me this, was a thorough robber himself, and I do not know whether any European will understand why the hardy fellow wept as he told of the glorious life and end of Kerim. Perhaps because his own head was not valued at fifty thousand roubles, and he could not give anyone that final happiness, or perhaps because the night was warm and romantic in Passanaur, and the mountains reared their heads cloudless and menacing to heaven, and the singers in the little inn were singing mournful songs. Perhaps. It is hard to tell.

This is the last story that I heard in the Caucasus. I travelled to Kislovodsk, and my time was at an end; the oil town on the Caspian Sea was waiting for me. The Caucasian railway brought me home, and I could only see the snow-peaks and mountain torrents in the distance, with their tiny settlements and the Caucasian horsemen trying to run races with the train. There once again lay the whole marvellous, unforgettable, fabulous land of the hills.

In those days the country was still at peace, as peace goes in the Caucasus. The Viceroy was a Grand Duke and still reigned in the palace at Tiflis, and nobody in the world could have foreseen that the last hours of the old Caucasus were at hand. That was in the year 1916, just before the greatest of all revolutions, before the time which called forth still more remarkable things than all the colourful people and romantic stories of the hills.

One more year went by, and then the Caucasus stood in flames. The innumerable races armed themselves again for the struggle for liberty. Battles were fought in the mountains with airplanes, machine guns, and knights in armour.

The Grand Ducal Viceroy fled in the night and was replaced by fantastic systems of government. For years the fight raged. And the Caucasus passed through all kinds of regimes, from theocratic monarchy to democratic republic, and, when the flames at last subsided after many years, the old tyrant who had been expelled, the Russian, returned again, from the north, and Soviet commissars descended as governors in the old palace of the Tsar.

And again it became evident that nothing in the Caucasus had changed. The years of revolution and the years of Soviet power have had but little influence on the Caucasian. Blood feud flourishes there as much as ever; the soldier of liberty, the Abrek, still rides upon the mountain trails; and the hill folk live as before, unexplored, with their incomprehensible languages, and their age-old customs and legends, which have increased abundantly since the revolution. Apparently nothing can change the Caucasian; he clings stubbornly to his fathers' ways of living; and there is no more superficial thing in the world than the much-vaunted Europeanization of the towns and villages of the hills. The mountain folk are not Europeans, and they are not Asiatic; they are Caucasians—that is to say, a special race of men that will endure.

Afterword

»The Orient of the Imagination«

by *Tom Reiss*

» E ssad Bey« was just 24, in 1929, when *Blood and Oil in the Orient*, his first book, was published with the promise blazoned on the cover: »More thrilling than any adventure novel, more instructive than any travel guide, as colorful as only life itself can be« Essad Bey's books took readers into a somehow reassuringly strange world of the mysterious orient at the darkest moment of the twentieth century. At a time when the borderlands of Europe and Asia were squeezed between two totalizing ideologies—Nazism on one hand and Soviet Communism on the other—his world promised that there were hills and valleys that could never be conquered.

By the time he died, twelve years later, in 1942, at age 36, Essad Bey, who always maintained he was »the son of a Muslim aristocratic father and a revolutionary mother,« had published at least fourteen more books—not counting two novels he wrote under the name ›Kurban Said‹—as well as unpublished manuscripts, hundreds of articles and letters written to a fascist salon hostess, his powerful protector, with whom he maintained an »intellectual love affair« that contains novels and worlds within worlds in its pages—letters ala Scheherazade, written to save himself from deportation to the Nazi camps. For, in fact, 'Essad Bey' was an invented person, the creation of a Jewish refugee named Lev Nussimbaum, who outwitted the Nazis by transforming himself into a Muslim desert adventurer and becoming a bestselling author in Nazi Germany. But what, if anything, was factual when it came to Essad Bey?

Born to a wealthy Jewish family in 1905 probably in Baku, Azerbaijan, the southernmost city in the Russian empire, Lev escaped the Bolsheviks by fleeing to Germany in 1920. (Raised by a Baltic German nurse, he was later most comfortable writing in German.) In Berlin he adopted the name ›Essad Bey‹ and converted to Islam at the Ottoman embassy in the last year of that old empire's existence. By age 25, he was an internationally famous author of sprawling historical romances filled with tall tales of his own personal heroism. Even as Goebbels was systematically purging Jewish writers from German publishing, Lev managed to publish 16 books, most of them international bestsellers and one an enduring fiction masterpiece—*Ali and Nino*—all by the age of 32.

As a 26-year-old Lev tackled biographies of Mohammed and Stalin simultaneously, and both were in bookstores before he was 27. They were international bestsellers and warmly received not only for their colorful writing style but for their insights into these two world-historical figures. The biography of Mohammed is the only one of Lev's books that has always remained in print in one language or another, and the original New York Times review of it sums up the idiosyncratic nature of his work:

> »The texture of this fine book is as a Persian carpet. There is material underfoot. But it is magic to the eye. We walk firmly on what we are bound to believe, we look at what transcends belief, and the question is how we can rend the credible from the incredible without tearing asunder the whole design.«

His books are readable seventy years after they were written, in no small part because Lev narrated even the driest analysis of oil-pricing mechanisms as though it were a Caucasian folk tale. In his books and his articles, as in his self-image, what Lev cared about was intellectual and emotional truths of the human heart and existential condition, amorphous things that could not be captured with the sharp angles of a scientist's or academic's tools. He would write in his deathbed memoir:

> »It is apparently difficult, particularly difficult for a ›literary man,‹ to ›photograph‹ instead of rendering. The temptations of literature are enormous. In the memory, perspective shifts. Involuntarily, the writer begins to prefer the truth of atmosphere to the simple truth of facts.«

But Lev's chief ongoing invention was always himself. With status of »Orient expert« of *Die Literarische Welt* (before he left the journal, at 28, Lev had published 144 articles in it, even more than his colleague

Walter Benjamin), he fashioned himself as a Weimar media star—a professional »Man of the Caucasus.« Though he received much attention in America, it was always German readers who mattered most to him. Yet almost as soon as *Blood and Oil* appeared, a few politically driven German reviewers took it upon themselves not merely to warn the public away from the book but, in a sense, to »out« the author. Lev, who by then was appearing on the Berlin café scene dressed in his »native« costume—sometimes a Caucasian warlord's fur hat and caftan, sometimes a turban with a gemstone set in the center—was perceived as a kind of ethnic cross-dresser, as well as something far more devious. Many Jewish journalists and scholars were writing books on the Middle East at the time, often out of a deep and sympathetic knowledge of the Muslim world, but they did not tramp around Berlin dressed in turbans, speak of their filial ties to warrior chieftains and call themselves by fancy Turkish names.

The following review of *Blood and Oil*, from the influential right-wing journal *Der Nahe Osten* is typical:

»This book is one of the most miserable publications of recent years. ... The author, who introduces himself as ›Mohammad Essad-Bey‹ and pretends to be the son of a Tartar oil magnate from Baku, has turned out to be a Jewish dissident named Leo (Lob) Nussimbaum, born in Kiev in 1905, son of a Jew named Abraham Nussimbaum from Tiflis. When one compares the accounts in the book, according to which the author was threatening Russian ministers at the age of ten, and in which the author pretends to be a relative of the Emir of Bukhara and an expert on Muslim customs, one gets a clear idea of the whole grotesquerie. . . . The Muslims will presumably firmly reject their alleged fellow believer ›Mohammad Essad-Bey.‹ (Essad= in Arabic asad, esed=lion=Lob=Leo?)«

The scandal had only a positive effect on book sales and it made Lev—or rather, Essad—famous, but when it came to the accusations about his identity, the critics did have a point: while never publicly deviating from his story that his father was a Muslim lord, Essad was sharing an apartment in Berlin with his father, who made no secret about being a Jewish businessman named Abraham Nussimbaum. »The many peoples that I have visited, the many events that I have seen, have made me into a complete cosmopolitan,« he wrote in a 1931 newspaper. In 1931 in Germany this was tantamount to admitting one was a Jew, but Lev did not seem concerned.

Some prominent Muslim refugees at the time did reject him, misreading the humor in his work as an attack on Islam or Muslim independence movements in general, when Lev's writing was anything but anti-Muslim. The leading point man in the Islamic faction of the assault on Lev was an Azeri nationalist living in Constantinople named Hilal Munschi. Munschi summed up the attacks on Essad Bey's character in a series of pamphlets he published in German and Turkish.

When I visited Baku in 2000, specifically to interview the various Azeri »partisans« of the Kurban Said debate, I was actually handed copies of Munschi's ancient attacks on Lev's character and »background,« in Azeri, as though they were contemporary news reports. I was shocked by the vehemence of the language—until I realized that I was reading attack literature from the early 1930's, resurrected seventy years later as »evidence.« »You see! You see!« shouted one prominent Azeri professor, waving his finger in the air, »it is all the proof we need! Right there in Munschi's article, he exposed the swindler for what he was!« My article on Lev in *The New Yorker*, which had appeared in 1999, apparently sparked a renewed debate, as prominent Azeris had to deal with the suggestion that *Ali and Nino*, their »national novel« had been written by a Jew named Nussimbaum. Luckily, since my book *The Orientalist* has appeared around the world, many younger Azeris have embraced the multicultural truth of their greatest novelist: that he was very much a cosmopolitan, and that if he was not a pure-bred Azeri, he was a quintessential Bakuvian, epitomizing that city's unique mix of modernity and tradition, Jew and Muslim, West and East.

While certain Muslim refugees and the right-wing press attacked Lev's inauthentic »Orientalist« writings, some on the pro-communist Left went after him for his unflattering depictions of the Soviets and the Revolution. *Vorwärts!* the leading left publication, simply dismissed his books *Stalin* and *OGPU*, saying that Essad Bey did not have »the necessary dialectical-materialist schooling« to understand events in Russia. Attacks from the right and left made him a controversial figure in Germany, and Lev's general response—to smile enigmatically and keep on writing more books—seemed to have the effect of keeping everyone guessing: What were his real politics? What was his racial background? What were the true motives of the »story swindler«? With his eclectic subject matter, odd clothes, sarcasm and purposely Caucasian-accented German, Lev simply didn't fall into any of the generally accepted categories of the day. The venom spat out at him became so potently inchoate that a Prague paper would eventually accuse him of pursuing »purely Bolshevist rather than Islamic interests,« while in Warsaw he was denounced as »a Marxist werewolf.« This accusation that the author of some of the most scathing exposes of Bolshevik terror was himself a »Marxist werewolf« suggest the extent to which Lev's mysterious persona had perplexed everyone. »Who is this Essad Bey?« Trotsky wrote in a letter in 1932, underlining the sentence. It was a question many people wanted answered, but was it even clear that Lev knew the answer himself?

Lev preempted »unfriendly« and humorless critics in the lighthearted introduction to his second book, *Twelve Secrets of the Caucasus,* announcing that he was »aware from personal observation, that there are such things as hospitals and secondary schools for girls in the Caucasus.« Indeed, coming from Baku, where many such innovations were first introduced to the Muslim world, he was more than aware of it. Readers of his articles would know that he held ambiguous views about Western »progress« in the East, not because he wished to insult the Orient but because he felt an overriding nostalgia and loss at the disappearing traditions he witnessed in the modernizing Baku of his youth.

»But things which would be in place in an encyclopedia will not be found here in a book which has no wish to be confused with the heavy artillery of scholarship.«

Twelve Secrets of the Caucasus is »a kind of curiosity shop of world history in its loyal preservation of all that is no more, all that is outlived and forgotten.« As a leading exposer of the Communist onslaught in the Caucasus, Essad was keenly aware that modern innovations could bring just as much destruction, but in his works on the Muslim Orient, he chose a comic-romantic tone. This tone was invariably misunderstood by Muslim expatriates as glibness about their situation, but his later personal correspondence, as well as a close reading of the books themselves, reveals that it was anything but glib. Lev's attachment to the »Orient«—his view of himself as an »Oriental«—was perhaps more real than his understanding of himself as a European or as a Jew. Of course, he was all of these things.

Lev's Orient was a different one from that of his detractors. One of the most striking chapters in *Twelve Secrets* describes a place Essad calls the »political Switzerland of the Caucasus,« the Valley of the Khevsurs, or Khevsuria: "There a man could at last be safe.« One stubborn American reviewer tried in vain to pinpoint Khevsuria on a map, regretting that better ones had not been provided in the book, but he did not realize that the answers were not to be found in his geography. Lev provided further guidance:

> »Khevsuria is quite near Tiflis, and yet the land is free, independent, and no policeman dares to follow his victim there. A gigantic wall of rock surrounds Khevsuria and separates it from the rest of the world. . . . From the cliff wall down into the void there hangs a long rope. Whoever has the courage can catch hold of the rope and let himself down to the Khevsurs. The police never follow. . . . Through it the first immigrants must have entered the land. Only the refugee dares use the rope, to be accepted if he is so inclined into the society of the Khevsurs and protected for ever from all dangers.«

This is the Orient Lev Nussimbaum is from: a mountainous realm insulated from political and ethnic conflict, a refuge where no secret policeman can follow, and where anyone with the courage to climb down a rope into the abyss is accepted—in short, the Orient of the Imagination.

Tom Reiss writes about international politics and culture for *The New Yorker* magazine. He has written for *The New York Times, The Wall Street Journal,* the *Financial Times,* and other publications. His work often focuses on how individual lives are affected by history, and is known for its rich juxtapositions of cultures and time periods that bring forgotten people and places to life. He was born in New York City, to an American father and a French mother, and he grew up in Texas and Massachusetts, where he graduated from Harvard College. A 1998 travel magazine assignment in Baku, Azerbaijan, led him to discover the unsolved mystery of Kurban Said, and to write *The Orientalist.*

For more information on Tom Reiss, Essad Bey and *The Orientalist*
please also check
www.theorientalist.info

BY THE SAME PUBLISHER

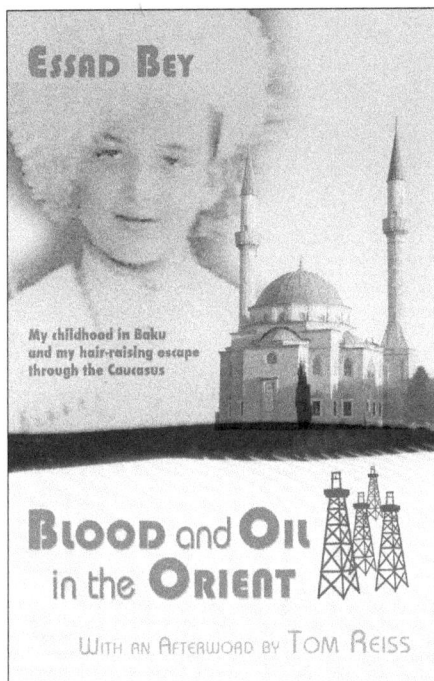

Essad Bey
Blood and Oil in the Orient
My childhood in Baku and my hair-raising escape through the Caucasus

With an afterword by bestselling author Tom Reiss

266 pages, paperback
ISBN: 978-3-929345-36-0

An Autobiography like Something Out of the Arabian Nights

In this lively and witty autobiography, Essad Bey, a.k.a. Lev Nussimbaum, tells us the story of his childhood in Baku, the capital of Azerbaijan, and of his flight from the Russian Revolution in 1917, which brought him first straight through the Caucasus, then to Istanbul – where this book concludes – and finally to Berlin.

When Essad Bey speaks of the people of the Caucasus and their customs so strange to us, a sort of anthropological cabinet of curiosities unfolds before our eyes, and we cannot help but be astonished. All the while, through his affectionate and sometimes openly ironic words, even the excesses of the Revolution sound like children's pranks and his hair-raising escape like an adventure novel.

Blood and Oil in the Orient is an informative and entertaining book; in the 1930s, it was an international bestseller.

www.bridges-publishing.de

www.ingramcontent.com/pod-product-compliance
Lightning Source LLC
Chambersburg PA
CBHW060018100426
42740CB00010B/1517